PENGUIN BOOKS

HOW TO RESCUE A HOUSE

David Ireland is adviser to the BBC series *How to Rescue a House*. He has worked in housing for the last fifteen years, directly helping people with their property problems, and now, through his job at The Empty Homes Agency, he is affecting national policy. He also puts his money where his mouth is: in 1997 he and his wife bought and restored a neglected cottage in south-west London. Passionate about how property can make our lives better, David's goal is to help everyone make better use of their own home, a new home, or an empty home.

Maxwell Hutchinson is a practising architect, a regular radio and television broadcaster and former President of the Royal Institute of British Architects. He has two weekly features on BBC Radio London covering London's architecture, landmarks and history, and has presented numerous television series, including *Demolition Detectives* and *No. 57, the History of a House* for C4. Humorous, opinionated and committed to architecture, Maxwell is the writer and presenter of the series *How to Rescue a House* on BBC2.

HOW TO RESCUE A HOUSE

Turn an Unloved Property into Your Dream Home

DAVID IRELAND

Preface and Case Studies by Maxwell Hutchinson

PENGUIN BOOKS

PENGUIN BOOKS

Published by the Penguin Group
Penguin Books Ltd, 80 Strand, London WC2R 0RL, England
Penguin Group (USA) Inc., 375 Hudson Street, New York, New York 10014, USA
Penguin Group (Canada), 10 Alcorn Avenue, Toronto, Ontario, Canada M4V 3B2
(a division of Pearson Penguin Canada Inc.)
Penguin Ireland, 25 St Stephen's Green, Dublin 2, Ireland (a division of Penguin Books Ltd)
Penguin Group (Australia), 250 Camberwell Road, Camberwell, Victoria 3124, Australia
(a division of Pearson Australia Group Pty Ltd)
Penguin Books India Pvt Ltd, 11 Community Centre,
Panchsheel Park, New Delhi – 110 017, India
Penguin Group (NZ), cnr Airborne and Rosedale Roads, Albany, Auckland 1310, New Zealand
(a division of Pearson New Zealand Ltd)
Penguin Books (South Africa) (Pty) Ltd, 24 Sturdee Avenue, Rosebank 2196, South Africa

Penguin Books Ltd, Registered Offices: 80 Strand, London WC2R 0RL, England

www.penguin.com

First published 2005
1

By arrangment with the BBC
The BBC logo is a trademark of the British Broadcasting
Corporation and is used under licence
BBC logo copyright © BBC, 1996

Designed and typeset by Smith & Gilmour, London
Set in GarageGothic-Black and Bell Gothic
Colour Reproductions by Dot Gradations Ltd, UK
Printed in Italy by Graphicom SRL

CONTENTS

FOR ALICE, AND JOSHUA

ACKNOWLEDGEMENTS

Lots of people have helped me in many different ways in putting this book together. Without their help and assistance, writing it would have been a much less enjoyable experience and the outcome would have been a distinctly inferior book. In no particular order I would like to thank Stefan McGrath at Penguin for seeing the potential of the book and taking a chance on it, Helen Conford for her valuable advice, help and skilful editing, Jonathan Ellis at the Empty Homes Agency for his ceaseless encouragement and optimism from the first twinkling of an idea for this book back in 2002 through to publication, David Offord for being a flexible boss when I needed it, Trevor Horwood for his meticulous and incredibly patient copy editing, Sarah Christie at Penguin for her enthusiasm and publicity skills, Jane Merkin and all the *How to Rescue a House* TV team for making the partnership with the BBC so enjoyable and fruitful, my mum, my dad John Ireland for his early encouragement and advice, and Maxwell Hutchinson for his excellent Case Studies and Preface. The biggest thank you has to go to my wife Jo for putting up with my many early mornings, late nights and frequent absences while writing this book – a period of our lives which was busy enough anyway, with the expectation, birth and first year on the planet of our daughter Alice. Thank you also to the many people who provided me with material and answered my many stupid questions whilst writing this book. They are too many to mention, but particular thanks go to John Earnshaw, Paul Campion, David Cropp and Emma Kuyper, all at Windsave, Solarcentury, the Forestry Stewardship Council, the Institute of Historic Building Conservation, Urban Splash, and *Regeneration and Renewal* magazine.

PREFACE

The United Kingdom has a desperate housing shortage. There are
around one million empty properties in the United Kingdom. This simply
does not compute.

As the second most densely populated country in Europe, after
Holland, how, in the name of good reason, can Britain afford to turn its
back on so many buildings with such demonstrable possibility? They could
create new and worthwhile homes with less effort than building from
scratch. As politicians of all persuasions fumble about trying to find a
solution to providing flexible homes for the new British demography, it is
remarkable that little or nothing has ever been said about the conspicuous
waste and neglect of thousands upon thousands of homes which seem
resigned to the scrap heap. Broken glass, leaking roofs, sagging gutters,
cracked downpipes, tired decoration and a jungle of a garden does not
mean that a house has passed its sell-by date and is for ever consigned
to the housing dustbin of history.

This mis-match between conspicuous need and obvious availability
is the product of the all too common community myopia. Just as we pass
by piles of festering rubbish, broken street signs, old refrigerators and
mattresses, graffiti and all manner of environmental junk without a care,
we seem just as able to turn a blind eye towards the corpse of a house,
which may in fact not be just that, but rather a sick home simply in need
of hard work, dedication, love and attention.

The British seem uncommonly able to ignore their environment.
I confess that I have often passed empty and semi-derelict houses without
asking the obvious and pressing question, why? It seems as if we are
destined to accept property dereliction and decay as part of the normal
urban or suburban experience. It goes like this. We build new houses and
are proud of them. We list historic buildings and boast about the value of
our heritage. We fiddle about with urban improvement schemes, closing
roads, putting up signs and bollards and congratulating ourselves on our
improving towns and cities. In the meantime, amongst all this worthy
improvement, the lonely and lost properties go all but unnoticed.

This condition is not limited to the urban environment. As I discovered,
the rural idyl of Aberdeenshire is peppered with empty houses all of which
present unique possibilities for new homes. They sit there atrophying into

the landscape like accidental romantic follies. Their owners, usually farmers, see them as nothing more than impediments to true straight-line ploughing or maybe a chance to house a cow or two.

For local authorities, empty homes are a burden. They diminish the community charge base and have a considerable negative impact on local property prices. Those who are unfortunate enough to live next to or around empty houses find that the value of their property is affected by the local wreck that becomes a playground for delinquents, arsonists, drug addicts and down and outs. Despite this, for no explicable reason, these blighted homeowners seem unable or unwilling to take command of the situation and do something about it themselves. It seems as if the overall position, nationally and at neighbourhood level, is beyond our collective wit and imagination. Just as a thousand crisp packets blindly blow down the high street, so broken sash windows rattle wantonly around our land.

All is not lost. As property prices rise and rise there is a pioneering breed of new potential home owners who are prepared to open filthy, creaking front doors, step gingerly among piles of junk, dead pigeons, human excrement, condoms and discarded hypodermic needles, and take on the genuinely honest and rewarding challenge of giving new life to an abandoned, decrepit and wretched house. It is not all as bad as that, but it can be. Anyone who is prepared to walk on the property wild side must be prepared for that and settle for something that is not as bad at all. Indeed many an empty house can be a pleasant surprise once inside. It can be just lonely and neglected, in need of love and life – and what a chance to realize a bargain. As this book so ably demonstrates, rescuing a house is not as difficult as it may seem. For a start the local community and the local authority will welcome any prospective rescuing pioneer with open arms as if breaking a siege of local despair, although some neighbours will think the dereliction frontiersmen foolhardy idiots who are prepared to risk time and money to turn 'that old wreck' into a worthwhile home.

So why are there so many houses that have been left to rack and ruin? The answers are as varied as the nature of the properties. A derelict pub in a prime location near Shadwell Docklands Light Railway station within five minutes of the Bank of England turns out not to be owned by a brewery in dereliction of their property duties, but by a local authority who who initially seemed unaware of their ownership. A house in Kennington was left to a pair of siblings who cannot make up their mind what to do with it, leaving it to be squatted, empty and decaying despite its prime location. The upper storeys above a shop in Islington, one of the most expensive parts of London, are left empty for family sentimental reasons. A pair of potentially elegant early nineteenth century houses in Bow, London, are empty, and it appears will remain that way, just because the owner says so. They are his, he will keep them and do what he likes. So go away and leave me alone. Who wants to live in rural Aberdeenshire, where high summer is as unwelcoming as late autumn in Liverpool? Someone does and suddenly an abandoned house or an empty barn risks a slight smile at the possibility of re-birth as a home for a new age.

The job of rescuing a house is not for the fainthearted. From the very first moment of trying to establish ownership and the buyability and viability, the enthusiast will have to summon up unbridled commitment, energy, enthusiasm, tenacity and hard work. Above all, search and rescue requires financial flexibility and compromise. In the property intensive-care ward compromise is a lifesaver.

This practical, down-to-earth manual is more than just a signpost to change. If we all woke up to the possibility and opportunity provided by the empty homes around us neighbourhoods could be rejuvenated, our housing-shortage list could be diminished and a small part of the personal and neighbourhood economy turned around for the common good.

This book accompanies an eight-part television series that shows that it can and is being done. The eight varied bands of house hunters all go into the process with wide-eyed enthusiasm and unbridled ambition. It is surprising how quickly they settle into the process, realize the potential rewards and become inured to what they discover inside the properties they find. After all, there is nothing wrong with a five-year collection of old newspapers, dirty and cracked windows, some washing up that has not been done for months and some dry rot at the bottom of the staircase. If it is cheap enough and provides the right accommodation, they snap it up. Where there is a will there is a way, and where there is a strong will there is a shortcut. Neighbours will cheer as you prise open a rotting front door and express your genuine enthusiasm at what you find. They may think that you are a little potty at first, but then jealousy may set in as they realize that you will become their neighbour at a fraction of the price it has cost them to live where they do.

When it comes to rescuing a house, make plans, set up a flexible financial arrangement, buy a good set of power tools, ideally learn to do some plumbing and plasterwork, make friends with lots of local builders who have nothing to do at the weekend, and determine to prove a point. As the movement of which this book and the television series are part gains momentum, there is no doubt that, just as the heritage lobby helped save many an important historic house in the early seventies, the dereliction lobby will do even more to eradicate the rotten teeth in otherwise smiling streets.

Mad as it may seem, house rescue is one of the few remaining genuine property opportunities left in this crowded and residentially ambitious land.

MAXWELL HUTCHINSON

INTRODUCTION

This is really not such a bad place to live. Positioned on the edge of the wealthiest continent on earth, bathed in the temperate warmth of the Gulf Stream, the British Isles is arguably one of the most beautiful archipelagos in the world. It boasts stunning mountains, moorland and lakes, a magnificent coastline, a host of idyllic villages and at least two world-class cities. Despite what some might say, it is still a rich, diverse, opportunity-filled and uplifting place to call home.

The trouble is, when somewhere is this good, we all want a bit of it. With a growing population and the trend towards living in smaller family groups, the demand for somewhere to live hasn't been as high since the end of the Second World War. Unfortunately, if we were just to build more and more new houses without proper planning, we would end up ruining the very country we all want to inhabit.

One of the simplest laws of economics says that when demand goes up and supply doesn't, prices increase. This is exactly what has happened across the UK and Ireland. The price of land and property has risen year after year at a far greater rate than our incomes have. Even when there is a property crash, prices soon recover and begin to increase again.

So if you want somewhere to live in and own, you face two problems. There aren't enough good homes available in the right places, and those that are available are too expensive. People have come up with all sorts of great ideas to try and square this circle. Some have suggested building kilometre-high blocks of flats; others want to convert old cruise ships into floating villages and moor them in our cities' rivers. A great new Dutch concept is to build houses out of recycled container crates. These are the sorts of ideas developers, governments and local authorities are seriously considering – and so they should. But this isn't much use to you. You don't want a concept, you want a home. Before you give up and decide to find some other country to live in, there is an alternative. Instead of building a new house, how about rescuing an old one?

We're becoming used to the idea of recycling newspapers, bottles and tin cans, and houses can be similarly reused. Unlike newspapers, bottles and tins, though, houses are built to last. Some last for hundreds of years (indeed, arguably the oldest house in the world is in Skara Brae, in Scotland), but time takes its toll and unless we're very conscientious about maintaining, updating and repairing them, houses tend to get a bit tired and tatty as they get older. After a while it shows, and they become not quite such nice places to live in. Our throwaway culture kicks in and we think, 'Oh, well, better get a new one, then.' So another once perfectly good house falls on hard times and another piece of land is swallowed up beneath a squeaky-clean development. The logic of renovating the old instead of building new is, in my view, inescapable. But not everybody agrees. Millions of new homes are planned for our countryside while at the other end of the scale a million homes have fallen out of use altogether.

Recycling simply means returning something to an earlier stage of its life. So yesterday's newspaper becomes pulp again to return as tomorrow's edition, or perhaps the pages of this book. The same can happen to a house. Rethought, reworked and repaired, a house can be rescued from the scrap heap and brought back to life as a place where once again you'd want to live.

But there's more to rescuing a house than simply not using more land. Lack of space is not the only threat facing these magnificent islands: there's pollution, drought, flooding, poisoning, a new ice age . . . OK, I know what you're thinking: 'Look, I picked up this book to learn about how to do up a house, not to read a lecture about all these depressing potential global disasters!' Well, yes, you're right, this *is* a book about doing up old houses, but it's the little decisions we each make about the way we live that collectively cause the big problems.

It's tempting to think that environmental concerns are so vast that anything we might do as individuals will have no detectable effect. But if everybody thinks like that, we're never going to improve anything. Everything that each one of us does has an impact. Environmental problems are global, national, regional and local. Making the right choices about how you design and build your home and what you build it out of will have a direct benefit to you and your family's health as well as the local wildlife in your garden and neighbourhood. You will also be playing your part in saving your country from the national and global challenges it faces. So by rescuing a house, not only can you get a nice place to live at an affordable price, you can also have it guilt-free.

The effect this can have really is significant. Buildings create a huge drain on environmental resources. An amazing 66 per cent of all energy consumed in the UK and Ireland is accounted for by buildings and building construction. When you add to that the toxins thrown into the air and the ground during building work, the pollution generated by their occupants once they are in use, to say nothing of the destruction of natural habitats, you'll see that how we design, build and use property has more impact on the environment than anything else we do.

Convinced? But surely, if it were so simple, wouldn't people be rescuing houses all the time? Well, they are, of course, but not in anything like the numbers they could. Most of us already live in second-hand homes – when we move in we just spruce them up a bit – but very few of us are prepared to take on a really neglected house. Local authorities, housing associations and a few specialist developers have been aware of this opportunity for years and are pretty successful at creating new homes out of neglected and empty property. But the main house-building industry has ignored them, so there are still a million or more potential homes out there waiting to be reused. There are also acres of unused commercial space that could, with a bit of imagination, be turned into homes.

Scruffy and neglected old houses don't do anybody any good if they stay like that. Derelict buildings make a neighbourhood feel down at heel, they attract vandals, fly tippers and worse. Empty properties distort the local economy and housing markets. Getting them all restored and occupied ought to be our national mission. And it could be. If this book contributes to that by putting information in the public domain and helping more people rescue houses it will have done its job.

How to Rescue a House brings together for the first time all the information you need to undertake such a project: how to find the right house, how to assess its viability, how to get the money to buy it and to develop it; how to redesign an obsolete building and how to renovate an old one; the people you need to hire and the materials you need to buy. Some of this information has never been published before, including many tricks and tips that property developers and local authorities have kept to themselves for years.

Armed with this book, a little bit of luck and a lot of self-will you can create a home for yourself by rescuing a house that nobody wants. Good luck!

PART ONE FINDING AND BUYING A HOUSE

While I was writing this book I always referred to it as a guidebook. But after I had finished it I did wonder for a time whether what I had written warranted the term. Perhaps a subject as varied and diverse as rescuing a house could never be covered sufficiently in a single volume. My mind was put at rest when I dug out an old book from a box in my loft. It, too, was a single volume, considerably smaller than this one, that rather confidently boasted of being 'the complete guidebook to South America'. A few years after buying it I visited South America and I can assure you that the guidebook was very far from complete. But looking at its now rather dusty cover again reminded me what function a guidebook should serve. It would be well-nigh impossible to write a book that covered every conceivable detail of its subject. But a guidebook doesn't seek to do this. It merely points out the important facts and offers some insight into them, allowing readers to make their own decisions about the route they want to take.

Every house rescue, like every trip to South America, will be a unique journey. But, equally, all those journeys will have much in common: finding and buying a house, deciding what to do with it, doing it, and finally, of course, paying for it all. With these broad headings in mind I have set this guidebook out in four parts.

This first part, 'Finding and buying a house', is all about . . . well, finding and buying a house. Yes I know, there are dozens of books, TV programmes and websites devoted to this subject and I sympathize with you if you feel you've had enough of these already. But before you skip on to Part Two, perhaps I can return to my old South America guidebook to explain what I'm trying to do. There is a very common, short and well-worn path to finding and buying a house that most people take. You know the one: registering with an estate agent, visiting a few houses and making an offer for the one you like best. For the moment I'd like you to think of this as analogous to a package holiday to a common destination such as Greece, France or Florida. Once you've been there once you don't need to read up on the place if you decide to go again. A visit to South America, on the other hand, might be a different matter; there may not be a package holiday that covers what you want to do. And the trip may involve locations and activities you're less familiar with. If you were going there you'd probably want to read the guidebook first. Rescuing a house is a bit like this; it involves going off the beaten track, doing a few things you might usually leave to others and knowing a few things that otherwise you wouldn't need to know. This part of the book aims to give you the inside knowledge that will let you plan a successful journey and purchase the right house at the end of it. Bon voyage!

For most of us our house is what
defines our wealth. So it seems amazing
that anybody would let something so
important fall into neglect, let alone
allow it to become empty and derelict.

1 FINDING THE RIGHT HOUSE

There are a million or more neglected or empty properties in
the UK and Ireland, so it shouldn't be too hard for you to find
one. But finding the *right* one might pose a greater challenge.
This chapter will guide you through the options. In Western
economies and societies home ownership is hugely important.
Great Britain and Ireland have two of the highest rates of home
ownership in the world. Not only are these homes places to
live, the equity within them underpins our ability to borrow
and spend. For most of us our house is what defines our wealth.
So it seems amazing that anybody would let something so
important fall into neglect, let alone allow it to become empty
and derelict. Hardly anybody makes a conscious decision to let
a house fall into disrepair and very few people want their house
to become empty, but life just happens to some people, and it
happens to some houses too.

Common reasons houses become neglected:

✚ Low demand

Certain properties simply cannot attract an occupant. Individual houses and even entire neighbourhoods can suffer from the phenomenon of low demand. In some streets there are whole rows of houses lying abandoned. People in these areas have lost confidence, not just in the houses but in the area's employment prospects, education services, facilities and security. House prices are so low in some inner-city districts that it's simply not economically viable for their owners to improve or even maintain them. At this point you may be wondering whether you want to rescue a house to live in at all. But don't give up yet; these are not the only reasons that houses lie empty.

✚ Prohibitive maintenance costs

Old houses are expensive to maintain. If you're thinking about buying a property for the first time you should think about this carefully. Houses need constant attention and money spending on them. Repainting woodwork, cleaning out the gutters, repairing damaged roof coverings – something seems to need doing every year. Things wear out, too. Every ten years or so you'll need a new carpet or two; you may need to refit the kitchen, put in a new boiler. Imagine owning a vintage Bentley; maintaining your house will cost you about the same amount of money and cause you about the same amount of grief. Of course, many people can't afford the upkeep, or they spend their money on the wrong things. As a result, the house deteriorates. The phrase 'a stitch in time saves nine' is very apt for old houses. If maintenance doesn't happen the cost of putting things right goes up and up. If someone can't afford to maintain their property, they'll never be able to afford the costs of refurbishment.

✚ Investments gone wrong

Property values increased by so much during the late 1990s and early 2000s that it became the best investment around. Anybody who could afford to bought a spare house or two. Many of these were then effectively abandoned. Prices were rising so fast that the profit the owner might have earned from letting seemed almost incidental compared to the capital growth. I remember speaking to one property investor at the peak of the boom in 2003. He had left his property empty for years, missing out on half a million pounds he could have made by letting it. He seemed unconcerned, pointing out that he had earned nearly twice as much as that in the rising market without any of the aggravation that comes with being a landlord. (I don't know about you, but I'd be prepared to put up with quite a lot of aggro for half a million quid.) This is all very well for the smart owners who sold at the peak of the property boom, but those who didn't were left with a scruffy old property that very few people would want to buy. Many of them decided to ride it out and are waiting for the property market to boom again. Not all of them can afford to.

✚ Obsolescence

Houses have a tendency to become out of date. When you consider how old many of them are, this isn't altogether surprising. Almost half of the houses in the British Isles were built before the First World War. Imagine if half of us were driving round in pre-1918 cars that we had patched up, modified and knocked about. There would be howls of protest that our car stock was ludicrously outdated. Houses, of course, are more adaptable and longer lasting than cars but some of them require a lot of money and thought to keep them usable.

In most cases the real story is that the house just isn't right for its current owner. But, it might be right for you. First though, you have to find it.

ESTATE AGENTS

Estate agents are the first port of call for most people when looking for a new home. Confusingly, in Ireland they are generally known as auctioneers, even though most don't do auctions at all. Whatever you call them, if you're looking for a house to rescue, it'll appear at first glance that they don't have what you're looking for. This isn't surprising: a window display full of derelict wrecks is hardly the image they want.

Most estate agents have many more properties for sale than those displayed in their windows, web pages or newspaper adverts. Their stock will often fall into three categories: *hot cakes* – new-on-the-market, quick-selling properties that are likely to have strong appeal; *plodders* – houses that will sell eventually, but may not be everybody's cup of tea; and *lemons* – properties that appeal only to a specific segment of the market (or nobody at all) and can take years to sell. Estate agents want to be associated with hot cakes. They want to give the impression they are selling lots of desirable properties very quickly, so these are the properties they market strongly. If they can't sell a potential purchaser a hot cake they may drag the odd plodder out of the filing cabinet. Rescue projects usually fall into the lemons category, and so rarely see the light of day. You won't get to know about them unless you ask. No estate agent will offer you a lemon unless you make it clear that a lemon is what you want.

Most agents know a few local developers and when a derelict or empty property comes along that looks like a good prospect they'll usually be given first refusal. Although estate agents aren't really supposed to behave like this, this is how it works in practice. You need to ensure that the estate agent thinks of you too when a suitable property comes on to the market. Let them know if you have your finances in place and are prepared to make a quick purchase. Most developers will be ready to move swiftly and if you're not, you'll be at a disadvantage.

Even if an estate agent doesn't seem to deal in the kind of property you're after, it's still worth talking to them. List every estate agent in the area you're looking at and visit them all. Keep in touch with them and, once they realize you're serious, they may well take on a property with you in mind that would otherwise have been rejected.

Established agents know the housing market as well as anyone. They'll probably know about plenty of houses on their patch with potential for rescuing even if they aren't actually selling them.

Take a notebook and
a camera with you.
You'll never remember
everything otherwise.

WALK THE STREETS

If you know roughly where you want to buy, have a wander round and see what properties are on offer. Don't try to save time by driving, you won't be able to look at them properly, or if you do you'll probably crash your car. It's amazing how much more you see when you're walking; most streets have a few rather unloved looking houses on them. Some might be empty, and there might even be the odd redundant commercial or agricultural building that will inspire you with its potential.

Take a notebook and a camera with you. You'll never remember everything otherwise. You'll probably attract suspicion from the locals by doing this, so it's good to have your story worked out in advance. What you say is up to you, but personally I'd opt for the truth. You may well meet the owner in this way. If you do you, it is a golden opportunity to open up a dialogue, but make sure you've read the section in the next chapter about negotiating with owners first.

AUCTION CATALOGUES

Potential rescue projects most often come up for sale at auction. Auctions are a quick and decisive way of disposing of property, which is why neglected ones that don't have immediate appeal are often sold in this way. Hundreds of properties are sold through auctions every week, mostly to developers and landlords, but buying at auction remains something of a mystery to the majority of us.

PROPERTY WEBSITES

The opportunities offered by rescuing houses have spawned some truly helpful websites featuring empty and neglected properties that aren't actively marketed elsewhere.

The first, www.empro.co.uk, is a not-for-profit website designed simply to put you in touch with the owners of empty properties. Register your interest in any of the properties featured on the site and your enquiry will be forwarded to its owner. The site is free to use, the start-up costs having been funded by a government grant. It works pretty well, although I have to declare an interest here as one of the site's co-founders.

Another site worth investigating is www.propertyrenovate.co.uk,

In Chapter 3 you will find a brief beginners' step-by-step guide to buying at auction. I'll also tell you how to find out what's coming up for sale.

which is a portal for properties in London in need of renovation that are being marketed by estate agents. These are the lemons mentioned above, and this site provides details of a whole basket of them without the hassle of visiting each estate agent in turn.

SELF-BUILD PLOT-FINDING AGENCIES

Self-build housing has become increasingly popular and a whole industry has grown up to provide information on plots of land for sale. Many plots are just that, – pieces of open land – but these are becoming increasingly scarce and most agency lists contain a large smattering of plots with empty and redundant buildings on them. Some of these are wrecks for which demolition is the only possible improvement, but a surprising number of rescue projects can be found this way. Most plot-finding companies require you to pay a fee in order to search their database for likely plots. The main web-based agencies are Plotsearch, Property Spy and Self Build Land UK (contact details for all of which are in the directory, p. 349). In addition, self-build magazines such as *Build It, Homebuilding and Renovating* or *Self-build and Design* (see directory, p. 350) have listings of available plots, although most of the information on them is sourced from agency websites.

DERELICT HISTORIC BUILDINGS

Several organizations working to save historic buildings publish catalogues of those they consider to be at risk, many of which are empty and abandoned. The catalogues make fascinating reading with everything from castles to greenhouses included. 'At risk' doesn't necessarily mean that a building is on the point of collapse; it can mean that the architectural features are in danger of being lost or damaged, or that the building's use has become ambiguous or redundant. That said, most of the buildings featured are in poor condition and a few are downright derelict. These are not sale catalogues, however, so if you're interested in a particular property you'll need to find a way of getting its owner to sell it to you (see the next chapter for more details on how to do this). The publishing organizations don't take a fee or commission if you do buy a property, but in most cases you'll need to either buy the register catalogue or take out a subscription to it.

Nearly all of the buildings featured in such catalogues are 'listed'. Briefly, the listing system for historic buildings in the UK works like this: grade I buildings are of national significance, such as St Paul's cathedral; grade II* (in words, 'two star') are of historic importance and both the inside and the outside of the building are protected; grade II buildings are also of historic importance but only the outside (and perhaps a few internally listed features) are protected.

The best register catalogues

✚ Risky Buildings

Published annually by Save Britain's Heritage (SAVE). This contains details of hundreds of properties across England and Wales (but not London). Properties in England are all grade 1, 2* or 2 listed while properties in Wales include buildings of every listing status as well as non-listed buildings of historical interest. You can obtain a copy from SAVE or view an edited version on their website for free.

✚ Scottish Civic Trust

For properties in Scotland there is a buildings at risk register run by the Scottish Civic Trust buildings at risk office, which publishes a buildings at risk bulletin available by subscription.

✚ English Heritage's buildings at risk register

This includes information on all grade 1 and 2* listed buildings known to English Heritage to be at risk in England and Wales. So far as I am aware, this is the only catalogue that covers London. The London section also includes grade 2 listed buildings. The register is available from English Heritage either by post or online.

✚ The Ulster Architectural Heritage Society

For Northern Ireland, and the An Taisce (the National Trust for Ireland) for the Republic of Ireland.

HOW TO BUY A HOUSE FOR 50p

I'm not kidding. Even in these property obsessed times you can still get a house for next to nothing! It's pretty rare, admittedly, but occasionally public sector authorities will dispose of properties for a nominal price. Homesteading schemes, as they are known, tend to be run only in areas that have very low demand for housing. Local councils and housing associations sell their unwanted empty houses to members of the public at a minimal price, the idea being to encourage people back into a run-down area to help regenerate it. In return, buyers must agree to pay some or all the cost of repairs and maintenance and to make a commitment to the local area. In most cases preference is given to people with local connections.

In 2001, Newcastle City Council sold four flats for 50p each to local families.

Just because a property isn't
on the market doesn't mean that
it's owner won't sell it.

2 PERSUADING THE OWNER TO SELL

There may be lots of ways of ways to find a house to rescue,
but you also need to know about the many ways of buying one.
As you might have noticed, by no means all of the properties
discussed so far will be up for sale when you discover them.
The rest may well be buyable, but first of all you'll need to
persuade the owner that they should sell.

  If you search this large, unmarketed property sector you'll
be giving yourself a far wider choice and you may be able to
negotiate a sale with no competition from other potential
buyers. Remember, just because a property isn't on the market
doesn't mean that its owner won't sell it. Most neglected
properties are earning their owners nothing and in all likelihood
are costing them a packet. Maintenance costs, council tax,
vandalism, squatters, arson, stress, stress and more stress. Play
this one right and you can seem like a knight in shining armour
to the beleaguered owner of a neglected property.

WHO OWNS THE PROPERTY?

Your persuasion techniques are only any use if you have someone to negotiate with, so the first step is to find out who the owner is. If the property is occupied, the matter is straightforward: ask the occupier. But if the property is rented the tenant might not be too keen to tell you, and if the property is empty there's nobody to ask. In Gateshead in 2000 a local community action group got fed up with owners abandoning homes and blighting their neighbourhood. They decided to name and shame. They adapted the historic 'blue plaque' idea and started putting up their own. 'Nobody lives here', it said, followed by the name and address of the guilty owner. The difficulty is that people don't like being associated with empty and neglected properties, so (unless you're buying in Gateshead) it won't be easy for you to find them. Take heart from this, though: in six years spent working on privately owned empty property I managed to trace the owner in every one of the 1,500 cases I dealt with. You can, too.

LAND REGISTRY

A good starting point is the Land Registry. Since 1990 the land register in the UK has been open to the public and for a fee anyone can inspect it and obtain a copy of any registered title. This is an official document that states who owns the property; it costs £4 by post or £2 online. This is a useful way to find an owner's name, but the address given is often the empty property in which you are interested. Still, at least you'll have a name. The details will usually include any charges registered against the property such as mortgages, loans and statutory enforcement notices. If the land is unregistered, the Land Registry won't have any information, but you could do a search of the Land Charges Registry (costing £1). This will reveal the owner's details if there are any charges against the property (e.g. a second mortgage) or if bankruptcy papers have been filed.

In Gateshead in 2000 a local community action group got fed up with owners abandoning homes and blighting their neighbourhood. They decided to name and shame. They adapted the historic 'blue plaque' idea and started putting up their own. 'Nobody lives here', it said, followed by the name and address of the guilty owner.

SEARCH AGENCIES

If you know the name of the owner but can't find any other details, you could use a private detective to track them down. This may sound rather extreme, but it's often the easiest way to trace an owner. Fees can be anything in the range of £100 to £1,000, depending on how elusive the owner turns out to be, so, unless you're desperate, try some of the other options first. They might work and they're free.

THE EMPTY PROPERTY OFFICER

Most local authorities have an empty property officer whose job it is to get empty properties back into use. They are your allies, so use them. Their activities are dictated by the local authority's housing strategy. Local authorities faced with high demand for housing will focus on providing social housing, so may prefer empty property to be acquired by a housing association. On the other hand, a local authority that encourages owner occupation is likely to provide more, perhaps even financial, assistance.

COUNCIL RECORDS

One place where an owner's name and address will almost certainly be recorded is on the local authority's council tax records (property rates in Northern Ireland). Different local authorities have different policies on disclosing information. Data protection legislation in this area is open to interpretation and many authorities will take the better-safe-than-sorry line. Your success here will depend as much on who you ask as what you ask for. Try the council's empty property officer. Explain what you want and why you want it. Alternatively, visit the local authority and ask to view the register in person.

Another line of enquiry at your local authority is its planning and building control department. If the owner has sought permission for alterations, for example permission to build an extension, there will be a record of their name and contact details. A bonus here is that anyone submitting a planning application is probably in a position to make decisions about the property, so even if they aren't the owner they may still be the person you need to deal with. To find out about any planning applications you'll need to visit your council's planning department and inspect the planning register for the street where the property is.

THE DIRECT APPROACH

You could adapt the Gateshead approach and post a notice on the door stating that you'd like to contact the owner, leave your contact number and wait. In the meantime, talk to neighbours, shopkeepers, the local neighbourhood watch group (details from the local police station), the postman. If the property is in a rural area, you could contact the local parish council. The parish clerk may be able to help. Don't forget, these people probably want to see the property back in use too, and so may well be happy to assist.

WHAT TO DO IF THE OWNER HAS DIED

Many properties remain empty while a will is disputed or heirs are traced, sitting in limbo until the identity of the new owner can be established. If you know the name of the deceased owner you could employ a firm of genealogists specializing in tracking down beneficiaries. Look in Yellow Pages (Golden Pages in Ireland) under genealogists. Sometimes you will be charged a fee, but more often than not such companies make their money from the person who benefits from the will.

Most neglected properties are earning their owners nothing and in all likelihood are costing them a packet. Play this one right and you can seem like a knight in shining armour to the beleaguered owner of a neglected property.

CASE STUDY_1 Maxwell's notes from the frontline

Mark Carroll and Stuart Tabbron are both in their early 40s. They have been living together for two years and are expert at improving houses and selling them on. They bought their current home only eight months ago; it is a charming Edwardian terraced house, on a quiet road five minutes from Kennington underground station in south London, and has just been valued at half a million pounds.

Their Vision

Wanderlust has got the better of them, and they want a new challenge: doing up a 'Georgian' house. They're keen on something with all the Georgian characteristics regardless of the precise period. They know they can only hope to achieve their dream on their budget by rescuing a wreck.

The Front Runners
Kennington, London

This large, unusual and almost certainly genuine Georgian property is a stone's throw from Mark and Stuart's current home. It is situated on a busy south London through-road and has been severely neglected for a long period of time.

Finding out about the home

Research in trade directories and electoral roles reveals that the property has been occupied by an entertaining variety of tradesmen, including: in 1849 James Purdey, a cheesemonger; from 1863 Samuel James Batear, a meat salesman of Newgate Market; in 1867 Daniel Earle, a woollen merchant who, it appears, would have used the property as a wool warehouse. Firearms were manufactured in the property from 1935, with no mention of the proprietor's name. From 1935 to 1941 the house was also used by the North Lambeth Printers and Skilled Employment Committee.

The property is a Grade II listed building, which makes it of historic interest – not surprising considering its age. For more on listed buildings, see p. 23.

The Land Registry Records show that the owner died in 2001. There is a notice of an inheritance tax charge but no record of whom the property was left to. Mark and Stuart eventually tracked down the son and daughter, who now own the property but have not decided what to do with it. The local authority, as well as registering it on their Empty Homes list, have also indicated that if the house is not renovated and returned to residential use in the near future they would consider exercising their powers of compulsory purchase. This is a last-ditch measure. They will not be successful with such an order if the owners can demonstrate that they are actively considering the property's future.

Islington, London

This building is situated on one of the most fashionable streets in central Islington, just off the popular restaurant mile of Upper Street, famously home to the establishment in which Tony Blair apparently did the deal with Gordon Brown. The ground floor of the property is occupied by the offices of a small television production company. The upper three floors are clearly empty and neglected. If this property can be bought, it would make a three-floored maisonette.

Finding out about the home

It is likely that the property became commercial in the late nineteenth century. By 1901 the property was occupied by a British gilder and decorator, John Savage, sharing with an Italian artist and his French family, an Italian professor of music and an Italian cabinet maker – a united Europe in the heart of Islington.

The current owner, who bought the property in the 1940s and used it to run a shirt-manufacturing business, leases the ground floor to a film company. According to the owner's son, who now looks after the property, it was previously owned by the Empire Pipe Company. His family apparently came to the country from Germany, successfully fleeing the Nazis.

The owner says that very little has been done to the property since it was bought, and he resolutely refuses to make any changes to the building. As a result, the building's original features are still intact; but the owner is intent upon keeping the property in the family, even though the upper storeys produce no income whatsoever.

What Next?

Mark and Stuart were finally able to get inside the house in Kennington, and were incredibly pleased with what they found. It is enormous, and has huge potential, despite the fact that the basement is uninhabitable. Mark and Stuart are still talking to the owners but it is going to be a long process.

For more on how to persuade an owner to sell, see pp. 37–45.

WHAT TO DO IF THE OWNER DOESN'T WANT TO SELL

Many rescuable homes are advertised for sale at auctions and estate agents, but these represent only a fraction of your potential purchases. The plain fact is that most empty and neglected property isn't on the market. How can you buy something that's not for sale?

There are two approaches: persuasion and force. Force isn't often an option. A word of warning: be prepared for a long wait; none of these mechanisms is quick and none will guarantee that you'll be able to buy the property in the end.

✚ Compulsory purchase

This is a power that all local authorities and some central government departments across the UK and Ireland have at their disposal. Compulsory purchase orders (CPOs) are a government's ultimate weapon in tackling neglected homes. They enable a local authority to purchase a property even against the owner's wishes. Of course, there must be a good reason to do so, and getting empty houses back into use qualifies as such. CPOs can be expensive and time consuming, however, and so are rarely used. The process can take a year or more and often involves a special inquiry. The authority will usually exhaust all other avenues before embarking on a CPO and will do so only if satisfied that a CPO is in the public interest.

Of course, a CPO transfers the ownership to the authority, not to you, but it may be possible to structure a legal agreement whereby you can purchase the property from them once the CPO has been confirmed. To do this you'll need to demonstrate a very clear plan of what you intend to do and a timetable of when you're going to do it. You'll have to convince the authority that you represent the best way of getting the house back into use. If the area has high levels of housing need it's unlikely that an authority would be prepared to sell the property into owner occupation (but you can ask). The authority is obliged to pay the owner market price for the property, so you can expect to pay the same amount if you buy it from them.

There are two approaches: persuasion and force. Force isn't often an option.

✚ Enforced sale

Enforced sale is a power British local authorities have to enable them to recover debt. It means councils can force someone owing them money to sell their property in order to settle the debt. Although the power was not designed as a way of getting empty properties back into use, it often has that effect as a spin-off. The owners of empty properties remain responsible for council tax bills and associated costs such as clearing up dumped rubbish, making dangerous structures safe and boarding up doors and windows to keep out intruders. The bills for such services often remain unpaid. Over time, with accumulated interest, these debts can become sizeable. A local authority can apply for a court order to force the sale of the property. If the court agrees, and it usually does, the property has to be made available to the open market for sale, often through auction.

> **Most local authorities employ empty property officers (see p.29); contact yours to discover whether any enforced sales are planned.**

✚ How to get an empty property on to the market if it's publicly owned

A powerful and largely forgotten piece of legislation still lurks on the UK's statute books. A Public Request to Order Disposal (PROD) enables you to request that any publicly owned empty property be put up for sale. The power was introduced in the Local Government Planning and Land Act 1980. If you're interested in an empty property owned by any central government department or agency, a local authority or the like, you simply need to write to the Director of Planning for your regional government office (in England) or Scottish executive or Welsh assembly and request that it be put up for sale. It's likely that many government offices won't have heard of PRODs, so you might need to explain and persist. You should be able to find out the contact details of your local government office from the Office of the Deputy Prime Minister's website www.odpm.gov.uk. The government office should investigate and find out why the property is empty. If there is no valid reason for keeping it empty, the secretary of state has the power to order its sale. You could try making a direct offer, but the usual method of disposal is sale on the open market at auction. At which, of course, you can try to buy it.

A POTENTIAL PROBLEM –
THE HOME INFORMATION PACK

The UK government is introducing legislation for England and Wales that may cause problems to would-be house rescuers: the home information pack. The thinking is that the house-buying process takes too long and many house purchases fall through as a result, not least because the longer the home-buying process takes, the more opportunity there is for gazumping.

In the near future, the responsibility and costs of gathering much of the information needed to sell a house will be transferred to the seller, who will need to compile such details before anybody even views the property. The information will be presented to prospective purchasers as a pack.

The home information pack will include:

➡ Title documents for the property

➡ Replies to standard enquiries, such as whether the vendor is aware of any problems with the property (these are currently requested by the buyer's solicitor)

➡ Copies of any planning, listed building and Building Regulations consents and approvals

➡ Copies of warranties and guarantees if the property is newly built

➡ Any guarantees for work that has been carried out on the property

➡ A draft contract

➡ Local authority searches

➡ A house condition report based on a professional structural survey of the property

➡ Seller's questionnaire

Packs for leasehold properties, such as flats, will also have to include:

➡ A copy of the lease

➡ Most recent service-charge accounts and receipts

➡ Buildings insurance policy details

➡ Any regulations made by the landlord or management company, additional to those on the lease

➡ Contact and legal details of the landlord or management company

There is a lot of sense in all of this, but it creates a lot more work for the seller. To a reluctant vendor, the pack will be just another reason not to sell, and you may need to increase your offer to offset the cost of obtaining one.

PERSUADING AN OWNER TO SELL

In general, I always think persuading people of the value of doing something is far more effective than forcing them to do it against their will. So it is with buying property. But when you find that real gem of a property that could become your ideal home, and the owner doesn't want to sell it, what do you do? How do you convince the owner that they should sell it to you? In most cases, what is a good deal for you could be a good deal for the owner too. After all, if the property is empty the owner isn't realizing any money from it, and if it's occupied and in poor condition the owner may be looking for a solution. Be warned, though, having the right deal is rarely enough: presentation is everything. Many prospective purchasers seem to think that persistence is the answer. Determination is an asset, but there is a thin line between this and badgering. I came across one case recently where the prospective purchaser of an empty property was so convinced of his case that he wouldn't take no for an answer. He took to phoning the owner late in the evening, writing letters to him on a daily basis and even waiting for him outside his house. All this carried on until he was arrested as a stalker. Needless to say, he didn't get the house.

Whatever approach you take, be prepared for the long haul. The owner of a neglected property who hasn't made a decision about anything for years is unlikely to be decisive over selling.

When choosing your approach, consider whether the owner would be likely to respond to a business case, or whether a softer approach is needed. Often individual owners have strong social and emotional ties to their property which cannot be broken even by the best-made case. (There are ways of persuading even these owners, but more on them later.)

MAKING A BUSINESS CASE

Generally, the business case works best for companies, and softer approaches are more suitable for individuals, but every case should be judged on its own merits and you must decide what will be effective in each situation. You shouldn't assume that, because allowing a property to fall into disrepair demonstrates poor business acumen, the owner won't respond to a business case. Most companies are interested in improving their profitability and shareholder value, and many individuals' minds work in the same way. If you can demonstrate that your plan contributes to these objectives, and, crucially, doesn't burden the owner with a lot of work or inconvenience, you could be in luck.

A business case explains what you want to do, when it's likely to happen and what the benefits are for the owner. There are no rules about how to do this, but the objective is to convince your quarry that you're serious, able to deliver and have a professional approach.

Most successful business cases include:

✚ A valuation of the property

There is no 'correct' price for a property, only one that the buyer is willing to pay and the seller is willing to receive. That said, people perceive property values similarly to share prices, and are worried that they might sell too cheaply. A third-party valuation from an estate agent can be an excellent way to avoid this, and provide a starting point for negotiating a price.

✚ Evidence that you can afford to buy

Demonstrating that you have a mortgage offer, cash, or some other form of funding already in place will help.

✚ Evidence that you're ready to buy

Having a solicitor or conveyancer in place would help too. (Yes, I know you can do your own conveyancing, but when presenting a business case, doing so will probably make you look less professional.)

✚ A timetable of how and when things could happen

Set out a realistic timetable. This isn't so much a fixed schedule that must be adhered to but evidence that you have thought about how and when you can deliver.

Once you have prepared your case, find out who is the right person in the company to deal with. Arrange a meeting and make your presentation as professionally as possible. Put your proposals in writing and leave a copy behind after the meeting. Follow up with a phone call once the owner has had time to consider your offer.

THE SOFTER APPROACH

This isn't so much a different approach as recognition that in many cases you need to deal with a whole raft of side issues before you get on to presenting your case and negotiating with the owner. Any number of approaches may work, but what follows is a proven persuasion technique.

Persuasion is the art of the possible. Once you understand how to do it, all sorts of seemingly unlikely projects will become possibilities. It has nothing to do with trickery or deception. Good persuasion is simply good communication, making your case so well that others can only agree with it. What you must do is convince the owner of the property that the best thing, the only thing, for them to do is to sell it to you.

Forget for a moment that you're a potential buyer; the advice to follow here is really the same as the techniques used in sales manuals. You need to sell a proposal; you want your prospect to buy it. There are countless guidebooks on sales techniques which you can read and adapt, but the basic rules are pretty much the same. What follows is an eight-step guide based on the method used by a highly successful London property developer. He has persuaded countless people to sell to him and has built up a portfolio of over 100 properties. He, of course, has his own personality and style that may be very different from yours, but look at the principles and see what you can use. Bear in mind that this is just one approach; property developers have many other techniques that you could borrow.

For another view take a look at Ajay Ahuja's excellent book _Beating the Property Clock_.

Persuasion is the art of the possible. Once you understand how to do it, all sorts of seemingly unlikely projects will become possibilities.

MAKE CONTACT

Persuasion works far better face to face. Think what works with you. When you receive unsolicited letters or emails you call them junk mail or spam and put them in the bin. The owner of the house you want to buy is no different from you, so if you want to avoid the bin treatment you need to get personal.

Contact the owner and say that you have noticed their house and identified a problem with it. Ask if they could spare the time to discuss it. You have some money/time/experience in this sort of thing, and you may be able to help. Don't say, 'I want to buy your house.' Chances are they haven't thought about selling it and will need to be persuaded of the merits of doing so. Showing your cards too early is a classic mistake; it could very well cut the conversation short. If they say no thanks at this stage your negotiation will have finished before it even started.

Arrange a meeting. A face-to-face encounter is much more likely to be successful than a phone conversation. Arrange to meet at a time and place that is convenient to them, not you.

KNOW YOUR OWNER

Get to know who you're dealing with by building up a rapport and preparing a basis for discussion. To do so, you need to find out a bit about the other person: what are their needs and what do they want? You also need to let them know something about you. If they understand what you are trying to achieve they'll probably be more prepared to listen to you. Be honest; people can spot a lie more easily than you might think. Explain your motives: all you want to do is to create a home and help the environment; you aren't a nasty property developer who is trying to make a fortune out of them.

Don't spend too much time on this get-to-know-you stage; after all, you're trying to buy a property not make a friend for life. As soon as the pleasantries have been concluded, move on to business.

Your body language can help to develop trust. A well-known technique is to observe the other person and synchronize your own body language with theirs. Talk at the same speed and pitch; move in the same way; adopt a similar posture. Turn yourself to face them and make frequent eye contact. These techniques help to put people at ease and make them feel you're on their wavelength.

Once your body language is synchronized, you can start to take the lead. If you have been successful you'll see the other person copying you when you change your posture or speech pattern. This technique is often used by sales people to inspire trust and confidence and you can employ it with equal effect.

UNDERSTAND THE SITUATION

During your negotiations you should try to appreciate the owner's point of view. The house you're trying to buy isn't up for sale, so you will need to present the owner with some fairly compelling evidence that selling is in their best interests. In a recent survey of owners of empty properties only one in ten said they'd consider selling. Their reasons aren't always logical but they need to be understood. Let the owner do the talking. Don't try to provide solutions at this stage. Here are some common reasons:

✚ Capital gains tax

In the UK, if a property isn't the owner's principal residence, any profit on their investment is subject to capital gains tax. This may act as a disincentive to cashing in. Most owners would have to pay tax on their profit, although there is a lot of misunderstanding about capital gains tax and people often make incorrect assumptions about what their liability would be. Either way, people don't like paying tax and sometimes make illogical decisions to avoid doing so. In Ireland the same applies, although the tax is levied at a lower rate than in the UK.

✚ Emotional ties

If the owner lives in the house there are bound to be some emotional ties to the property, to say nothing of the logistical problems involved in upping sticks. Things should be simpler for empty properties, but emotions can run through these too. About a quarter of owners of empty properties once lived in them themselves. A home, even an ex-home, has all sorts of personal memories attached to it which often override logic.

✚ Admitting defeat

Unless your owner inherited the property, the fact that it is now empty and neglected indicates an investment that has misfired. Selling now may make apparent the size of the mistake and amount to a public admission of failure. Some people prefer denial.

✚ 'Property is an investment'

The British (and occasionally Irish) property-owning obsession clouds people's judgement. We're conditioned to think of property as an investment, not a liability. Owners of empty properties, even those with big mortgages, sometimes think of money spent on an empty property as they would deposits in a savings account, believing that a rising market will always more than compensate their loss of income or extra costs.

✚ Pipe dreams

Many owners have plans to do great things with their property. Sometimes these are realistic and may come to pass; other times they stand no chance of getting off the ground. The owner is unlikely to make the distinction. Their plan to create the eighth wonder of the world on Peckham High Street is to them a reality. Challenge it and they may take it as a personal attack.

✚ Inertia

Many people like things to stay the same, even when they could be made better. Some are fearful of change while others just can't be bothered. You may even find an owner agreeing that it would make sense to sell their property to you, but still refusing to do so.

CREATE INTEREST IN YOUR PROPOSAL

Move on to a businesslike discussion. The best way to keep the owner's attention is to keep them thinking. Ask questions and look interested in the answers. Try to agree with what the other person says as often as you can. If you can't agree entirely, then agree in principle.

Don't be afraid to take notes, although it's courteous to ask the owner's permission to do so. Most people won't mind. It can be quite flattering to think that what you're saying is worth writing down.

CHECK YOU'VE GOT IT RIGHT

The best way of showing you understand is to repeat things back. Not parrot-fashion, but a brief summary to show you have been listening. It also gives the owner an opportunity to correct you if you've got anything wrong.

Make sure that the owner has your phone number, address or any other contact details you have. Leave your home phone number as well as your mobile, otherwise you'll come across as a fly-by-night character, in the same mould as dodgy salesmen and cowboy builders. Agree when and where you're going to meet again and leave with a handshake. (Contrary to popular belief, handshakes have no meaning in contract law, but they do convey shared agreement and trust, which is exactly what you want.)

MAKE YOUR PROPOSAL

In this stage you need to reach agreement on the benefits of your proposal. Now, and not before, you should offer your solution to the problems brought to light during your discussion so far. Think about what is the biggest issue for the owner and present your solution to address it. Emphasize the benefits to them, and offer evidence that you can deliver what you promise.

Don't offer something you can't deliver. People are instinctively wary of exaggerated promises and would prefer to be offered something that sounds reasonable and deliverable. You don't need to finalize the deal at this stage, only to reach agreement that the benefits of what you have suggested would help resolve the problems that have been identified.

CHECK AGAIN

Just as you checked earlier that you understood the owner's problems and needs, now check that the owner understands the benefits of your proposal.

AGREEMENT

You now understand the owner's problems and you're agreed that your proposal will help resolve them in a satisfactory manner. If you have got this far, you have sold your proposal. The owner has agreed in principle to sell the property to you. Well done!

The next step is negotiation. You may both want to move straight on to this from the agreement stage, but it's often a good idea to take a break and return to the negotiations a day or so later. You don't want to make the owner feel that he or she has been pressured or rushed into things. A night or two to think about what you have agreed is no bad thing.

Owning a neglected property is a stressful experience for most people. If you ask the right questions you should be able to find out what is causing the owner the biggest headache and what effect it's having. Start thinking about how you can help address the problem with your solution.

NEGOTIATING A PRICE

Phew! Finally you have found a house that somebody is prepared to sell to you. But this is no time to rest on your laurels. You need to move on quickly to negotiating the price and other details. Many potential property sales collapse at this point, but by bearing in mind a few simple points you can increase your chances of success.

I find it helpful to think about things this way: You want to buy the property for as little as possible and the owner wants you to buy it for as much as possible. But if you're both reasonable people, you'll both accept that some compromise is necessary. Obviously, there is a maximum price that you would be prepared to pay and a minimum price that the owner would accept. Part of the charade of negotiating is that both parties try to keep these figures secret whilst trying to find out what the other party's limit is.

The important point about limits isn't what they are, but whether they overlap. If they do, you will almost certainly reach a deal; if they don't, you almost certainly won't. You need to find this out quickly to avoid wasting everybody's time.

Most negotiations open with an offer from the buyer to the seller which is either accepted or rejected. Usually several offers and counter-offers are made before agreement is reached. Bearing in mind that you want to find out about the owner's minimum price it's a good idea to pitch your first offer well below your maximum. Don't expect this to be accepted, it's only a shot across the bows, but don't pitch it so low that it is seen as an insult. If your initial offer is refused (and it probably will be) you should ask the owner to name a price. You will then have two figures on the table. If you're going to reach a deal the eventual price will be somewhere between them.

Tactics come in at this point. If you put in a second offer only slightly higher than the first you're sending a message to the owner that you're nearly at your limit.

Though tempting, it isn't always wise to screw the owner down to the lowest price you can. A good negotiation should end with both parties feeling they have got a good deal. If you emerge triumphant with a low agreed price and the owner feeling defeated, there is good chance that the deal will go wrong later. House buying and selling can bring out the worst in people, and humiliated people have a horrible tendency to try to get their own back.

Each offer and counter-offer narrows the range of potential prices for the deal. You could go on shaving pennies for ages, but there comes a point when you really need to close the deal and move on. A better tactic at this stage is to split the price between the last offer and counter-offer and call it a final offer. This is surprisingly effective and helps both sides feel that they have done equally well in the negotiation.

The important point about limits isn't what they are, but whether they overlap. If they do, you will almost certainly reach a deal; if they don't, you almost certainly won't. You need to find this out quickly to avoid wasting everybody's time.

Remember: it's not just the sale price you need to consider. Other factors such as how quickly you can take possession, the size of your deposit, which extra items are included (garden sheds, white goods, carpets etc.) are also important. All must be finalized before the deal is done.

Most people who buy a house do so without really understanding what is happening. If you don't understand the process you can't be in control of it.

3 BUYING THE HOUSE

Most people who buy a house do so without really understanding what is happening or why. If you don't understand the process, you can't be in control of it, which is not an ideal position to be in when so much of your money is at stake. I've written this chapter in order to demystify the property-buying process so that you can take control of it and make it work for you.

In an era when we're becoming increasingly used to the idea of buying instantly with the click of a mouse button, the property-buying process is beginning to look very long-winded and old fashioned. Despite new legislation and improved technology, it still takes as long to buy a house today as it did fifty years ago. Property costs a lot of money, so it's important to check out all the potential problems, and it's this that takes most of the time.

BUYING BY PRIVATE TREATY

The term 'private treaty' is these days rarely used outside Ireland, and this section could equally well have been titled 'Buying in the normal way' (whatever that means).

   The process starts when you and the owner have agreed a price. You might think that once you reach this stage everything is in the bag, but over a third of property sales fall through after an offer has been accepted. Many of these failures are avoidable if you're in control.

CONVEYANCING

The correct though almost never used term for this process is 'conveyance', but whatever you call it, most people employ an expert to do it for them.

➧ Traditionally, solicitors are used, but you can appoint a licensed property conveyancer (another made-up word) instead. Some solicitors are very good at conveyancing, but there is no doubt that it lacks glamour. Preparing a defence case for a juicy criminal trial is much more exciting than your boring old house purchase. Consequently conveyancing jobs tend to be farmed out to the office junior or pushed down the order. Licensed property conveyancers have no such distractions and tend to be a bit cheaper, too. Many are web based and communicate via email or text. This speeds things up a bit, although not by as much as you might think.

➧ One way of saving money is for both sides to use the same conveyancer – fewer people involved should result in a less adversarial approach, a quicker turnround and lower fees – but it's a bit risky. A conveyancer working for both parties may find themselves with a conflict of interest if they discover a problem that could cause the sale to fall through. Many conveyancers operate on a no-sale, no-fee basis, so when push comes to shove most of them would prefer a sale to go through.

➧ There is nothing to stop you doing the conveyancing yourself; it's not that difficult, especially if the property is freehold. But the consequences of messing it up are severe and you could lose an awful lot of money. You can buy a pack containing all the necessary paperwork from most legal stationers, major bookshops or H M Land Registry (contact details are in the directory). If you take this route, follow the forms and make sure you don't leave anything out. You could also get a solicitor to check what you have done; they might be a bit sniffy about doing so, but they'll charge you considerably less than they would have for the conveyancing.

Once you have agreed the sale price with the seller you need to tell your conveyancer, who will then produce a 'memorandum of sale'. This is a letter to the owner's conveyancer confirming the details of the accepted offer.

In England and Wales most of the initial stages of conveyancing will be covered by the home information pack (see above, p. 36). This will put the onus of supplying all the information up to the contract of sale on to the seller. The original process outlined here will continue to operate elsewhere in the UK and could even return in England and Wales should the home information pack system prove unsuccessful. The differences in the Scottish and Irish buying processes are outlined later in the chapter.

Home information packs will include a survey of the property, the title deeds, a copy of the land registry entry, the lease (if applicable), local authority search results, completed pre-contract enquiry questionnaire and a draft contract of sale. Your conveyancer's job is to check all this and advise you how to proceed.

Where home information packs aren't in operation your conveyancer will need to:

✚ Check the title deeds of the property and land registry entry, largely to make sure that the seller is actually in a position to sell. Outright fraud is rare, but property can, for example, have joint owners, or be owned by a trust, by a company, by receivers after a company has folded or be in probate after an owner has died. Any of these could mean that the person selling the property has no legal right to do so.

✚ Check the legality of the lease if the property is leasehold. Most leases are fine, but some can put unreasonable responsibilities on the leaseholder.

✚ Carry out a local authority search to ensure that, for example, there are no plans to build a road through the property. More frequently, dilapidated properties may have outstanding notices, orders or charges on them served by the local authority requiring the owner to repair or improve the property. If the seller has not done so and the requirement is still in force you will inherit it. Sometimes, if a notice hasn't been complied with, the local authority do the work themselves and charge the owner. If the bill wasn't paid, a charge may be put on the property. The search will also reveal any planning restrictions. Although most local authorities will reply to searches in a couple of weeks some can take up to two months. If you want to hurry things along you can opt for a manual search, whereupon the conveyancer, for an increased fee, will contact each council department individually to obtain the information.

✚ Send pre-contract enquiries to the seller's conveyancer. This is usually a standard questionnaire that aims to find out details such as: What is included in the sale and what do the owners intend to take with them? Where are the boundaries of the property? Who owns perimeter walls, fences or hedges? You will need the answers to these questions before you can proceed with the sale.

✚ Receive and check the contract of sale. This is the document that transfers ownership of the property to you. The seller's conveyancer prepares it. At this stage it's just a draft and is often amended later. It has two parts: the particulars of sale and the conditions of sale. The particulars describe the property, states who the buyers and sellers are and gives details of any leases. The conditions of sale contain information about the agreed sale price and details of what is included in it. It also specifies the date on which the sale will take place (the completion date).

From this point on the process is more or less the same irrespective of whether home information packs are in operation or not.

SIGNING CONTRACTS

When buyer and seller are satisfied with the contract of sale the conveyancers send it to both parties for signature. At this point the moment is fast approaching when you'll be contractually obliged to buy the property so you need to make sure that you're in a position to proceed. It would be foolhardy to go beyond this point without a full written mortgage offer, a survey report of the property accepted by you and your lender and an agreed completion date for the sale in the contract, or without having resolved any issues about who is paying for what.

EXCHANGING CONTRACTS

When you're happy, you return your signed contract to your conveyancer who will exchange it with the contract signed by the seller. You then need to sign the contract from the seller and return this to your conveyancer, so that both conveyancers have identical versions of the contract signed by both parties. This is called exchange of contracts. At this point you need to provide the money for the deposit on the property (normally 10 per cent although a different amount can be agreed between the two parties). Your conveyancer may want to be paid at this point too.

COMPLETION

The final stage is completion. This is when the exchange of ownership actually takes place. It can happen on the same day as contracts are exchanged or can take place weeks or even months later, depending on what has been agreed in the contract. If the sale is complicated and there are lots of things to sort out it's better to give yourself a good length of time between exchange and completion so that there are no last-minute hitches. The better organized your conveyancing the less potential there is for disaster. Completion takes place when the funds are transferred from you and/or your lender to the seller; the conveyancer and the estate agent take their fees and at the same time ownership of the property is transferred to you. When everything is done your conveyancer or the estate agent will get in touch and tell you so. You can now go and pick up the keys from them as the proud owner of your new property.

ODDS AND ENDS
There are a few loose ends to tie up after completion. Your conveyancer will arrange for the title deeds to be transferred into your name and sent to your lender, or to you if you bought the property without a loan. They will also arrange for the land registry entry to be suitably amended and if the property is held on a lease they'll make sure that your name is on it.

BUYING AT AUCTION

Most people have got at least one good story about somebody making a life-ruining decision at an auction. The one I like best is the lady who put a large luxury house up for sale with a guide price of just £10. Everybody was a bit suspicious and in the end only one person bid. After handing over his tenner the lucky new owner asked the seller why it was so cheap. 'The terms of my divorce settlement were that I was to sell the property for whatever I could and divide the proceeds equally with my ex husband,' she said. 'I don't really need the money – but he does.'

Most of us know very little about buying at auctions. What we do know has been gleaned partly from fact and partly from anecdotes and TV sitcoms. Not surprisingly, people are rather wary of them. Despite this, auctions can be a good way to buy property. Certainly, if you don't know what you're doing you could get yourself into a big mess in a short time, but the same could be said for any method of buying property. Prepare properly and there's no reason why you can't buy a good property at a good price with minimal risk.

If your sole experience of auctions is from *Only Fools and Horses* you may be under the impression that bidding at an auction is all about spontaneity and impulse. This is fine for the school fête when it's only a box of biscuits falling under the hammer, but when you're buying property things become rather more serious. Prior to bidding, you need to be certain what you want and what you can pay, research the properties, sort out your finances and be ready to progress with the sale quickly.

If your sole experience of auctions is from *Only Fools and Horses* you may be under the impression that bidding at an auction is all about spontaneity and impulse.

FINDING YOUR AUCTION

Even if there appear to be no auctions near to you, it doesn't follow that no properties in your locality are sold in this way. Some auction houses sell properties right across the UK. These national auctioneers are mostly based in London, but there are one or two in Manchester and Edinburgh. A greater proportion of properties are sold by auction in Ireland than the UK, but these tend to be at the top end of the market (UK auction lists comprise mainly cheaper properties). The big Irish operators are based in Dublin. Once you have decided which auctioneers best suit you, ask to be included on their mailing lists. You will then receive their catalogue early, giving you longer to research potential properties you may want to bid for. Some auction houses provide online catalogues and there are specialist sites that monitor all the auction catalogues and will, for a fee, inform you about any properties that are coming up for auction that meet your criteria.

WHAT ABOUT THOSE RISKS?

In many ways preparing for an auction is like preparing for any other kind of property purchase. It's just that the time scale is much stricter, and things are done in a slightly different order. These differences throw up two areas of risk. First, and unavoidably it you're buying in an area where home information packs are not in force, you have to spend some money up front on a survey and some conveyancing work before the auction. If the survey or the research by your conveyancer uncovers something that puts you off, or you get outbid at the auction, that money has been spent for nothing. But this is not really so different from buying a home by the conventional method in which, although you don't part with any money until your offer has been accepted, you can still get gazumped or be deterred by an unfavourable and expensive survey. Second, and more avoidably, if you fail to prepare properly for the auction, you could end up being liable for 10 per cent of the purchase price.

A comprehensive list of auction houses in England and Wales, together with some in Scotland, can be found on the Empty Home Agencies website www.emptyhomes.com.

Before you bid for a property, I'd suggest that you make the following preparations:

✚ Attend an auction

With so much at stake it's not a good idea to start bidding for a property at the first auction you ever visit. You'll be wondering how it all works and working out what to do and suddenly your lot is next. To make things easier, why not visit a property auction beforehand, just to get a feel for it? You'll come to the next one far more confident if you do.

✚ Obtain the catalogue

Catalogues give details of properties that are coming up in the next auction. You might be surprised to find out that they are often published only three or four weeks before the auction day. This doesn't give you much time to prepare, so you need to be organized in advance. Catalogues don't go into great detail beyond a photograph or two, a location map, maybe a floor plan, some details of the type of tenure and an indication of the guide price. The guide price is nothing more than that, an estimate of the eventual sale price. This isn't the same as the reserve price. The reserve is the lowest bid that would be accepted and will often be set lower (usually by at least 10 per cent) than the guide price. Although it would be very helpful to know the reserve price, nobody is going to tell what it is since you would then have an unfair advantage. However, you could try making a private offer in advance of the auction. It's not unusual for a seller to accept a bid in this way if they consider it sufficiently attractive – around 15 per cent of properties in the auctioneers' catalogues are sold prior to auction day.

✚ Work out what you can afford

Think about the total costs of your project, including purchase, renovation and conversion costs, architects' and solicitors' fees. Then calculate the absolute maximum you can afford for the whole project. Take away all the costs except the purchase of the property and set your ceiling price just below this. Don't over-stretch yourself, you can be sure that some unexpected cost will arise at some stage during your project and it's wise to keep some money back just in case.

✚ View the property

Bidding for a property on the strength of the catalogue details alone is just plain silly. Amazingly, though, some people do exactly this. You wouldn't consider buying a property from an estate agent without visiting it first, and an auction is no different. It's a good idea to arrange to view a property that you like as soon as possible after seeing it in the auction catalogue. Usually the auctioneers set up a viewing day when everybody who is interested in bidding can attend. You simply book your slot (the day may even be advertised in advance in the catalogue). Alternatively, the auctioneer may nominate a local agent to show you round, or even lend you the keys in exchange for a deposit.

✚ Put your finances in place

If your bid is successful, you'll have to pay a
10 per cent deposit immediately after the auction
finishes, so take 10 per cent of your maximum
purchase budget with you. Auction houses will
usually accept a banker's draft or building society
cheque. Ask your bank or building society to issue
one for 10 per cent of the maximum you want to
bid. If you manage to buy the property for less
than this then the auctioneer will refund you the
difference. Don't try to pay in cash; not only
will you look like a gangster, you may very well
get treated like one. Auction houses have to
guard against being used in money-laundering
operations and your wad of used notes is bound
to arouse suspicion.

You need to have a firm mortgage offer
from your lender before the auction (see Chapter
13). Don't forget to tell your lender that you're
buying at auction. Most lenders will probably be
happy to help, but won't like it if you announce
to them you have just bought at auction without
first obtaining their agreement. Be sure that
you borrow enough. Your mortgage offer and
any cash deposit must cover the maximum cost
of the purchase. If you manage to get a bargain
at the auction and end up borrowing less than
you arranged there is unlikely to be a problem,
but if it's the other way round you could be
in trouble.

✚ Appoint a conveyancer

You need to have made your conveyancing
arrangements before you turn up at the auction.
As with private treaty, you can use a solicitor or
a licensed conveyancer or you can do your own
conveyancing. If you're buying in an area where
the home information pack is in operation, all the
information you need should be available to you
in advance. All you need to do is check it and
make sure that your lender is happy to lend you
the money. Elsewhere you might not get as much
information, but the auctioneer can usually
provide at least the title deed for you to inspect.
You'll probably need to carry out local authority
and other searches as well as checking out the
land registry entry. (You may need to do a manual
search at your local authority if time is tight.
See the conveyancing section earlier in this
chapter for more details.)

✚ Arrange a survey

Your lender will require a survey and valuation
to be carried out before making a mortgage offer.
Where home information packs are in operation,
the seller should provide these for you. Elsewhere
you'll need to arrange for your own survey
through your lender. As with any other property
purchase you must decide whether to opt for
a basic valuation, a homebuyers' report or
a full structural survey.

Once you have completed your preparations, follow these steps on the day of the auction:

➡ Before you set out, ring the auction house to make sure that the property you're interested in is still for sale. Properties are sometimes withdrawn at the last minute, usually because the owner is one of those 15 per cent who accept a private offer before the auction.

➡ The auction house will usually give out update sheets to the catalogue as you arrive at the auction room. This will tell you about any alterations to the properties for sale, including those that have been withdrawn. Occasionally new properties will be added at the last minute, but you'd be very brave to consider bidding for these unprepared.

➡ Get to the venue early so you can collect yourself before the auction starts. Most people operate better if they aren't flustered by a rushed journey.

➡ Register your interest before the auction starts. The auctioneer's clerk will take your details and usually you receive a card with a number on it. This is for you to wave at the auctioneer if you want to make a bid. The number identifies who is bidding, so don't swap with anybody else. If there is no card system, just use your hand.

➡ Bid. The auctioneer will usually explain the rules and procedures first, then begin the proceedings by describing a property and naming a starting price. Bids usually increase in £5,000 increments. (For very cheap properties the increments will be less and for very expensive properties, more.) Although most people go along with the auctioneer's increments, there is nothing to stop you bidding for a different amount. To do this you need to raise your hand and say how much you bid.

➡ Win. If your bid is the highest and the reserve price has been met, you've won! The property is yours. The auctioneer's clerk will ask you for your details and the details of your solicitor or conveyancer. They'll also ask you for proof of identity, so make sure that you take some with you.

If the reserve price isn't met, then the lot is usually withdrawn from sale. If the highest offer the auctioneer receives meets or is above the reserve price then the sale has to be completed. You'll normally be able to tell when the bidding passes the reserve price because the auctioneer will say something such as, 'I am here to sell'. Different auctioneers have their own phrases, which is one reason it's a good idea to watch a few lots first before you start bidding.

➡ Pay your 10 per cent deposit immediately. Once you have done this you'll be asked to sign a document called the auction memorandum. In return you'll be given the contract document. This is more or less the same process as signing and exchanging contracts in a normal property purchase. Needless to say, the contract document is a vital piece of paper, it proves you have agreed to buy the property. Don't lose it.

➡ Move on. Send the contract to your solicitor or conveyancer within a day or so. This will enable them to proceed straight away.

➡ Pay the balance of the payment. Usually it needs to be transferred within a month of the auction. This is one reason you need to make your financial arrangements beforehand; if you can't raise the balance by the deadline you could well lose your deposit as well as the property.

SOME TIPS TO HELP YOU BID

✚ Decide which property you're going to bid for and your absolute maximum price. Most problems arise when people have last-minute changes of mind or allow themselves to be carried away by the excitement of an auction. It's very tempting to stray above your price limit if you think that by doing so you will secure your property, but try to be disciplined. If you miss this one, there will always be another.

✚ If you don't want to bid yourself you could get somebody else to do it for you. Your solicitor or conveyancer will probably be happy to do this for you but, of course, they'll charge you for their time.

✚ Don't worry if you scratch your nose or get a fly in your eye; it's unlikely that the auctioneer will mistake it for a bid. If somehow you manage to bid accidentally for something you don't want, tell the auctioneer or another member of staff before the hammer goes down.

✚ If the property fails to make its reserve price and is withdrawn from sale, you could approach the seller after the auction and make an offer.

✚ If you do miss out, don't be tempted to go for another property you have done no preparatory work on.

✚ Don't be too disappointed if you don't get the property that you were after. There will be other days.

If you're interested in finding out more about buying property at auctions, Howard Goodie's *Buying Property at Auctions* is a comprehensive guide.

BUYING A HOUSE IN SCOTLAND

There are significant differences in the way properties are bought and sold in Scotland, primarily relating to the order in which things are done. These differences apply to both private treaty and auction sales. What follows concerns buying by private treaty, but it should be easy enough to see from this and the previous section what you need to do when buying at auction.

PREPARING TO MAKE AN OFFER

The first thing to do, even before you start looking at houses, is to arrange your finances. If you require a mortgage you need to get an agreement in principle from your lender saying how much you can borrow.

Next you must arrange your conveyancing. You can use a licensed conveyancer or do it yourself; most people in Scotland use solicitors. They are more involved in the process than their counterparts in England and Wales, and carry out many of the estate agent's functions south of the border. (Although it could be argued that this makes it a less boring job, many of the comments I made on p. 49 apply here too.)

You can now go property hunting. When you have found one that you want to buy, tell your conveyancer. Your conveyancer will then contact the seller's conveyancer and 'note interest'. Once you have done this the seller will be obliged to let you know if anybody else makes an offer for the property. This gives you the opportunity to put in your own offer should you wish.

Before you make an offer you need to make a full application for your mortgage. This will involve the lender getting a survey and valuation carried out. If other people are interested in buying the property this might seem like a painful delay at a critical time, but don't forget that all your competitors will be in the same situation as you. Getting the valuation carried out before you make an offer does actually make sense. In Scottish law once you make an offer you have entered into a binding contract. This means that if the seller accepts your offer you're obliged to complete the sale. This could be very difficult if your lender refuses to advance you money after receiving the results of the survey and valuation. The downside is that you'll have to pay for a survey and valuation before you know whether you're even going to make an offer for the property. If you decide not to proceed, you won't get your money back for the survey.

MAKING AN OFFER

Once the valuation and survey have been carried out, your lender will make you a formal mortgage offer. With this in place you can make an offer for the property.

The seller sets and advertises what is sometimes called the upset price. This is similar to a guide price at auction in that prospective purchasers are expected to treat this as a minimum and bid above it. Only in areas of low demand and in times of depressed house prices will a seller accept an offer below the upset price.

If there is more than one person making an offer for a property the seller's conveyancer will start a round of sealed bids. A deadline will be set by which time all bids must be received. Once the deadline has passed the conveyancer will open all the bids that were received before the deadline for the seller to consider. Usually the seller accepts the highest offer, but is under no obligation to accept any of them. In fact, if they feel so inclined, the seller can open another round of sealed bids. Your offer should include any other information you think important. You should state the date on which you can complete and say if there are any extras you want included in the price (a garden shed, for example). One trick is to offer an amount slightly over a round number. For example, if you were considering offering £120,000, put in an offer for £120,002 (not £120,001, just in case somebody else is on to the same trick!).

One trick is to offer an amount slightly over a round number. For example, if you were considering offering £120,000, put in an offer for £120,002 (not £120,001, just in case somebody else is on to the same trick!).

FINALIZING THE DEAL

If your offer is accepted the sale is very unlikely to fall through. That old English pastime of gazumping is virtually unknown in Scotland. There are, however, things to do. The first of these is to complete the 'missives', which is the equivalent of exchanging contracts in England and Wales. The two conveyancers exchange letters to finalize a number of details that have not already been agreed. Chief amongst them is setting the completion date (often referred to as the entry date). This is usually set about a month after the letter, but you can agree on whatever day suits you. Once both parties are happy with all the details, the missives are said to have been concluded.

A week or two before the entry date your conveyancer will send you a bill covering your deposit, stamp duty and their own fees. Sometimes the seller will allow you to have the keys at this point, especially if the property is empty.

The day before entry day your lender will transfer the necessary funds to your conveyancer. (If you're buying a property without a mortgage you'll need to pay the balance to your conveyancer on this day.) You'll then have to sign the title deed. Your conveyancer will then either send this to your lender, or will give it to you if you're buying the property without a loan. On entry day you'll have to sign another document called the disposition, which transfers the property ownership to you. You'll need a witness with you for all these signings, to verify that you are who you say you are. Once you have done this the conveyancer will give you the keys (if you haven't got them already) and the property is yours.

BUYING A HOUSE IN IRELAND

The process of buying a house in Ireland has much more in common with the (pre home information pack) process in England and Wales than the process in Scotland. Again this guide is for buying a property by private treaty but much the same applies when buying at auction.

First, find your property and agree a price with the owner. Where there is a lot of interest in a property an auctioneer (the term includes estate agents in Ireland) may start a closed bid or private tender. This is a less formal version of the sealed-bids system used in Scotland. A closing date is set and anybody who is interested can enter a bid either in writing or verbally. Usually the person with the highest bid wins. In other cases the system works much as in England and Wales. However you arrive at it, once you have agreed a purchase price with the seller, let your conveyancer know.

Conveyancers in Ireland are usually solicitors, but as elsewhere you can use a licensed conveyancer or do it yourself. Whoever you use, conveyancers in Ireland tend to go straight into preparing the contract of sale first. Usually the contract is a conditional one, which means that you can sign it early, but you can get out of it if one or more of the conditions aren't met. Conditions often include your obtaining a mortgage offer and the survey and searches being satisfactory. As you can imagine, this encourages people to sign contracts with rather more abandon than they do elsewhere in the British Isles since they have much less to lose. Sellers and auctioneers have become less than enamoured by such thinking and it's not uncommon for an auctioneer to insist on the buyer having a loan offer before contracts are signed. Irish lenders have responded to this development quite well and it's possible to get a provisional loan offer in two or three days. Whichever approach is taken you'll need to come up with your deposit at this stage and pay it to your conveyancer.

Meanwhile, the conveyancer will carry out much the same checks as anywhere else, although there are a few minor differences. Usually they will:

Check the title deeds of ownership and the land registry entry to ensure that the owner is entitled to sell it.

Check that the property was built in accordance with planning regulations, building standards and building by-laws.

Carry out a planning search with the local authority to check any planning restrictions on the property and see if any proposed developments are planned near by.

Carry out a compulsory purchase order search to make sure that the property isn't in the path of a proposed new highway.

Check that there are no outstanding debts (encumbrances) such as mortgages, loans or unpaid bills secured against the property. If there are, under Irish law, you as the new owner will inherit them.

Check whether capital gains tax (CGT) has been paid. The seller is obliged to pay this on sale of the property and will usually provide a CGT certificate to prove that it has been paid. If this doesn't materialize you'll have to pay the CGT yourself and then try to claim it back either from the Revenue Commissioners, if the CGT was paid but the seller couldn't produce the certificate, or from the owner personally if it was never paid. CGT is currently running at 15 per cent of the purchase price in Ireland (for most properties), so this will be a significant expense.

When your conveyancer has received all this information, they'll ask whether you still want to go ahead with the purchase and, if you do, they'll draft a deed of transfer. This document, when agreed and signed, transfers the property to you. Then starts the most extraordinary game of legal ping-pong. If you're happy with the deed of transfer you sign it, your conveyancer then sends it to the seller's conveyancer for the seller to sign (if they are happy with it). It's then returned to your conveyancer for what is grandly called engrossment. This actually just means getting it typed up. You sign it again in duplicate (you only signed the draft version last time) and it is then returned to the seller's conveyancers to sign again. One of the two identical versions comes back to your conveyancer, who sends it to your lender along with the title deed. At the same time the remaining balance of the money is transferred from your lender (or from you, if you're buying without a loan). This completes the purchase. Finally, you can collect the keys.

Just because you're planning to rescue
a house doesn't mean you should ignore
all the usual considerations when
choosing somewhere to live.

4 IS THIS THE RIGHT HOUSE FOR YOU?

Rescuing a house is like negotiating an obstacle course; the
path is littered with pitfalls and barriers, all of which can be
traversed provided that you know how. An athlete wouldn't
start running the course without knowing the nature of those
obstacles, and neither should you. So think of this chapter as a
bit of pre-race training before you decide whether you want to
run with the property.

IS THE LOCATION ACCEPTABLE?

Later in this book I'll talk you through the various ways in which you can change and improve a house to make it right for you, but there's little you can do about its location. You might get lucky and buy into one of those mythical 'on the up' areas that change into a fashionable district before your very eyes, but, sadly, that these are much rarer than you might think. Most grotty areas were grotty a hundred years ago and will probably stay grotty for years to come. Different amenities are important for different people. Good local schools won't be of much interest to you if you have no school-age children, but there are plenty of other things to take into account.

THE WEATHER

The climate varies hugely from one part of these islands to another. On the whole the further east you go the drier it gets and the further south the warmer it gets. But just as significant is altitude. The higher you are above sea level, the harsher the winters will be. Some areas are regularly cut off by snow in winter. This may not be obvious if you're viewing a property in August.

VIEWS

Nice views really can subconsciously sell a property. Don't ignore your emotions, these things are important. You'll very quickly get fed up with a view of a brick wall, but you'll never tire of a panoramic vista.

COMMUTING

How easy will it be for you to get to work? Or, if you're planning to change jobs, is the area one in which you can find employment? How congested are the roads and public transport at the times you'll need to travel?

PARKING

Is there adequate off- or on-street parking? In some cities you may have to park a considerable distance from your house. How will you feel about this when you're laden down with shopping bags or screaming children?

SHOPS, PUBS AND RESTAURANTS

How good and how close are local facilities? A good pub in walking distance is a major boon to some people. Swanky restaurants and designer shops are a good sign of the prosperity and desirability of an area, but how often will you use them? Having a branch of Tesco five minutes down the road may be more important.

NOISE

You can't choose your neighbours, but you can choose a property that isn't too near busy roads, noisy factories or pubs and clubs. Of course, not everybody enjoys peace and quiet; some like to live where there is a bit of life and bustle. In the next chapter there is a section explaining how you can, to some extent, enjoy the best of both worlds.

FLOODING

Check to see whether the property is in an area that is prone to flooding. There are published flood-risk maps for all of England, Scotland and Wales that give every area a low, moderate or significant flood-risk rating according to location, predicted water levels and type and condition of flood defences. The maps are published by the Environment Agency in England and Wales and the Scottish Environmental Protection Agency in Scotland. There is talk of producing a similar map for Northern Ireland but for the moment the Rivers Agency can provide information. There is no risk map covering the Republic of Ireland at present. These maps are very useful, but you should consider them only as a guide. Talk to locals about recent flooding events and what happens to local rivers and streams at times of high rainfall. Floods are very destructive to property, and if the house is at risk you could be in for a lot of work. Not only will it cause real hardship to have to deal with a flood, you may also find that no insurance company will be prepared to insure your house.

SCHOOLS

Obviously important if you have or are planning to have children, but also bear in mind that good local schools have a big impact on house prices. Most state schools limit their intake to local catchment areas, the boundaries of which vary from one year to the next depending on the number of children of the intake age living in the area. Being close to a good school will dramatically increase your chances of being able to get your children into it. It will also make your house more desirable (and expensive) when you come to sell.

HEALTHCARE

National Health Service care standards are far from uniform across the country. In many areas local G Ps and dentists have full lists and are taking no new patients. Hospitals vary in both quality and facilities. If you have special health needs this could be a very important factor.

CRIME

The truth is that the vast majority of people are law abiding and only a small proportion of crime is targeted at private individuals. Nevertheless the incidence of crime varies enormously from one area to another, and living in a place with a high crime rate can make both your life a misery and your insurance premiums higher. In areas with high burglary rates it can be all but impossible to get contents cover. The Home Office publishes local crime statistics, but almost as revealing can be to telephone a few insurance companies and see what you are quoted for buildings, contents and motor insurance.

There is more information on flooding, and dealing with the effects of it, in Chapter 7.

ARE YOUR PLANS FEASIBLE?

There could be numerous people you need approval from before you can go ahead with your plans to rescue a house. Planning permission is an obvious barrier, but there are lots of other consents you may need to obtain before you can do what you have in mind. Many of these take the form of legal rights that others may have over the property. The need to obtain consents introduces a degree of risk into any project; if permission is refused you could be left with a property you can't use.

Just because you are, or may become, the legal owner of a property doesn't mean that other people have no legal rights over it too. If this is the case you may have to seek their permission before any alterations can take place. Failure to do so might scupper the whole project, but you should never risk going ahead anyway. The other party could take out an injunction to halt the work, you could be sued for damages and in extreme cases you could face criminal charges. Fortunately, such dramatic encounters are rare. More frequent are simmering disputes that lead to frayed relations with your neighbours. Such problems occur most frequently in urban situations, particularly when the property is a flat.

There are a number of legal rights that may exist over a property, the most common of which are detailed below.

+ A lease

Even if a property is empty occupancy rights may still exist. The ultimate owner may have granted a lease, that leaseholder may have granted a sublease and so on, so there could be a string of people benefiting from occupancy rights. You may be proposing to buy one of the leases, but you need to check if there are others.

+ An easement

An easement is an agreement with another party giving right of way or the right to restrict the use of the property in some way. A common easement is for an occupier of an upper-floor flat to have access through the front garden of the ground-floor flat. Easements restricting use are often referred to as restrictive use covenants. Easements are common and not a reason for abandoning a purchase. Just make sure you understand the implications before you proceed.

✚ A tenancy

A tenancy is an agreement that a property owner makes with somebody else to allow them to occupy their property. Even if nobody is living in the property it doesn't follow that there is no tenancy in place. If there is, you'll have to take action to gain possession. If the tenancy has, in effect, been abandoned, this should be relatively straightforward, but what action you take will depend on what sort of tenancy is in place. In the UK there are many types of tenancy, but in the context of otherwise apparently empty property there are only three you're likely to come across: an assured tenancy, an assured shorthold tenancy and a regulated tenancy.

Put simply, an assured shorthold tenant has the fewest rights and a regulated tenant the most. To find out what sort of tenancy somebody has you need to find out when they moved in. After 27 February 1997: probably an assured shorthold tenancy. Between 15 January 1989 and 28 February 1997: it will be an assured tenancy unless the landlord specifically stated at the time that it was an assured shorthold tenancy. Before 15 January 1989: a regulated tenancy.

The situation in Ireland is similar, but a further complication is that a tenant who has stayed in the same tenancy for more than a year has the right to convert the tenancy into a four-year agreement, effectively giving them security of tenure for three more years. If you're buying a tenanted property you should check out the tenancy arrangements to make sure that the owner really can sell to you with vacant possession. Unless you have a comprehensive knowledge of tenancy law, a solicitor is the best person to do this.

✚ Mortgage conditions

A previous owner may have borrowed money secured on the property, either when he or she acquired it or later on. Under the mortgage agreement the lender is likely to have secured various rights such as re-entry or repossession. You shouldn't presume that the mortgage or these rights would automatically be removed if the property ownership were transferred to you. The best course of action in these circumstances is to speak to the lender and ask if they would be prepared to remove them. Usually they will, and things can be sorted out quickly. Never proceed with a purchase until these issues have been resolved.

✚ Implied rights

Owners or occupiers of neighbouring properties may have rights implied by law. For example their agreement is needed before work can be carried out to party walls. Right of access to your property may be implied for maintenance. Another common implied right is the right to natural light. This may restrict any potential development of your property that reduces the natural light available to your neighbour. Again not usually a reason for abandoning a purchase, implied rights exist in practically every situation where there is a neighbouring property. Be aware, though, that this could restrict your development plans.

The issues surrounding planning permission and Building Regulations approval are so important that I have devoted almost the whole of Chapter 8 to them. For now, this section concentrates on other possible issues and what to do about them.

PLANNING RESTRICTIONS

Planning permission is a huge subject. There are two or three planning issues to consider at this stage.

✚ Permitted use

Most buildings and land have a planning use class assigned to them; for example agricultural, residential, retail. You can use the building for any purpose falling within this use class, but if you want to use it for something else you need to apply for planning permission to do so. For example, if you buy a barn to convert into a house, you'll need to apply to change the permitted use from agricultural to residential. If your application is rejected, that barn you bought may turn out to be a complete waste of money.

Some properties have no permitted use assigned to them at all. This is usually because the property has been used for the same thing for so long that it predates planning law. There is nothing unlawful or even unusual about this.

✚ Established use

If your house has no permitted use assigned to it, but has been used as such for a good few years, it'll be the same. A property that has been used for the same purpose for ten years or more has effectively decided its own planning use class. You can apply for planning consent to confirm and regularize this use, but you don't have to; the only real advantage is that it might make things easier when you come to sell the property in the future. Problems can arise when a property has an ambiguous use, or indeed no use at all. A space above a shop with no permitted use class assigned to it that has lain empty for the last ten years would be a case in point. In such an instance you would need to apply for consent to change the permitted use to suit your plans.

✚ Planning permission

This is required for all development, so if a previous owner carried out alterations they would almost certainly have needed to obtain planning permission first. If they didn't do so, you could well find it difficult to raise a mortgage. (Irish lenders seem to be particularly strict on this.) Happily, the problem is usually solvable. In both the UK and Ireland it is possible to apply retrospectively for planning permission, often called regularization. You should ask the seller to obtain regularization as a condition of the sale. In the UK the established use rule applies here too, so if something was built without planning permission more than ten years ago then the requirement for planning permission lapses. In other words, if the owner has got away with it this long, they're off the hook.

✚ Planning conditions

When planning applications are approved it's quite common for them to be approved with conditions. If you buy a property with planning conditions attached you will be bound by them. Conditions can relate to all sorts of things, for example how many families can live in the house, how many car parking spaces you need to provide or even who is allowed to own the house. Some conditions can make it difficult for you to raise a mortgage, so consider them carefully.

SQUATTERS

Squatters have certain legal rights and just because they have occupied a property without the owner's consent doesn't give the owner the right to remove them or even enter the property without their agreement. It would be foolish to buy a property with squatters already in it, but of course they could move in after you've bought it. Although you may be told it's easy to remove squatters, it isn't always. You shouldn't presume that somebody living in a once-empty property is a squatter. In some cases a tenancy may exist.

If you have squatters in your property you have two options: negotiate with them and seek a voluntary solution or apply to the county court for a possession order. It's best to seek legal advice before doing anything. If your lawyer can't resolve the problem, see if you can find somebody else to give you some independent advice. In the UK you could try the charity Shelter. Although Shelter's primary concern is to help people who are homeless or threatened with homelessness they do offer good impartial advice to property owners as well (their contact details are in the directory). They publish some excellent advice on their website and can help with enquiries over the phone. Many squatters are well aware of their legal rights and a botched attempt at eviction could leave you with a bigger problem than you started with.

There is nothing wrong with negotiating with squatters, most will be expecting the owner to take possession proceedings and so talking to them about what you're doing can help everybody to appreciate where they stand. If you intend to seek a possession order you need to apply to the county court. A fast-track procedure now exists in the UK that allows you to apply for an interim possession order, pending a judge's final decision.

This means that you should get vacant possession of the property much more quickly – twenty-four hours instead of twenty-eight days for the traditional approach.

If you intend to use the accelerated procedure you need to make your claim to the court within twenty-eight days of becoming aware that squatters are occupying your property. If you don't do this, the judge will take into consideration whether you should have known about the occupation sooner than you did.

The court will ask for an undertaking that you'll allow the occupier/s back on to the premises (with compensation) if the court later decides you were not entitled to a possession order, and that you will not re-let or sell the property or make it uninhabitable until the court makes its final decision by granting a full possession order. (This would probably mean that you couldn't start major building works.)

If the court grants an interim possession order the squatters will be required to leave within twenty-four hours and not return within twelve months. If they refuse they are committing a criminal offence and risk arrest by the police or eviction by a court bailiff. They may also be fined or imprisoned or both.

Breaking and entering isn't squatting, it's trespass. If somebody damages your property whilst gaining entry it's likely that the police will be able to deal with the situation. They have powers to remove trespassers immediately. However, it is very important to act quickly whilst the evidence of forced entry is still present. It also harms your cause if you put off reporting a break-in for days. If you exhibit no sense of urgency, you can hardly expect others to.

✚ Wildlife

A different type of legal right, but no less important. Bats and certain other species are protected by law. It's an offence to kill, injure, disturb, or capture them. It's also an offence to cause damage to bat roosts or obstruct access to or from them. It's your responsibility to find out whether there are bats in your property. Look carefully in loft spaces for droppings. It's no defence to say you didn't know they were there or that your actions were unintentional. If you do find bats you can get advice from the Bat Conservation Trust (see directory for contact details) or your local wildlife conservation trust on what to do. Some clever conversion schemes have actually taken place around bat roosts, leaving them undisturbed, but in most cases a bat roost could well scupper a loft-conversion scheme. Other species are also protected by law. Barn owls and swallows often nest in empty buildings and if you find their nests you should seek advice on how to avoid disturbing them. The people to contact are English Nature, Scottish Nature or the Countryside Council for Wales (see directory). There are other harmless creatures that may inhabit old empty buildings, too, and although they aren't all protected it's important to take them into account when planning building work. If there are nesting birds don't disturb them until after the young have fledged.

✚ What to do if there are legal rights over your property

Most properties have some legal rights over them; flats in particular will have several. The important thing isn't whether they exist or not, but whether they have the potential to affect the feasibility of your project. To decide this you must establish what legal rights exist then determine their potential effect, and, finally, see if you can address any of them.

The first move is to find out who is benefiting from the rights. This should be fairly obvious. In whose name is the tenancy? Who is the mortgagor (i.e. the company who funded the mortgage)? Contact them and see if it's possible to reach agreement on removing the legal right. Mortgagors will often be quite flexible – after all, it's in their interest to maximize the value of a property upon which they have a loan secured. Getting an empty property back into use will benefit them as well as you. If the person benefiting from the legal right is unwilling to remove or relax it, or cannot be traced, you can take legal action to remove the right by demonstrating that it no longer fulfils its original purpose.

Or you may decide that all the hassle involved alters the viability of the whole project.

IS IT FINANCIALLY WORTHWHILE?

There are any number of sound environmental reasons for rescuing a house, but for most of us the whole project needs to stack up financially as well. How much is it likely to cost to turn the property into what you want it to be and can you buy it cheaply enough to make your refurbishment cost effective? If the answer is no, you might as well spend the money on a property in better condition and save yourself the hassle. It might even be cheaper to demolish and rebuild.

Have a look round the property yourself; even if you aren't a building expert you should be able to get a rough idea of what you're letting yourself in for. If the layout of the property doesn't meet your needs and you intend to adapt or redesign it, think about how easy it would be to do. You should soon be able to tell the difference between those with real potential and the no-hopers that are best avoided.

Consider taking a surveyor along with you to give you a rough idea of what renovation works are needed and whether any alteration plans you may have are practicable. The surveyor should also be able to provide a ballpark figure of how much it's all going to cost. A builder could do much the same thing, of course, and for free, but unless you know and trust them there is a risk that their estimate may be pitched too high or too low, depending on whether or not they want the job. If you pay somebody a fixed fee for a survey they have no reason not to be objective and their report will prove invaluable if and when you need to obtain quotes for the work.

Even properties in good condition can be expensive propositions. A redesign and conversion can easily cost as much as or more than a refurbishment. Think about what you want to achieve and what alterations you may want to make (see Chapter 5).

Chapter 7 below details some of the problems commonly encountered in neglected buildings, so look out for the tell-tale signs.

If the layout of the property doesn't meet your needs and you intend to adapt or redesign it, think about how easy it would be to do. You should soon be able to tell the difference between those with real potential and the no-hopers that are best avoided.

The following issues are common ones that you might easily overlook.

✚ Utilities

It's always possible to get utilities (water, drainage, gas, electricity, telephone line) installed, but if you have a top-floor flat in a block with no gas supply it could be prohibitively expensive. There is an urban myth about a BT promotion campaign shortly after the UK telecom deregulation offering free connection to any property. One resident of a remote Hebridean island took them up on it and BT was obliged to install a new undersea cable at a cost of millions. It is unlikely you'll be this lucky. Although deregulation of the utility industries has increased the number of suppliers from which you can choose, there is often no choice regarding the infrastructure. For example, Transco is responsible for the installation and maintenance of gas pipes in the UK, but since they do not supply the gas itself, there is no incentive to attract new customers with free or heavily subsidized installation. If you want gas installed, Transco will charge you the full whack.

✚ Meters

Whether there are separate metered supplies for the utilities is usually an issue only for flats or for commercial properties that could be converted to residential use. Clearly, you don't want to be sharing gas or electricity bills with another flat or the shop downstairs, but separation of supplies can be expensive. For example you would need to install separate mains water supplies and stopcocks for each flat in a conversion. Many flat owners have been left literally high and dry when their neighbour has turned off the water and gone on holiday.

✚ Radon

Radon is a naturally occurring gas formed underground by the decay of radioactive minerals. It is potentially harmful to humans and has been linked with various cancers. Radon is most often present in Cornwall and Devon, but there are also hot spots in the limestone areas of Derbyshire, Northamptonshire, North Oxfordshire, Lincolnshire, and Somerset in England, Clwyd, Powys and Dyfed in Wales, Deeside and Gordon in the Grampian Region and Caithness and Sutherland in Scotland, the Mourne and Sperrin Mountain regions of Northern Ireland, and parts of counties Carlow and Sligo in Ireland.

It is not difficult to eliminate radon gas (see pp. 167–8), but unless you are planning a full-scale refurbishment the procedure could be both disruptive and expensive. For further information and advice on how to test for and eliminate radon contact the BRE radon helpline in the UK or the Radiological Protection Institute in Ireland (details in the directory).

✚ Japanese knotweed

Seriously! If the property has this aggressively invasive plant in its garden you should ask yourself whether you want to take it on. This monstrous weed is almost impossible to eradicate and can completely take over a garden. It has also been known to grow up through the floorboards of buildings and take over the inside too. Some estate agents say that a heavy infestation of the plant can devalue a property by 25 per cent, so either steer clear of properties that have it, or use it as a bargaining chip when negotiating the purchase price. For further information on Japanese knotweed see p. 163.

IS THE LAYOUT RIGHT?

First of all, is it big enough? This sounds obvious, but you need to consider the *potential* of the property, not just the prima facie evidence. If you want to extend or adapt the property you need to ask yourself some questions.

✚ Are the services in the right place?
Are the bathroom and kitchen in the best locations, for example? If the answer is no, all the water, waste pipes and drains will need to be rerooted, and that could cost a fortune.

✚ Have the utilities got sufficient capacity?
If you're intending to extend the property you might need a more powerful boiler and larger water tanks or an upgraded consumer unit (fusebox). An older property will almost certainly require rewiring, at least.

✚ How high are the ceilings?
If they are really high you might be able to squeeze another floor in. If they are really low a tall person might need a crash helmet. Is the loft space suitable for conversion?

✚ Where are the load-bearing walls?
Does your planned layout affect them? It's usually possible to replace a load-bearing wall with a suitable steel joist, but this is expensive.

✚ Are staircases in the right place?
If you want to change the layout, staircases can be relocated, but again this is neither easy nor cheap.

✚ Is there sufficient natural light?
If you need to add windows, will they overlooking neighbouring properties? (You'll need planning permission, and overlooking is a common reason for refusal.) For more on this problem and its solution see pp. 88–90.

✚ Is there an adequate fire escape?
What happens if the shop below catches fire? Would you know about it? Could you still get out? Do you need an automatic fire-detection system? If the property is multi-occupancy and is three or more storeys high the answer is probably yes. See pp. 96–7 for more on fire hazards and their prevention.

✚ Where's the dustbin?
Not usually a problem for houses, but in flats rubbish can be a real nuisance, especially if the occupants have no choice but to leave their smelly bin bags in the hall for a week.

✚ Is there wheelchair access?

Even if no one in your household has special needs you should bear in mind that the provision of wheelchair access is often a legal requirement in conversions and new properties, so it would be prudent as well as considerate to include it in your plans. Also, of course, none of us is getting any younger – it's as well to plan for the long term.

✚ Is there potential for a garden, a balcony or a roof terrace?

It may be hard to picture on a cold and blustery February day, but when the long, warm evenings arrive you'll envy those with even the tiniest balcony. If you have a family or are planning one, you'll need somewhere safe for children to play, but even you live alone, outside space is important. We all need somewhere we can get a lungful of fresh air and restore our sanity.

You will probably need to visit the property several times, preferably at different times of the day, before the answers to these questions become clear in your mind. This is another situation in which a surveyor's advice and opinions could prove to be invaluable. You could also ask your surveyor to give you a full set of measurements for each room and an opinion whether the rooms are of adequate size for your proposed use. This is important. Your own judgement will be subjective, and for some reason a room in a derelict house always looks smaller than one in good condition.

Outside space is important. We all need somewhere we can get a lungful of fresh air and restore our sanity.

For more on hiring a surveyor and having a property surveyed, see Chapter 9.

PART TWO PRACTICAL PLANNING

Rescuing a house isn't a new idea, and not one that the human race has a monopoly on. Hermit crabs predate humans by millions of years and they have been happily moving into second-hand mollusc shells for as long as they have been hermit crabs. Sand martins migrate to these shores from Africa and nest in cliff burrows that have been used time and again by generations of their forebears. But my favourite animal house recycler is the rabbit-eared bandicoot, partly for its wonderful name but also for its bizarre looks. A bandicoot is an Australian marsupial that looks like a cross between a kangaroo and a cartoon mouse. It lives in deep burrows like a rabbit and, although it's a competent burrow digger, it's happy to reuse and adapt an old one.

We humans do much the same. Fortunately, though, we are able to weigh up the alternatives and decide whether to restore a house to its former glory or change it into something that better meets our needs. This part of the book examines these options and the practical issues and problems surrounding them. Chapters 5 and 7 cover two very different approaches: redesign and restoration. In practice most rescue projects will be a mixture of the two, so you'd better read through both. Chapter 6 looks at ways to extend your living space

An existing building shapes as well
as restricts the design. With a little
imagination and a creative designer,
all sorts of things are possible.

5 DESIGN AND REDESIGN

A lot of housing in the UK and Ireland is very old, much older
than any of us. Just think how differently life is lived now from
a hundred years ago. We live in much smaller family groups; we
have electricity, own cars and enjoy hot and cold running water;
most of us are home owners rather than tenants; we live longer,
commute further and relocate more often. Then think about the
things we expect from our home: somewhere that's affordable,
cheap to run, continuously increasing in value and a showcase
for our possessions and good taste. Is it any wonder that our
ageing housing stock sometimes struggles to cope? This chapter
shows you how to decide what you want from a home and
redesign an old property accordingly.

With constant attention and investment many houses manage
to adapt very well to our changing lifestyles and expectations,
while some fail to keep up and their occupiers move on, leaving
the house behind.

But properties can be rescued and turned into places that
people are pleased to call home.

WHAT IS DESIGN?

Design is one of those words we all use yet find difficult to define. The 'designer' designation implies that something is desirable and expensive – a Giorgio Armani suit or, if you're a real style fanatic, maybe Philippe Starck's lemon juicer.

Good design begins with a good idea, becomes a good plan and ends in a good product. A well-designed house is in this sense no different from a hand-made pair of shoes. Good design doesn't need to be new, different, or fashionable, but it must meet the needs of the user. A well-designed house is both easy and pleasurable to inhabit.

Putting time, thought and (unavoidably) money into designing your new home is the most important factor in making it somewhere you want to be. It might sound glib, but get the design stage right and the rest becomes relatively easy. There is a tendency among many who start a rescued-house project to consider that design doesn't apply to them. After all, the building already exists and it's simply a case of 'doing it up'. This is rarely true. Of course, some projects simply require refurbishment, and a historic building is often best left unaltered, but in most cases your project would benefit from modification.

An existing building shapes as well as restricts the design. With a little imagination and a creative designer, all sorts of things are possible. If you need to trim your budget it's tempting to skimp on the design costs (much less painful than saying bye-bye to that sexy designer kitchen you'd promised yourself), but please don't. Good design will make the whole project worthwhile and will probably pay for itself in the long run. A well-designed house should be economical to run and will probably be worth more when you come to sell it.

Design is one of those words we all use yet find difficult to define. The 'designer' designation implies that something is desirable and expensive – a Giorgio Armani suit or, if you're a real style fanatic, maybe Philippe Starck's lemon juicer.

WHAT IS A WELL-DESIGNED HOUSE?

The simple answer is one that meets its occupant's needs and wants. Although we all make different demands on our homes, there are a number of requirements common to us all that old properties are traditionally bad at providing. These are the issues that most often need to be addressed when redesigning an obsolete building. Five of the most important are peace and quiet, good lighting, security, fire safety and use of space. In this chapter we will look at each of these areas in detail as well as looking at the design implications of the home room by room.

Urban Splash, an innovative regeneration developer based in Manchester, has, in conjunction with equally innovative architects Shed KM, brilliantly rethought the old Victorian terrace. It's probably the best recent example of modern design revitalizing old housing. The house is turned upside down: two bedrooms and the bathroom are on the ground floor while the upper floor has become one large multi-functional space incorporating all of the first floor and the roof space. The rear wall of the house is replaced with floor-to-ceiling glazing and the back yards are knocked together to form a communal outdoor recreational space for the whole terrace. The design has taken all that is good about modern flat living and applied it to resolve all that is bad about old Victorian terraces. The house makes full use of its space and its natural light, placing the areas used in the day where they receive light and leaving the darker parts of the house for rooms used at night. This example shows how design can turn something that nobody wants into something desirable – the very essence of rescuing a house.

MAKING A NOISY HOUSE QUIET

We live in an increasingly noisy world. If you have seen a noise map (a map that plots the average background noise levels across the country) you'll know how noise levels have increased almost everywhere in the last few decades. New roads, airports and housing have spread out from our major towns and cities. Almost everywhere you can hear at least a distant background hum of mechanical noise. In many urban areas that hum can become a roar. On top of this, locally produced noise from extractor fans, air-conditioning units, bustling pubs and clubs and boisterous neighbours can make things almost unbearable. Indeed, noise is one of the reasons that many urban properties have become abandoned.

But all is not woe. Advances in the understanding of the science of sound (acoustics) and in sound insulation and absorption products mean that we can, in theory, once again enjoy domestic peace and quiet in even the noisiest locations. Perhaps soon in practice, too, since recent changes in the Building Regulations in the UK have made pre-completion testing for noise transmission a legal requirement. For many properties, especially a conversion to flats, this could have a major impact on your project budget. Noisy locations usually have lower property values, and curing a cheap property's noise problem may prove to be a good investment.

HOW SOUND WORKS

Very simply put, sound is a wave of energy. As it passes through mediums such as air or building materials, they vibrate and pass the sound on. Our ears cannot hear all types of sound. Dog whistles and bats emit very loud, high-frequency sounds, but most of us can't hear them. Noise is simply unwanted sound that we *can* hear.

Noise can be stopped or reduced (attenuated) in two ways: it can be absorbed or it can be blocked. Materials that absorb sound do so by converting the energy into tiny amounts of heat. Metal foil is good at absorbing sound, for example, which is why recording studios used to be lined with the stuff. Other materials block sound, by shutting it out and reflecting it back. This is what we call sound insulation. Dense materials such as concrete and stone are good sound insulators. The best way to reduce noise transmission is to include both absorbers and insulators.

One of the difficulties of reducing noise in buildings is unpredictability. You can do everything you should, installing state-of-the-art insulation and absorption materials, and then when you come to do the test it doesn't work. The usual reason for this is a breach in the insulation. For insulation to work properly it has to be complete. If you have ever lived or worked in a building on a busy road, you'll know that opening a window just a crack can allow noise to flood in. It's a bit like a boat. Even a little hole in the hull will sink it.

HOW TO REDUCE NOISE

This is a specialist area and, although it's useful to understand the basics, if you're refurbishing a flat you'll need some expert advice. Many good surveyors are very knowledgeable about acoustics and know where to buy in specialist advice. Money spent on investigating the problems and planning your approach is usually well spent. Even the best sound-attenuation products will be wasted if they aren't in the right place or used in the right way.

You should expect schemes to concentrate on the acoustically weak areas of the property, usually be the floors and ceilings (particularly those separating your flat from your neighbour's) and the windows.

The approach to floors and ceilings is to increase their mass, often by installing a suspended ceiling. This is fine unless you have low ceilings or want to preserve a decorative one, in which case you'll need to insulate the floor above. A floating floor (the opposite of a suspended ceiling) will do this, or there is a seemingly very effective lining product called Acoustilay, but either way you'll need the agreement of whoever lives in the flat above yours. This could be easier said than done, particularly if they've got nice polished floorboards that you're proposing to cover up.

Noisy locations usually have lower property values, and curing a cheap property's noise problem may prove to be a good investment.

Windows are the weakest point in a building, acoustically speaking. Double glazing helps, but there's a problem in that the optimum gap between panes for thermal insulation is 20 mm while for acoustic insulation it's 100 mm. The best solution is triple glazing with both 20 mm and 100 mm gaps, but it's expensive, and you'll still have to do something about ventilation. If your property is near a noisy road, though, it's a good investment.

BRIGHTENING UP A GLOOMY HOUSE

There's nothing quite like natural light to improve your mood, and one of the things that make so many old or neglected houses feel so miserable and depressing is their lack of it. One of the features of modern interior design is to allow in a lot of natural light. Not only does it make us feel better, it makes rooms seem bigger, it shows off our possessions and decoration to their best and (something that is rarely appreciated) it's safer – fewer accidents happen in well-lit houses. Older houses were built with fewer and smaller windows than properties today, but often neglect has made things appear worse than they really are. Before you start knocking out internal walls, consider these ideas:

➥ What's happening outside? Are overgrown trees and shrubs blocking the light? Could they be pruned or cut down?

➥ When were the windows last cleaned? Dirty windows can reduce natural light by 70 per cent.

➥ What about the decoration? Dark colours absorb light; pale ones reflect it. Even wall surfaces that appear to be decorated in pale colours can actually be quite dark with years of accumulated grime. All that how-to-sell-your-house advice about clean neutral colours making rooms look bigger really is true.

➥ Can you borrow light? Houses built close together sometimes used to have a feature called a courtesy panel – a block of exterior wall painted white opposite a window. The result is surprisingly effective. Most of these have weathered away now, but you might be able to paint a new one opposite your windows.

➥ Similarly, white chippings or limestone paving stones outside will reflect the light upwards. Think how bright your house feels in the morning when it's snowed the night before. This creates the same effect all year round.

➥ Use big mirrors in dark hallways. Not only can you have the pleasure of looking at yourself every time you walk past, mirrors reflect back light even more effectively than a white wall.

➥ Use glazed internal doors (any glass panes more than 250 mm (10 in) wide or high will need to be of safety glass). You could even build some internal 'windows' using glass blocks. They are not to everyone's taste, but they are certainly effective and in the right location can be quite stylish.

If the property is still too dark, there are many structural changes you can make to brighten things up.

Daylight quality is improved by having it come from more than one direction. It means you get sunshine for a longer part of the day, and it helps to eliminate dark corners and shadows. Artists' studios almost always have windows in at least two walls for this very reason. There are two approaches: put more windows in, or take some walls out. Some layouts will lend themselves better to one kind of arrangement than others.

✚ Put in more windows

If you're going to put in more windows, think about the external appearance, too. The positioning of windows (fenestration) has a huge impact on what a house looks like. Handsome houses are like handsome people; all their features are in the right proportion and in the right place. Look around for old bricked-up window openings. If the lintel or arch is still intact you could easily open it up again.

✚ Enlarge existing windows

If you do this, bear in mind that making the opening a non-standard size will necessitate making a bespoke (and therefore expensive) window frame. You may also need planning permission, especially if the window overlooks another property. Overlooking issues can sometimes be resolved by using obscured glass (patterned, acid etched, sandblasted or just plain old frosted). Also be aware of potential hazards. Low windows on upper floors are easy to fall into or out of. You'll also need to make sure your replacement windows meet the latest Building Regulations standards (high performance double glazing and safety glass in potentially dangerous locations).

✚ Take out internal walls

Open-plan layouts can make homes appear much lighter. Although they don't increase the overall amount of light entering the house, they do get rid of some light-absorbing wall surfaces. Of course, an open-plan layout isn't for everyone. Once the internal walls are gone, it's not only light that can travel around unimpeded; so can noise, smells, children, pets and anything else you may want some occasional privacy from.

✚ Let in light from above

Consider a top-lit solution for dark corridors, halls and stairwells. Skylights can be fitted to both flat and pitched roofs, and don't usually require planning permission. Alternatively, you could go for a tubular skylight – a small dome located on the roof attached to reflective polycarbonate tubes. The light reflects down the tube and can bring natural light into a room up to 5 m away. These are ideal for small shower rooms or rooms without windows.

Velux windows can be fitted into pitched roofs; they are often the cheapest solution, because they are designed to be fitted from the inside, and can usually be installed without planning permission. Another increasingly popular choice is a flat glass roof. This works well on many types of property, and since it can't be seen from the ground you're less likely to have problems with planning permission than for domed or pitched glass roofs. A flat glass roof must be double glazed, with a laminated glass outer layer and an inner layer of toughened glass for safety.

✚ Designer solutions

If you're still in the dark there are some really swanky designer solutions available if your budget will stretch to them. Glass flooring can be used to allow more light into a basement, and you can even find glass staircases. All this may make your house look like a goldfish bowl, but technological help may be at hand. Privalite is an interesting new glazing product from the USA. Tiny LCD cells are embedded in it and at the flick of a switch it will turn from a black screen to a transparent sheet of glass. Brilliant, unless you're a curtain manufacturer. For more on all of this see the excellent book *An Introduction to Architectural Science* by Steven V. Szokolay, which explains the science behind how light, sound and heat work in buildings.

MAKING YOUR HOME SECURE

We all like to feel safe behind our own front doors. Household surveys show time and again that people's fear of crime is as inhibiting as the effects of crime itself. A regeneration project in east London recently found that many elderly people were clinically malnourished because they were too frightened of being burgled or mugged to leave their homes for long enough to shop properly, so lived off processed foods from the local convenience store.

But not all is doom and gloom. Crime is actually decreasing, most burglaries are committed on commercial property, not residential, and you can dramatically reduce your chance of being a victim. Most residential burglary is opportunistic, so by considering security in your design you can lengthen considerably the odds against suffering one. You don't have to turn your property into a residential Fort Knox. In fact, if you do, the local crooks will no doubt wonder what it is you have that warrants so much security. All that is required to deter most would-be burglars is to get him noticed and slow him down. Your local police crime prevention officer will be happy to advise you on security, but here are the basics.

GOOD LAYOUT

So far as is possible, try to eliminate dark corners and passageways where intruders can lurk unseen. Also try to restrict access to the less-visible areas of your property. If your back garden isn't overlooked, make sure it's difficult to get in to. Have good high fences or walls and a secure gate and keep them in good repair. Grow boundary hedges of something dense and prickly such as holly or mahonia.

SECURITY LIGHTING

The external variety is usually linked to a PIR (passive infra-red) detector which activates the light when movement is detected; it then turns off after a few minutes. Internally you can buy switches containing light-sensitive cells that turn the light on when it gets dark and switch off after a predetermined time, so giving the illusion of an occupied property.

LOCKS AND BOLTS

External timber doors should be of good quality and secured with a 5-lever mortise deadlock (commonly, though not always accurately, called a Chubb lock). You can also buy fittings that lock when you pull the door closed but can then only be opened with a key from inside or out. This has two benefits: first, it is impossible to gain entry simply by breaking a window and reaching round to the latch to open the door; second, it inhibits the intruder's escape. Most intruders plan their escape route before they actually make entry. If there's a chance they'll be trapped inside they may well not bother. If you have any external doors that open outwards the hinges will be exposed and vulnerable. The answer to this is to fit hinge bolts. These brass or steel bolts lie on the hinge side edge of the door and fit into an opening in the frame when the door is closed. To strengthen doors against being kicked open you can fit security bars along the internal face of the lock edge of the doorframe. Usually called London bars, these hold the door frame together and stop it splitting if the door is forced.

BURGLAR ALARMS

Burglar alarms, of course, detect intruders, and then either set off a local alarm or silently alert the police. There are hundreds of different alarm packages available and most companies offer a free survey. If you're having a lot of internal work done it can be a good time to install one. Even if you don't want or can't yet afford a complete system, you can still have the wiring concealed behind the plaster. All the messy (and most expensive) work will then already be done. Wireless alarms are also available, operating on batteries and sending a radio signal to the main control panel if triggered.

WINDOWS

Some burglars will be prepared to break and open a window to get in, but very few are prepared to crawl across the shards of glass in a fixed pane, so fit window locks to all ground-floor windows, and any others that are easily accessible from the outside. Most new windows have locks fitted as standard, and most existing windows can have them retro fitted. On the continent most houses have wooden shutters or external metal blinds. These really do make entry difficult, but in a country like ours where hardly anyone has them, they do rather advertise the fact you're away from home. Another option is toughened glass. Laminated is probably the best from a security point of view, but is expensive. Also you won't be able to break it yourself in the unlikely event that you need to do so in an emergency.

Eli Seath, a mosaic artist, Rachel Forster, an interior designer, and Sally Fletcher, who trained as an architect, are all single mums. They have three six-year-old boys, Jude, Carl and Dujarn, who attend the same school.

They all currently rent, and are all good friends. They want to stop renting, and have decided that the solution is to pool their finances, use their various skills and resources and buy a property together.

Their Vision

They believe that they can each raise £150,000, giving them a total budget of £450,000. They are prepared to invest their own time, and because of their various professions they will bring an enormous amount to the project. They know that it will be very difficult to find a house to accommodate three families, and have come to the conclusion that they need to take on an empty property. They have already started looking.

Thinking of new solutions

Although the women are keen on communal living, they also want some self-contained areas. They think they could share certain elements, including the garden, a central-heating system, a large industrial freezer, and so on. They also started to discuss a shared playroom for the boys, a place where all three families could relax, a shared laundry room, and communal storage to limit the amount of duplicated space within each of the units.

The Front Runners
The Railway Arms, Shadwell

This old, truly derelict public house is just east of Shadwell station on the Docklands Light Railway. It has clearly been empty for some considerable time. There is evidence of vandalism, squatting, and a series of fires – but despite all of this the brickwork looks sound, the roof is repairable and the building is not beyond redemption.

Victorian Warehouse, De Beauvoir Town

The building of De Beauvoir Town in Hackney began in the 1830s on land belonging to the De Beauvoir family. The area has never been fully redeveloped as a smart London quarter, as it is poorly served by public transport, though it is close to the busy Kingsland Road and the prosperous streets of Islington.

To the south, the Town is bordered by the Regent's Canal. The area around the canal and its basin is solidly industrial, with some splendid two-storey brick-built Victorian buildings. It was one of these which filled the women with excitement.

The building in question looked abandoned and in derelict condition, but like most Victorian industrial buildings it has weathered extremely well. This is a truly beautiful building. Externally it is muscular and dignified, clearly designed and built to stand the test of time. Internally it boasts all the usual Victorian industrial structure that is now so popular: cast-iron columns, substantial cast-iron beams supporting huge floor joists that carry fine plane-edged boarded floors, all with around fifteen feet floor-to-ceiling heights on both storeys.

Finding out about the home

Although the pub sign proudly declares that it was once run and operated by Watney Coombe Reid, enquiries at the Land Registry and elsewhere reveal that the property does in fact belong to the local authority, the London Borough of Tower Hamlets, who, when contacted initially seemed to be in some confusion regarding their ownership. As the local authority they would be advised either to pass it on to a housing association or offer it at auction. If the latter course of action were adopted, the women would still have an opportunity to buy the pub, which could be extended into the beer garden and possibly vertically to provide the amount of accommodation they require.

What Next?

After discussion the women felt that the derelict pub was far too much for them to take on, so it had to be the industrial building in De Beauvoir. However, the ground floor was occupied by a busy firm of upholsterers in the southern half, and a joinery works in the northern half. The women's hearts sank, only to be revived when they saw the vast empty first floor, which was certainly large enough for three self-contained apartments, with the possibility of a terrace on the flat roof.

The proprietor of the upholstery business told the women that the property had recently been acquired by a housing association. Yet again, it seemed that they could not realize their dream. However, discussions soon developed into a fascinating and unusual proposition: the plan is to form some corporate entity – a limited company, a company limited by guarantee, a partnership or similar – involving the three women, the upholsterers and the joiners. The two manufacturers would remain on the ground floor, with three self-contained apartments for the families above. All five parties would share the freehold and would set up a mechanism for converting and maintaining the building.

It was decided that Sally and Rachel would carry out a full measured survey of the building, obtain cost advice from a quantity surveyor, and put together a business plan so that they could make a firm and viable proposition to the housing association, whose aim will undoubtedly be housing with charitable intent. This could be a real goer.

MAKING YOUR HOUSE SAFE FROM FIRE

Fire safety, like security, is an unglamorous facet of house design. We tend to think of our homes as a safe refuge, and unless we've experienced it, it's very difficult to imagine a fire in our own home. So we view money spent on ugly fire doors and ceiling upgrades as wasted. But there are over 70,000 house fires resulting in nearly 500 deaths in the UK each year. Quite apart from the risk to you and your household, the potential of losing everything you own ought to make fire safety at least as big a concern as security.

If you're making only minor alterations to the property, it's likely that you won't have to comply with all Building Regulations requirements, although common sense dictates that you should follow them anyway. Your local fire prevention officer will be happy to offer advice.

ONE- AND TWO-STOREY PROPERTIES

In bungalows and two-storey properties the requirements are fairly minor. (The number of storeys doesn't include the basement because, like the first floor, it's only one floor away from safety.) You'll need to ensure that the windows are big enough to get out of, which excludes most centre-pivoting and bottom-hung windows and all fixed-pane windows. And you'll need mains-operated smoke detectors with a battery back-up system. These are widely available and not expensive. They can be easily incorporated into an electric lighting circuit at about the same cost as putting in an additional light fitting. Smoke detectors should be fitted throughout no further than 3m from each bedroom door. In most houses this means one in the hall and one on the landing.

The Building Regulations require fire-safety features in all residential buildings. In addition there are stricter requirements under other legislation for houses in multiple occupation (HMOs). These are properties originally built as a single dwelling but later subdivided. The principle behind the regulations is twofold: people can be fairly easily rescued from a ground-floor or first-floor room, so on these two floors the emphasis is on external exits. Above the first floor rescue becomes increasingly difficult, so the emphasis is on a safe evacuation route. This means putting in fire doors and upgrading walls and ceilings so that fire cannot spread to the escape route.

THREE-STOREY PROPERTIES

Three-storey houses should have a protected escape route, usually the main landing/staircase/hall, and all rooms should open directly on to it. This means not having a layout where one room can be accessed only by going through another; an en-suite bathroom is OK, but a living room accessed through a kitchen isn't. All walls along the route must resist fire for 30 minutes and any internal doors must resist fire for 20 minutes.

Most walls will resist fire for much longer than 30 minutes. A 9mm plasterboard stud wall in good condition has 30-minute fire resisting properties, and brick holds back fire for hours. Probably the only areas you'll need to worry about are poor-condition lath-and-plaster walls and chipboard partitions.

Doors are a different matter. Old panel doors have poor fire-resisting properties and most glazed doors are even worse. Fire doors are widely available, although the cheaper ones are quite plain. Most are the same thickness as external doors (44mm) and all need self-closers – no door will resist a fire if it's open. The least obtrusive solution is the Perko door closer. This fits inside the door, leaving visible only a small chain connecting the door to the frame on the hinge side. Check with your building control officer first. Some councils don't accept Perkos and require overhead-arm hinge closers instead.

So much for the theory. In practice, most people find door closers so inconvenient that they either disable them or wedge fire doors open. Some builders even keep a stock of closers that they'll fit temporarily until the building control officer has carried out the final inspection. This is both foolish and illegal. If you cut down a fire door you'll weaken it and cause it to lose its fire resisting properties so order them in sizes as near as possible to that of the door opening.

As an alternative to fitting new fire doors, you can upgrade your existing ones. If the internal doors in the house are original you really should consider this option first. 'Intumescent' means 'expands when exposed to fire', and all sorts of intumescent products are available to help you upgrade doors. The first thing to assess is the condition and make up of the door and frame (the door set). You can't properly upgrade a weak or damaged door. Don't forget the doorframe. Loose or damaged door linings and architrave must be repaired or replaced before you upgrade the door. As with lower-rise properties you should, of course, install mains-electricity smoke detectors as well.

DESIGNING YOUR SPACE ROOM BY ROOM

THE KITCHEN

The current importance of the kitchen means that it's top of the list when considering the design of any house. A kitchen is no longer solely a place in which to prepare and cook food. It's a multi-purpose room and function, more than anything else, should dictate its design.

On p. 18 I talked about how many old houses have become obsolete. Nowhere is this more true than in the kitchen. Think of all the appliances you now expect to find there: a cooker, a fridge, a freezer, a dishwasher, a washing machine, a kettle, maybe an extractor, a tumble drier, a food processor, a bread maker . . . the list could go on. Socially, things have changed too. Many people now regard their kitchen as the heart of the house. How many times when you have visitors do you find you congregate in the kitchen, even though there are far more comfortable rooms to sit in? A century ago, the kitchen was somewhere to be tucked out of sight, where the woman of the house would slave away preparing the food which would be transported to the dining table at set meal times. Today cooking has become less of a chore and more of a social occasion. Whoever is preparing the food no longer wants to be hidden away. The trend is towards large open-plan kitchen/dining areas. As our kitchens have become more visible we've become more interested in what they look like. Aesthetics are now as important as function.

A century ago, the kitchen was somewhere to be tucked out of sight, where the woman of the house would slave away preparing the food which would be transported to the dining table at set meal times. Today cooking has become less of a chore and more of a social occasion. Whoever is preparing the food no longer wants to be hidden away.

FOOD STORE

Old houses had cool larders or pantries in which food was kept. Some houses still have them. These small, unheated rooms do make good storage space, so think twice before you knock them out. Naturally, you'll also need to plan space for a fridge and a freezer, but if you're lucky enough to have a cellar or a garage you could put a second freezer in there and a smaller one in the kitchen for everyday use. You'll also need space for dry goods, which will probably take up two or three of the built-in units in a fitted kitchen.

EQUIPMENT STORE

In addition to the olive stoner, pasta maker or fondue set that most of us seem to accumulate but never use, you'll need somewhere to put all your useful cooking pots and pans, cutlery, crockery, food blenders, kettles and the like. Whether you're happy to have these on show on shelves and racks or whether you prefer them to be hidden away will dictate what sort of units or cupboards you want.

SLUICE

Kitchens tend to be where most household cleaning operations start and finish. If you don't like the idea of mucky things sharing the space in which you prepare food, you need a utility room as well. If there's not enough space, at least get a double sink to separate the muck from the food.

BOILER HOUSE

The kitchen is the most common place to find a boiler, but there are strict regulations about where you can site a boiler flue. Unless you opt for a fan-flue boiler, your choice of boiler location will be limited. Flues must be at least 300mm from an openable window and at least 600mm from an exterior corner.

DINING ROOM

You might want to eat every meal in the kitchen, or only use it for breakfast and snacks. Think about how you can plan the kitchen to accommodate your preferences.

ENTRANCE HALL

Back doors often open directly into the kitchen. The way many people use their house means that the kitchen is the first room visitors enter. Make sure you leave sufficient space for then to do so without falling on to the cooker. Muddy boot prints are much easier to remove if the floor surface is washable, but if space permits, a lobby where boots and shoes can be left will keep your kitchen much cleaner.

RUBBISH TIP

Most of the rubbish we produce at home ends up in the kitchen, so buy a decent sized bin. Glass, paper, cardboard and cans can all be recycled. A waste-disposal unit may prove useful, though a compost heap in the garden is a better and cheaper alternative. A little thought at the design stage can prevent your kitchen becoming a mini landfill site.

Your kitchen will probably fulfil all these functions and more, in addition to its intended use as a food preparation and cooking area. To make sure your kitchen works, you need to put the right things in it and lay them out in the right way. The classic design principle for kitchens is the work triangle. The locations of the cooker, sink and fridge should form a triangle and they need to be joined by worktop. This means that everything you need for cooking is within easy reach. The triangle layout is not essential, but you should at least try to keep these three things fairly close together. Don't just choose a standard kitchen out of a brochure; think about what uses your kitchen will be put to and buy the individual items that best suit your needs.

FITTED KITCHENS

Kitchen units come in various standard sizes that increase in 100mm intervals. You can pretty much fill your kitchen with as many wall and floor units as you think you'll need, and with a bit of planning have no more than a 100mm gap at the end – perfect for a wine rack. You can pay from a few hundred pounds for a basic flat-pack DIY installation kit to tens of thousands for a top-of-the-range designer effort. What is amazing isn't so much the variety, but how similar they all are.

COOKERS

For a cooker, the important consideration is where to put it. Don't site it in a corner (you won't be able to reach it properly), near a door (dangerous) or against an internal wall (makes a cooker hood difficult to install). Most cookers are available either built-in or freestanding.

The other decision you need to make concerns fuel. If you have a mains gas supply you have a choice of gas or electricity; if not, you can still choose gas, but of the LPG (liquid petroleum gas) variety.

All-electric cookers have the advantage of fast-heating ovens and the disadvantage of slow-heating hobs. Halogen hobs overcome this to some extent, but they're still not as quick to react as gas burners. The main drawback with electricity is its inefficiency. It costs four times as much to cook with electricity as it does with gas.

Gas and LPG have the benefit of instant heat from the hobs but the ovens are slower to warm up and give out moist exhaust gases that contribute to condensation. Another problem is that heating temperatures aren't as uniform as for electric ovens, although fan assistance can overcome this to a degree.

Dual fuel cookers combine a gas hob with an electric oven, giving you the best of both worlds.

WORKTOPS

Worktops should be more than simply what you just plonk on top of whatever base units you've chosen. It's often better to decide how much worktop area you need and then think about filling the space underneath. Nothing will influence the usability of your kitchen more than where and how extensive the worktops are. You really need at least 3m in length, although this can be divided into several sections. You'll certainly need worktop on either side of the sink.

As with kitchen units, the price of worktops varies enormously depending on their composition and design. Cheaper worktops are made of laminated board, dearer ones of wood, granite, marble or other materials. Square edges are cheap, moulded round ones more expensive. You could use ceramic tiles instead, although the grouting between them gets grubby and is hard to keep clean. A new material is synthetic resin, which can also be used to make sinks. Formica has been out of vogue for a while, but it's making a comeback, as are similar products under other names. Softwood worktops lack durability, but hardwoods such as beech and maple do very nicely, though if you don't keep them regularly oiled they'll absorb liquids and stain. The best and most expensive materials for worktops are granite, marble and glass. They are strong, easy to clean and look great, but they also cost up to twenty times as much as cheap laminate. The choice is yours.

SINKS

Some cutting-edge kitchen designs don't incorporate a sink, the theory being that if you have a dishwasher you need only a tap to supply water. In the real world, however, the idea of the sinkless kitchen is unimaginable. (Dishwashers never seem to cope with scrambled-egg pans anyway.)

Even the most basic house usually has a sink in its kitchen, more often than not under the kitchen window. Unless you plan to relocate the kitchen this is usually the best place to leave it. The window provides both a source of natural light and something to look at while you're scrubbing the scrambled-egg pan. In any event, the sink will need to go against an outside wall close to the external drains. Don't put wall units above the sink; you'll clonk your head.

The primary choices are double or single (go for double if you've got the space) and which material. Most sinks are made of stainless steel and although this might not be fashionable, it's an excellent material for its purpose. Stainless-steel sinks are also surprisingly cheap. If you don't like the look of them, the alternatives are synthetic resin and ceramic. The best thing to be said for resin is that it comes in a choice of colours that can match a co-ordinated kitchen design. Ceramic, by which I really mean a butler's or Belfast sink, has shifted its status from plant trough to style icon in recent years, and many companies now produce them again. They fit in well with all sorts of period houses, although in truth they were never really stationed or used in the way we use them today. You can even get double butler's sinks now, which I'm sure was never in the original plan.

OTHER APPLIANCES

Like cookers, most other appliances can be either freestanding or fitted. Most fitted models come in standard sizes so you can pick and choose among models and manufacturers. Faulty washing machines are the most common cause of domestic house fires, so don't be tempted to buy a badly reconditioned or second-hand one.

Fridges can use an enormous amount of electricity, up to a third of the average household bill. New fridges and freezers will display an energy rating, 'A' being the best and 'G' the worst. High-rated fridges are normally (although not always) more expensive than low-rated ones, but the energy saving potential is significant. Not only will you create a smaller environmental impact, your investment will be more than repaid over the life of the appliance through lower fuel bills. (Bulk discounting schemes operated through your local energy advice centre or local authority might mean that you can buy high-rated appliances at a discount. See Chapter 13 for more details.) If space allows, the best configuration is a small larder fridge and a separate chest freezer. Larder fridges are more efficient than fridges with freezing compartments because the coils don't ice up (and they don't need tedious regular defrosting). Chest freezers are more efficient than upright freezers because they lose far less cold air when they are opened.

Please dispose of your old fridge or freezer responsibly. Take it to the council tip, or make sure that, if the supplier of your new fridge takes the old one away, it is drained properly. Most old models use CFC (chlorofluorocarbon) refrigerants. These are destructive to the ozone layer and emit powerful greenhouse gases. More modern fridges use (hydrofluorocarbons), although these are only marginally better.

BATHROOMS

This is another room where people's expectations have changed enormously in recent years. Most pre-twentieth-century houses didn't have one at all, and only since the 1950s have most houses contained as standard a bathroom that we'd recognize today. These days, we don't ask whether a house has a bathroom but how many.

Once again, your choice will be dictated by your own needs and the space available. If you have teenage daughters and need to get to work on time, multiple bathrooms will be an absolute necessity. Also, plan ahead. You may be fit and agile now, but as age takes its toll a downstairs bathroom could avoid you having to move later. If you do sell, an extra bathroom really does pay dividends. There's no doubt that bathrooms sell houses. An estate agent told me recently that 'Bathrooms are the new kitchens'!

If you're planning a major refurbishment, look carefully at the current bathing arrangements. Are they adequate? Is the current bathroom large enough for all the sanitaryware you're planning to put in? Is it in the right place?

HOW TO MAKE A SMALL BATHROOM FEEL BIGGER

If the existing bathroom feels too small, these simple ideas might help:
➤ Increase the visible floor space by installing a wall-mounted hand basin. You can even get wall-mounted WCs. Get things off the floor, and keep anything you don't need such as a laundry basket in another room.
➤ Make the walls and floor the same colour (pale colours work best). This can fool the eye into thinking that the floor (and therefore the room) is bigger than it really is.
➤ Corners are wasted space, so you could fit a corner basin or WC. (Some of them look rather odd to me, buts that's just my personal taste.)
➤ Re-hang the door so it opens outwards, or replace it with a sliding door.
➤ Make it a wet room, thus avoiding the need for a shower tray (see p. 105).

Recent changes in the UK Building Regulations have made a downstairs toilet mandatory for new-build properties to accommodate the needs of wheelchair users. If you're renovating an old house this requirement won't apply to you, but if you're converting a commercial property into a residential one it will.

Your choice will be
dictated by your own
needs and the space
available. If you have
teenage daughters and
need to get to work
on time, multiple
bathrooms will be an
absolute necessity.

INSTALLING A NEW BATHROOM

If you're relocating a bathroom or installing one from scratch, you'll need to find a suitable place to put it. This could well mean sacrificing space from somewhere else. The ideal location, of course, is adjacent to an outside wall and close to the existing drainage pipes. It's possible to create an internal bathroom (i.e. one with no external walls), but although the water supply can be re-routed easily, a macerator and pump will probably be necessary to dispose of waste. In theory this is a clever solution – the macerator blitzes the waste and pumps it away through narrow-bore pipes – but the installation can be awkward and expensive, and the cheaper macerators are noisy.

Other considerations are ceiling height and floor strength. A popular place for a new bathroom is in a converted loft. This might look great on an architect's plan, but many people are disappointed by the lack of usable space after it's built. Build a mock-up in the loft first; you might find it feels like a cramped swimming-pool changing cubicle rather than the bathroom of your dreams. If the ceiling slopes, put the shower and the basin under the highest part. Upper-floor ceiling joists are usually not as robust as floor joists. Even if they are adequate to support a simple loft conversion, a 200 kg cast-iron bath full of water is another matter entirely, and you should obtain the opinion of a surveyor or structural engineer before your proceed.

Once you've found your space, the next step is to decide what to put in it.

The current fashion for suites is definitely white. This makes mixing and matching much easier than it would have been in the 1970s with its pampas and avocado shades.

The current trend in houses is towards bigger bathrooms at the expense of smaller bedrooms. If you're conscious of resale value, most estate agents will say that it's better to have several smaller bedrooms than a few big ones, and that losing a small bedroom may not be the best solution. That said, it's you who has to live in the place not the estate agent, so decide what suits you.

FITTING OUT YOUR BATHROOM

✚ Showers

As a nation, our taste in personal hygiene is becoming more continental. A shower can be anything from a cheap rubber attachment on your bath taps to a fully dedicated wet room. In practical terms there are two major considerations when buying a shower: temperature and power.

When installing a shower, the major consideration is avoiding leaks. Leaking showers are one of the commonest causes of internal flooding. Running water, especially water under pressure, is very good at finding its own level, and the quickest route isn't always down the plughole. When lining a shower, wall tiles stuck straight onto the wall really aren't up to the job. You need to use good quality marine plywood as a base lining, and liberal quantities of good-quality waterproof tile adhesive. The joints on the plywood lining are vital because, although they'll be covered in mastic, that doesn't last very well. Alternatively, you can buy proprietary panels made from glassfibre or plastic-laminated plywood that can be fitted straight on to the walls; two leading brand names are Respatex and Norske Interiors' 'Mermaid' range of panelling.

If you want to go really continental, you could install an open shower in a wet room. Instead of having a shower tray, the water flows into a drain in the middle of the floor. The floor must be made completely watertight and the drain unit must be one designed for the purpose. The floor has to slope towards it at a gradient no shallower than 1 in 40, so you'll need either to raise the floor or to carve out the floor joists if they contain sufficient timber for you to do so safely. You can use floor tiles as a covering, but the same comments apply as for shower cubicle walls. Alternatively you can buy moulded sheet floors; Altro marine is a popular brand.

✚ Ventilation

All bathrooms benefit from some form of mechanical ventilation, and for internal bathrooms it's an absolute necessity. A basic fan can be controlled by a light switch, but for internal bathrooms you'll need one with an automatic over-run timer. An alternative is a humidistat fan that automatically adjusts its setting depending on the humidity of the air. The best fans have heat recovery units on them, extracting most of the heat energy from the air before it's pumped outside.

✚ Bathroom suites

These come in two, three or four pieces (wc, basin, bath and bidet). Two-pieces suites are used in cloakrooms and usually have smaller basins. Three- and four-piece suites are for full-size bathrooms. The current fashion for suites is definitely white. This makes mixing and matching much easier than it would have been in the 1970s with its pampas and avocado shades.

To avoid complications you can buy an all-in-one shower cubicle made from moulded plastic. They don't look as bad as they sound, but they are quite expensive.

BEDROOMS

Bedrooms have fewer design considerations than other rooms, but don't assume that you have to use every room in the house in the way it was originally designed. An important consideration for a bedroom is noise. If the house faces a busy road, you'll probably sleep better in a back room. One thing that matters less is light. The Urban Splash house (see p. 83) took this idea and located the bedrooms on the ground floor. One thing you may want to rethink is access. A lot of Victorian town houses have long narrow additions at the rear with one bedroom accessed through another. This arrangement is hardly practical, but the far room could make a good en-suite bathroom or an office.

Bedrooms in older houses often contain just a single electrical socket. If you're rewiring, think about how the room will be laid out, and provide more outlets in convenient places.

LIVING ROOMS

The living room, like the kitchen, serves many functions. A place to sit and relax, to entertain friends, watch television, eat, drink, play video games or surf the net. In most homes it's the most heavily used room. Most living rooms work best with a central focal point, and it's probably for this reason that so many fireplaces have survived here and not elsewhere in many old houses. A focal point doesn't have to be a fireplace, though. A window with a good view, a picture, a piece of furniture or (save us all!) a giant plasma screen T V can all do the same job.

More than any other room in the house, the shape of a living room really makes a difference. When deciding on the layout of your property, pick a square room. Long thin or L-shaped living rooms can feel awkward. If your living room is big, square, has lots of electrical outlets and a nice focal point, you won't go far wrong.

HALLS AND LANDINGS

Otherwise known as circulation space, halls and landings are seen by one school of thought as a waste that should be minimized, while others argue that they impart spaciousness and airiness to a house. By carefully repositioning internal partitions you can push the design of your property down one or other of these routes. Before you do, it's worth bearing in mind that most property designs are tried and tested and that the original design is often the best configuration. Unlike the other rooms in the house, our use of circulation space hasn't altered. We still need to move easily from one part of the house to another, and so long as you can do so there is probably no need to change things. One exception is the provision of wheelchair access. Wheelchairs need wider doorways and turning circles than were specified in most second-hand houses.

It's worth bearing in mind that most property designs are tried and tested and that the original design is often the best configuration.

Some properties, however
you rearrange them, simply
aren't big enough.

6 EXPANDING YOUR LIVING SPACE

Lack of space is the most common reason people give for moving house, so it must be pretty important when choosing a new one. It stands to reason that getting the space right for you and your household is a top priority when designing your home. Some properties, however you rearrange them, simply aren't big enough. The solution is to extend them. Extensions are very often incorporated as part of a refurbishment programme. It makes sense to get all the dirty work done in one go and also means that you can properly incorporate the new space into your overall design for the property.

There are three main options: go out, go up or go down.

GOING OUT — BUILDING A CONVENTIONAL EXTENSION

The viability of a conventional extension will depend on how much land you have available to build on. The boundary of your plot is also crucial, as is the proximity of neighbouring properties. If you can extend, the two usual options are a single-storey or two-storey addition.

A single-storey extension satisfies the need for an extra or larger room, or it may make possible a rearrangement of the ground-floor layout. A single-storey extension will appear to be cheaper than a two-storey one, but it'll almost certainly work out more expensive on a pound-per-square-metre basis. After all, the costs of the foundations and the roof will be much the same for either, but two-storeys have twice the floor area.

PERMISSION

Planning permission isn't needed for all extensions. On 1 July 1948 'permitted development rights' (PDR) were introduced which allow the extension of a property without consent within certain limits.

PDRs exist for most properties except listed buildings, unless they have been removed by what is known as an Article 4 directive, a power sometimes exercised in conservation areas to give the local authority more control over development. In most cases, though, PDRs apply and you can extend the volume of the original house by up to 15% or 70 cubic metres, which-ever is the greater, up to a maximum extension size of 115 cubic metres.

Lower limits apply to terraced houses, where the volume of the original house may be increased only by up to 10% or 50 cubic metres, whichever is the greater, again up to a maximum extension size of 115 cubic metres, and to all properties in national parks, conservation areas and areas of outstanding natural beauty. In these areas the allowance takes on a different meaning: you'll need to make a planning application for an extension of any size, but if you apply for anything outside the PDR limits it will almost certainly be refused. Don't forget the 1 July 1948 cut-off date, which means that if the building has been extended at any time since then, a portion, or perhaps all, of your allowance will already have been used. You could demolish any post-1948 extension to regain your full allowance, or apply for planning permission for a larger extension.

In Scotland PDR is 20% or 24 sq. metres in floor area up to a maximum of 30 sq. metres. Volume is measured externally and should include the roof space. For terraced houses it's 10% or 16 sq. metres up to a max of 30. In Ireland the same principles apply, although the law is less complicated. In essence you need planning permission to build any structure, including an extension, with a floor area of 23 sq. metres or more.

THE PRACTICALITIES OF BUILDING AN EXTENSION

Many of the things you need to take account of in building an extension are the same points you'd need to consider if you were building a new house. Like a new-build house, you should start with a site investigation. Whether you can build an extension and how much it's going to cost will depend to a large extent on the nature of the site. You should investigate the following.

SLOPES

Extensions are best built on flat land. If the proposed site is at the bottom of a slope, excavations could make the land unstable. If it's at the top, the extension could possibly subside. The most important factor is soil type. Moisture-retaining clay soils are the most prone to instability. A slope of more than 30° presents a real problem, and you'll need advice from a surveyor or structural engineer.

SERVICES

Some outside walls of houses are covered in pipes to convey wastewater, sewage and rainwater. You may also have various meters, pipes and cables fixed to the wall you intend to build the extension against. If these have to be moved or rerouted it will add to the cost. If your proposed extension includes a bathroom or kitchen you'll need to plan for drainage. If the existing drains are a long way away, and especially if they aren't very deep, this could pose a problem. Drains need a fall (slope) to work properly and shallow drains will make it difficult for you to achieve the right fall with new drainage.

BASEMENTS

The purpose of foundations is to spread the load of the extension to the soil below. If your property has a basement, much of the load will fall on the basement wall instead, so you need to check if it's strong enough.

TREES

Extensions are best not built too close to trees. Tree roots can exacerbate soil-shrinkage problems and get in the way of the foundations. As well as the risk to your property you need to have some consideration for the trees, too. Before you go chopping them down or lopping bits off you should check to see if they are the subject of a tree-preservation order. (If your property is in a conservation area, all trees are protected and you'll need conservation-area permission from the council even to prune them.)

RIGHTS OF WAY

Your extension mustn't obstruct any public footpath or right of way. This applies even when an old path hasn't been used for years. If you already own the property, the local land search carried out by your conveyancer should have revealed any public rights of way. If you don't, then you shouldn't assume that no right of way exists simply because there is no obvious footpath.

NEIGHBOURING PROPERTIES

If your proposed extension is within 6 m of your neighbour's property it's likely that under UK law you'll have a duty under the Party Wall Act to notify them. (For more information see p. 185.)

FLAT ROOF OR PITCHED ROOF?

The arguments for a pitched roof are numerous: it looks good, it helps the extension blend into the house, it gives you extra loft space, it's more likely to get planning permission, it'll last longer, it gives better options for thermal efficiency and it's less likely to leak. The arguments for a flat roof, on the other hand, are less numerous if equally compelling: they're cheap.

If you're on a tight budget, choosing a flat roof may be a saving worth making. Be aware, though, that many local authorities are less likely to give planning permission for a flat-roofed extension, especially if it's two-storey. Weather acts more harshly on flat roofs than on pitched ones and the materials used (usually metal or asphalt) are more prone to weathering than slates or tiles.

Most houses have a pitched roof, and extensions to them look better with a pitched roof too. This applies as much to a single-storey as to a two-storey extension. In most cases it's possible to adapt the existing roof to cover the new extension. This involves adding to the timber support work and providing matching slates or tiles. In cases where the roof structure is in poor repair it may be easier to fit a new roof.

If you're building a whole new roof, the most common method is to use prefabricated timber rafters that are criss-crossed with struts. These are called roof trusses. The load is spread evenly throughout the truss, which are therefore much lighter and thinner than traditional cut-and-pitch roof rafters. Because the timber itself is less strong, the accuracy of the design and installation of the truss is critical. You should expect the manufacturer to require highly detailed measurements and plans of your proposal. This information is used to design the truss with the help of a computer program. If your builder proposes to make up trusses in your back garden, you should be worried.

FOUNDATIONS

Foundations provide a solid base for the extension to sit on. They should prevent the extension settling into the ground, and avoid it being affected by ground movement. Old houses often have quite shallow foundations by today's standards and you may find that you have to build deeper foundations for the extension than exist for the main house in order to comply with Building Regulations. This can lead to some differential movement between the two, although any cracking is usually limited to the junction between the extension and the main house. Usually it's best to accept this and tie the walls of the two together using flexible wall ties. If you try to eliminate it entirely you could end up causing the movement to occur elsewhere, resulting in cracking in the walls of the main house.

If the subsoil is liable to shrinkage or you're aiming to build on a sloping site you may have to build deeper foundations or even drive piles into the ground to provide a sufficiently firm base.

The most common type of foundations are strip foundations, which are simply strips of concrete normally 150 mm to 300 mm deep poured in a trench below ground level. The wall is then built directly on to the foundation. In clay soils (which are liable to shrinkage) trench-fill foundations are more commonly used. These use the same principle as strip foundations but the concrete layer is much thicker, ideally extending down to firm soil and extending up to just below ground level. Where the risk of subsidence is particularly high other forms of foundation are sometimes used. Pad-and-beam foundations consist of a series of deep concrete blocks joined together with lintels and just below ground level. The wall is then built onto the lintels. Raft foundations, as their name implies, consist of a reinforced concrete raft that covers the whole floor area of the extension and extends a little beyond it. The walls are built on a reinforced ridge around the edge of the raft, spreading the weight of the extension over the whole floor area. Pile foundations were until recently used only for commercial buildings, but improvements in the technology for driving them into the ground has made them a realistic option for residential building. In extreme conditions, steep slopes and unstable soils, piles may be the answer. They can be drilled deep into the ground, transferring the load of the extension down below the unstable ground. Like pad-and-beam foundations they are joined with a lintel or reinforced bar and the wall is built on to this.

CONSERVATORIES

The term conservatory comes from the original use of these structures, as a place to conserve delicate plants through the winter. If that's your aim, build a three-sided greenhouse attached to the south- or west-facing side of your house. For most people, though, a conservatory is, in theory, an extra reception room. In practice, though, just like a greenhouse, a conservatory heats up very quickly in the sun and cools very quickly when it's cold outside. In fact there are relatively few occasions when the temperature is right to use an unheated or un-air-conditioned conservatory in comfort.

Conservatories can, however, make a quick and cheap extension. If you keep the floor area below 30 sq. metres you should be able to avoid the need for both planning permission and Building Regulations approval. (In Ireland it's below 23 sq. metres and I'm afraid you'll probably still need building by-law permission. But bear in mind that conservatories have their limitations and are of less practical use than other types of extension.

If you want a conservatory reception room:

    Site it against a west or south-east facing wall. South-facing conservatories can turn into ovens in the summer.

    Have a separating door between the conservatory and the rest of the house. Open-plan conservatories just pass on their extreme temperatures to other parts of the house and will cost you a fortune in wasted heat in the winter. (A separating door is a requirement in Scotland.)

    Install a roof blind to make the room usable during the day in summer months.

    Install a roof vent at the highest point, this relieves the worst of the high temperatures on sunny days and reduces the risk of wind lift. Without it a strong gust of wind through an open conservatory door can practically lift the conservatory into the air.

    Build good foundations if you have clay soils or the site is close to trees. Many designers will insist that because conservatories are light-weight they don't require proper foundations. This is true enough in well-draining soils, but foundations also prevent damage from soil heave (soil swelling and lifting), which can easily occur where the soil is liable to swell and shrink as it gets wet and dries out.

CASE STUDY_3 Maxwell's notes from the frontline

Natalie Sharpe is 28, and a college lecturer. She has a six-year-old son, and now lives with Lee Fawsitt, her partner of three years. Lee is a window and conservatory fitter. The family want a dog. They filled in an internet doggy questionnaire which revealed that their ideal canine companion is . . . a Great Dane.

They recently bought a new, two-bedroom flat in a quiet estate in a Nottingham suburb. The flat is immaculately well kept and tidy, but it is clear that it is far too small.

Their Vision

With the money from their current flat, together with savings and borrowings, they have a budget of around £120,000 – not much even by Nottingham standards. However, Lee is an accomplished do-it-your-selfer, and Natalie is very happy to roll up her sleeves and help. They believe that the only way to maximize their available cash and capitalize on their building skills is to find and renovate an abandoned property.

Natalie is clear about the image and appearance of the house after renovation: she wants a large comfortable family house decorated in a contemporary manner with a garden big enough for her boisterous partner, a child and the Great Dane. There is a strong chance that they will be able to achieve their dream as, shockingly, Nottingham has 4,650 vacant homes.

The Front Runners
Carlton Hill

This bungalow, called Villers Faucon, is in Carlton and is set on higher ground above a short, unadopted and unmetalled road, with wonderful views over the surrounding area. Although it looks 1930s in appearance, it could well have been built after the Second World War.

The bungalow was owned by Bruce McMellon, who died a couple of months ago in a nursing home. Apparently, he had a lady friend who is very elderly. The nursing home believe that she was the beneficiary. The property has been empty for at least eighteen months. Both front and back gardens are a jungle.

Local estate agents have indicated that a bungalow of this size in this location would sell at around £110,000–£120,000: within the family's budget. Given

the size of the rear garden and the fact that the bungalow has never been extended, there is a real opportunity to add extra accommodation at the back. The existing garage is an integral part of the property and could be converted into a further bedroom and bathroom. There is sufficient space in the front garden for the building of a new garage.

Internally the property is almost exactly as Mr McMellon must have left it when he went into the nursing home. As it stands, the property would be more than adequate for the existing family, and conversion of the garage would fit the bill for the enlarged household. Lee could also build a substantial conservatory at the rear.

The area

Carlton Hill is a lively area with shops, a library, a post office and all local amenities. There is a straight, clear road into the centre of the city, and Mapperley Plains Primary School is only two miles away. The population of this part of Nottingham increased dramatically in the second half of the nineteenth century. Between 1851 and 1881 the population doubled to 4,600 and had doubled again by 1901, when it grew to 10,300.

South Mapperley

This two-storey detached house was built towards the end of the 1920s or early in the 1930s. It has a huge, very overgrown garden. Although the structure of the building is mostly in good condition, there are a few slipped slates and leaking gutters, and the windows are in a poor state, much to Lee's delight. This is a large house with immense possibilities, and the couple loved it. Local estate agents value it at around £95,000–£100,000: again within the family's budget.

The property is owned but not occupied by an elderly lady. She and her late husband were both market traders and lived in the property for over fifty years. Following an appalling attack by an intruder she left the property, and now lives an active life in a local sheltered housing community. She visits the property infrequently and has recently decided that it is time to sell.

What Next?

Villers Faucon in Carlton Hill was just the family's ticket. Unfortunately, the beneficiary of Bruce McMellon's will suddenly decided to put the property on the market and instructed solicitors to ask for bids of over £120,000, with an impossibly short deadline. Sadly, the solicitor indicated that she had already received cash offers from property developers in excess of that amount, and Villers Faucon had to be ruled out by Natalie and Lee.

However, Natalie and Lee met the owner of the house in South Mapperley on their first visit to the property, and it was clear that she wanted to sell, they wanted to buy, and a deal could be done.

The family were proved right: a derelict wreck would fulfil their dreams.

GOING UP – BUILDING A LOFT CONVERSION

Loft conversions make a lot of sense. You don't lose any of your garden space, you don't lose natural light from existing rooms and you preserve the basic original shape of the building.

Some loft conversions avoid the need for planning permission. As with conventional extensions there are permitted development rights for most properties. You're allowed to extend the volume of the house by 50 cubic metres. If your extension is inside this limit, doesn't change the shape of the roof as it's seen from the road and doesn't increase the overall roof height you don't need planning permission. You will, however, need Building Regulations approval, because a loft conversion puts additional load on a building's structure. In a robust building the conversion can be relatively simple; for others, major structural work is needed to make the roof strong enough to take the additional load.

THE PRACTICALITIES OF A LOFT CONVERSION

Not all lofts make good loft conversions. When deciding whether yours would, there are two important points to consider: its size and how it's been constructed. Small lofts obviously make small loft rooms, but the crucial measurement is the height of the loft. This determines not only the height of the room but also its width. Don't forget, it's not just a case of whether you can stand up in the middle of the loft, it's the area in which there is sufficient height for you to walk around. Measure the distance between the top of the joists and the apex of the roof. If this is 2.3 m or more, you're in business. Any less and you'll probably end up with a very small or unusable loft room.

Loft conversions make a lot of sense. You don't lose any of your garden space, you don't lose natural light from existing rooms and you preserve the basic original shape of the building.

✚ Another way: dormers

A way of increasing the usable ceiling height of a loft conversion is to build a dormer into the design. (A dormer has a flat roof extending from the pitched roof.) This takes after the form of a dormer window. All types of dormer increase the amount of floor area below a usable ceiling height. The disadvantage of a dormer is that it allows less light into the loft room than using pitched roof-light windows and will almost certainly require planning permission because it will change the external shape of the house. In many areas, particularly conservation areas, planning permission is unlikely to be granted. The usual configuration is to build the dormer extending from the rear roof pitch and incorporate a roof-light or two in the front pitch. This retains the orginal appearance of the house when viewed from the road. Dormers can increase the cost of a loft conversion significantly.

✚ Remember the joists

Ceiling joists are the lengths of timber that hold up the ceiling below them, but if you convert the loft they'll need to support the new floor above them, too. In modern houses, ceiling joists normally measure 50 mm x 100 mm in section. These are too weak to support a floor and will require replacement before converting the loft. In older buildings, ceiling joists were sometimes over-specified. Any joist measuring 50 mm x 200 mm or more should be strong enough to take the weight of a floor. Some building designers suggest that undersized joists be upgraded by screwing new pieces of timber to them to increase their bulk. This can work, but you should be aware that such methodology is frowned upon by the loft-conversion industry and it's quite likely that your buildinging control officer would also disapprove. Another consideration is the way in which the roof timbers

have been constructed. Older houses had their roofs constructed on site from large pieces of timber, but since the late 1950s roofs have been built in a way that makes them harder to convert. The timber parts of the roof are prefabricated off site from thinner sections. In order to make these stronger, more diagonal trusses are put in. These get in the way when you want to create a loft conversion, but if you remove them you need to provide other forms of strengthening to compensate.

If the existing ceiling joists aren't strong enough the best solution is to attach new beams to the external walls of the building. This creates a frame that takes the whole weight of the new floor and transposes it to the external walls of the house, though at a dramatically increased cost. In a detached house you can hide these new beams within the unused spaces around the sides of the new loft room, but in conversions in terraced and semi-detached houses or where a dormer is incorporated, the beams will protrude and you need to somehow incorporate them into the design.

However you build your loft conversion, you'll need a set of stairs to get up to it. This can be one of the most expensive parts of a loft conversion. Staircases can be bought off the shelf and if your design allows for one of these to be used, your costs will be reduced considerably.

GOING DOWN – BASEMENT CONVERSIONS

Going underground is a great idea for contemporary houses. Many modern eco houses are built at least partly into the earth. It's hardly a new idea – historic sites in Turkey, China and Mexico show that throughout history people have seen the benefits of living underground. Underground rooms are cool in the summer and warm in the winter; they are quiet and have a very low visual impact. Restoring an old house might give you little opportunity for avant-garde architecture, but as an option for extending the space a basement conversion is something you should consider. A basement conversion gains much more space than a loft conversion because the ceiling height is the same throughout. There are unlikely to be noise problems, and unless the property is listed or in a conservation area or you'll be making visible external changes, you won't need planning permission, just building control approval.

Like lofts, basements are often underused storage areas (most Georgian, and many Victorian and Edwardian houses have them). Some Victorian houses have a cellar rather than a basement, often built for coal storage. It's possible to change either a basement or a cellar into underground living areas, although basements are normally much easier and cheaper to convert.

Underground rooms are cool in the summer and warm in the winter; they are quiet and have a very low visual impact.

✚ Windows

Depending on how your property was built, it may be possible to install windows in the basement to allow in natural light. If you can do this without building a light-well you should do so. A room with natural light and ventilation can be used for any purpose, whereas one that has only artificial light and ventilation will have more limited uses. The reason for this is legal as well as practical. Rooms with low levels of natural light and ventilation aren't considered habitable. This precludes their use as a living room, dining room or (arguably) a bedroom. Provided they have sufficient artificial light and ventilation, however, you can use them for any other purpose. They make great kitchens, bathrooms and utility rooms. If you want a habitable room you need to let in as much natural light as you can. As a rough guide you should try to make the window area at least 10 per cent of the floor area of the room, and have at least half the window area capable of opening. It's often possible to dig out a low-ceilinged cellar to make it usable, but excavating anything more than a few inches of subsoil will be very expensive. Depending on your soil type and the depth of the foundations, there may also be structural implications. Never contemplate digging out a basement without advice from a structural engineer, surveyor or architect or you could, quite literally, bring the house down.

✚ Layout

The layout of rooms in the basement conversion is critical if you're really going to make the best of it. A traditional design would view the basement as simply another floor of the house. The staircase down would lie under the main staircase and at its foot would be a lobby replicating the hall above, and all rooms in the basement would lead off it. This is a good layout and maximizes the space in the property. It also makes the new basement feel part of the original design of the house. Another option is to access basement rooms from related rooms on the ground floor: a utility room in the basement accessed from a ground-floor kitchen, a cloakroom accessed from the ground-floor hall or a playroom accessed from the main living room. This is an expensive arrangement because it requires more than one staircase and loses a lot of space to access points, but if done well it can make the basement a much more usable and useful addition to the house. Of course, you don't have to convert the whole basement at once. A single room in the basement can be a very worthwhile conversion, though more expensive on a cost per sq. metre basis than a complete overhaul.

✚ Remote rooms

Avoid the so-called 'remote room', a basement room that can be accessed only through another basement room. You may well be refused consent if you have one in your design. A remote room is awkward to use and can easily become the forgotten room in the house, a likely candidate for the junk store, not to mention almost impossible to escape from in the event of a fire.

✚ Floors

Some basements already have a sound floor, but most have something pretty rough and many are just bare earth. Even a reasonable-looking floor will need some work. It will probably not be completely level and will almost certainly not have a damp proof course or any insulation. If you are installing a new floor a concrete one makes most sense. A suspended timber floor will take up a lot of vertical space and impinge on your ceiling height. In any case you won't be able to get enough ventilation underneath to prevent it from rotting. A new floor should include a damp-proof membrane (dpm). Insulation is best applied above the floor and below the floor covering.

If there is a good existing floor in the basement you can apply a liquid (bitumen) dpm to it. If it needs levelling off you can apply a layer of levelling compound to give a smooth flat finish. As with new floors you will need some insulation, and a layer between the floor surface and the floor covering is probably best. Put in as much as you can without losing too much ceiling height.

The basements of some Georgian houses had brick or stone slab floors. If you have one of these you really should try and retain it. Not only is it an important architectural feature of the building, but you get a great floor covering effectively for free. You can lift the bricks or stones and install a dpm and some insulation before relaying them, but if they are in good condition you might be better leaving them as they are and enjoy their rough charm. There's more information on how to insulate a floor like this in Chapter 11.

✚ Walls

The thought of damp walls is what puts most people off underground rooms. Bricks and most other building materials are porous, and most soil is damp for at least part of the year. If you don't do anything, inevitably the damp is going to soak through into the basement. The degree of the problem is directly related to the soil and topography of the area. In areas with rocky soil, especially chalk or limestone, dampness will probably be quite mild. In an upland location in the South Downs it may be almost non-existent. Clay soils on the other hand, especially in low-lying areas, and near to rivers, lakes or the sea are prone to high levels of dampness. The solution is to build what is in effect a vertical damp proof membrane over the walls. This is called tanking. There are several different methods of tanking, and you should get a surveyor's advice on what is best for your situation. The most common and the cheapest method is bitumen. It is supplied either as a sticky paint or in self-adhesive sheets. The problem with these products is that the wall needs to be clean and dry before they can be applied, otherwise they will just peel off. This may seem to rather defeat the object. After all if it's dry enough to stick why exactly do you need it? The answer is that some dampness is seasonal, and bitumen can be applied easily in the dry part of the year. The other option is what is sometimes called a dry wall system. This uses a rigid membrane that is screwed onto the wall. A small cavity is left to allow the wall to breath. And a plasterboard covering is applied to the inside of the membrane. The success or failure of these products is all down to how well they are applied. I've used the boat hull analogy elsewhere in this book but it applies in a literal sense here. Even a little hole is no good.

An alternative to tanking is a system called French drains. The name may not conjure up pleasant thoughts, but installed properly this is probably the best way of waterproofing a basement. It's a system of free draining channels applied to the outside surface of the underground wall that drains water away from the house. A waterproof barrier can be applied to the outside wall surface at the same time. This is the most expensive waterproofing option, although if you need to excavate the walls for any other reason the cost is reduced and it's well worth considering. You need a skilled contractor to do this work properly, and it's really important that you take up some references from previous clients to see if they did it properly.

CONVERTING GARAGES AND OTHER OUTBUILDINGS

Rural buildings and some older town houses often have one or more outbuildings – coal, wood or feed stores, outside WCs, workshops, barns or stables. In more modern houses the outbuilding most often found is a garage. All these are potential conversions to residential use, although the amount of work, expense and ultimately the viability of any such conversion will depend on the design of the outbuilding, its condition and what use you intend to put it to.

Garages are usually the easiest outbuildings to convert, especially if built into or next to the house. Most garages are too small to hold a modern family car and usually become a glory hole for all the junk you can't be bothered to take up into the loft. If your house has a garage, it could in all probability be better used for some other purpose.

PERMISSION

Your biggest obstacle is likely to be planning permission, especially if the area you live in has a parking problem. Planners won't want you making a change that in theory adds to the problem (even if in practice you can't fit your car in the garage). The issue will revolve round whether the house was originally built with planning permission that had conditions stipulating the number of off-street parking spaces that must be provided (this is only likely in houses built or substantially altered from the 1970s onwards). You should write to or visit your local authority planning department to see the original approval documents. If there are no parking conditions on the approval, you may not need planning permission at all (but you should check first). If there are conditions, you'll need to find some other space to be designated as off-street parking. If you have a large front garden it should be possible to create a hardstanding.

Single garages are almost invariably built with internal measurements of 2.4 m x 5.5 m, this being the minimum demanded by most planning authorities, all of whom presumably drive Minis, to allow the garage to be counted as a parking space. Cost-conscious house builders rarely do more than they have to.

Some planning authorities require that the parking area is spacious enough to turn the car round if the alternative is to reverse out into a busy road. Additionally, some larger houses may need more than one parking space, which is another potential trap. By extending your house you could push it above the threshold and be obliged to create another off-street parking space because, according to local authority thinking, people with big houses have more cars. Indeed, you could even fall into this trap simply by adding a conventional extension. And after all that fuss, you can still park your car on the road if you want, anyway!

WALLS

Most garages and outbuildings are built with a single-skin brick or breezeblock wall. This has very poor insulating properties and will need to be upgraded if it is to become a habitable space. You'll need to build an additional inner skin wall inside the building, of either block-work or timber. A block-work wall requires foundations or footings, though if you're lucky the original wall will have been built with double-thickness foundations that you can use. If not, build the inner wall from timber. A timber inner-skin wall is constructed in a similar way to a studwork partition wall with the addition of a breathable vapour barrier behind it. However constructed, the new wall will require proper insulation (see Chapter 11 for further details).

FLOORS

Few outbuildings were built with damp-proof membranes under the floor. You'll need to do some work to it, or even re-lay the floor. The same principles apply here as for basement conversion floors (p. 120).

ROOFS

Roofs on outbuildings are generally not built to the same standard of weather resistance as house roofs, and in any case there may well be some repair work to do. The roof will need to be overhauled or perhaps even replaced if it's in really poor shape. Outbuildings usually contain no insulation at all, so the roof will need to be insulated to at least the Building Regulations standard (see chapter 11), and preferably beyond. The marginal cost of adding more insulation is small and the extra expense will be repaid in lower fuel bills in no time.

7 RESTORATION

This chapter demonstrates how to implement repairs in such a way that you don't just renovate your property but restore it. This might seem at odds with the advice of Chapter 5, 'Design and redesign', and the two approaches are certainly different. Redesign changes a badly functioning building into somewhere you want to live whereas restoration preserves a building and returns it to its former glory. Which approach is right for you will depend on your own taste and the building that you're working on.

   It's hardly unusual for an old house to need doing up. Properties require constant maintenance and attention.

ROOFS

The primary purpose of a roof is to keep out the rain. Most roofs are pitched to allow water to run off quickly. Flat roofs are very slightly pitched too, and have special waterproof coverings. Once a roof fails and water finds a way through things can go downhill very quickly. Water damage to timber, ceilings and plasterwork can be irreparable and may allow fungus and wood-boring insects to gain a foothold, so if your property has a dodgy roof, this is the best place to begin your renovation work and stop the rot before it starts.

If the roof's defences are already breached, make temporary repairs as soon as you take possession of the property; the cost of repairing the damage done by water entering through a leaking roof will be far greater than putting a tarpaulin over it. Once the roof is weathertight you can relax a little. You have probably stabilized the deterioration.

Most pitched roofs have two components: a timber-frame structure and an outer covering of impervious material such as tiles or slates. Disaster can strike either.

THINGS THAT GO WRONG WITH ROOF STRUCTURES AND WHAT TO DO ABOUT THEM

ROOF SAG

If the roof and the covering of an old house are original it's quite possible that the roof was constructed using 'green' (i.e. unseasoned) timber. Roofs made like this sagged very soon after construction. The timber then dried out and hardened and the roof settled in a stable but swaybacked form. If this is the case it's often best just to leave it. Trying to straighten things out can redistribute loads and cause problems elsewhere in the building. And anyway, a wonky roof can look quite charming.

A more prosaic reason for sagging concerns replacement roof coverings. In the 1960s and 1970s concrete tiles became widely available. At a guess, something like a quarter of all Victorian houses on these islands had their roofs re-covered in these interlocking, heavy (and frankly pig-ugly) tiles. A concrete roof tile weighs about four times as much as a slate, but many builders failed to take sufficient account of this and the roof structure, inadequately strengthened or not strengthened at all, soon began to sag. The timber on these roofs was already old and well dried out, so the sagging weakened and sometimes fractured it. If your wonky roof has concrete tiles, these rather than green timber are the probable cause. Sags caused by bodged repairs are bad news. A structural engineer will advise you, but depending on the severity some major repair/replacement work may be necessary. (The Institution of Structural Engineers' website has a search facility to enable you to locate its members. The I S E 's contact details will be found in the directory.)

INSECT AND FUNGAL ATTACK

This problem can occur wherever there is timber in a property, but it is closely linked to damp problems, so the roof timbers are often the first to suffer in a neglected house. The contents of this section should be borne in mind when examining floor and ceiling joists, timber beams and any other vulnerable components of a house you intend to rescue.

Sound, original timber in old houses is too hard and dry to make a tempting meal for an insect. However, when timber gets wet, and especially if fungal attack starts, it will soon soften up to the extent that a few insects with iron teeth and lead-lined stomachs will treat it as a free meal. First of all let's look at fungal attack. There are two types, wet rot and dry rot.

Wet rot is a general term used to describe a whole range of fungal species that cause timber decay. All wet-rot fungi require higher moisture contents than the dry-rot fungus, and are much more common. They don't have dry rot's ability to colonize a building rapidly, so are much easier and less expensive to eradicate.

Photo: DAVID CROPP

Dry rot, contrary to popular belief, is actually very rare. This is just as well, because it's the most serious type of timber decay. It can live with a lower moisture content than wet rot fungi, and has the ability to grow through damp masonry and brickwork and behind plaster. It can spread like wildfire, making treatment both complicated and expensive. Dry rot occurs throughout the U K and Ireland but is most prevalent in areas with high rainfall: northern and western England, Northern Ireland, Wales, Scotland and western Ireland.

If the timber in your building is being attacked by wet rot you must:

➡ find the source of the problem (it's usually to do with a leak or lack of ventilation);
➡ fix the fault;
➡ let the dampness dry out;
➡ remove the fungal growth and repair the damage caused; and
➡ isolate or treat timbers at risk from continuing dampness with a protective fungicide.

If you find rot in load-bearing timbers, or if you find any dry rot, you need to take specialist advice before attempting anything other than fixing the original building fault. The timber-preservation industry has its fair share of sharp operators, so stay away from slick salesmen and try to find an independent expert. Good people in this business aren't always easy to locate, but a good place to start is the industry's professional body in the U K, The British Wood Preserving and Damp Proofing Association (see directory for contact details). Your surveyor can then design a solution based on the expert's advice. On the whole, you should be looking to use as few chemicals and replace as little timber as possible.

Woodworm is a term so often heard that you might be forgiven for believing that there is a species of creature wriggling around that goes by the name. The truth is that 'woodworm' describes a whole range of species, none of which are worms and all of which are insects. By far the most common is the **common furniture beetle**, which bores pin-sized holes in floorboards and furniture. It's found most often in southern England. The magnificently named **death watch beetle** is another that prefers warmer climes. Found in southern England and Wales, parts of the Midlands and occasionally in southern Ireland, it prefers hardwood timbers such as oak, ash and chestnut that have been softened by water and rot. As these woods are seldom found in modern domestic buildings you're unlikely to come across it unless the property is pre-1900. The **house longhorn beetle** is quite rare but causes severe damage to softwood timber (which doesn't need to be wet or rotten). It's not native to the U K or Ireland and at present is mainly confined to parts of Surrey and Hampshire, although climate change may encourage it to extend its range. Another import is the **powder-dust beetle**. As you might guess from its name, it pulverizes wood to a powder from the inside, causing irreparable damage. It prefers starchy woods such as ash, elm and oak. Although there is evidence to suggest that it's increasing in numbers this insect is still very rare, and you'd be unlucky to encounter it. **Weevils** are cute-looking little beetles with long pointy noses. Lots of weevil species attack wood, but only when it has already been damaged by fungus. Weevils are more an indicator of a problem than its instigator.

Identifying the insect that is causing the problem will lead you to the solution. In most cases dealing with the rotten timber and dampness is enough. The insects' food source literally dries up and they move on. If all else fails you may need to resort to an insecticide. There are plenty of cowboy firms that will happily dose every square inch of wood in your house with noxious poisons, but this is almost always unnecessary and might leave residues of chemicals that could be harmful to you and your household. Common chemicals used include P C P (pentachlorophenol) and Lindane. These poisons have been banned in many European countries and the U S A because of their dangerous effects on people, though they are still used in the U K. (For more details see pp. 240–43). The responsible end of the industry uses species-specific insecticides that aim to break at least one stage in the insects' life cycle. The infestation then dies out over time. But beware – such companies may look for repeat business; they may recommend 'continuous control', meaning that you should have them back every year to spray again. Don't let yourself become obsessive about this; we don't live in a sterile world, and the odd insect wandering about in the roof probably won't do any harm. If your roof is watertight and adequately ventilated fungal and insect attacks won't recur.

We don't live in a sterile world, and the odd insect wandering about in the roof probably won't do any harm.

ROOF COVERINGS

Most pitched roofs are covered in slates or tiles, although there are other traditional coverings local to particular parts of the country: stone slates in Yorkshire, the Cotswolds and parts of Scotland, thatch in south-west England and East Anglia, and wooden shingles in the Home Counties. All these coverings are made from natural materials, and they weather over time. Indeed, part of the appeal of an old house is that natural materials often look better the older they get. Of course, there comes a point when 'weathered' becomes 'knackered', and remedial work is needed.

Slate is a natural stone quarried in the UK, Ireland and many other countries of Europe, Africa, Asia and South America. Until the advent of the railways its use was very localized, but once it could be easily transported around the country it became an almost ubiquitous roofing material from the mid nineteenth century until the 1920s. The most common (and arguably the best) roof slate comes from North Wales and is distinguishable by its bluey-grey colour. The quality of this slate means that it can be cut thinner and to a smoother finish than other slate. Slate from other areas such as Cumbria and Cornwall is cut thicker and often has a greeny-grey to brown colour. Being a natural material, slate avoids many of the damaging global environmental consequences of other materials. But there is a cost, and parts of North Wales have paid heavily. The Blaenau Ffestiniog valley there is literally covered in the spoil of slate quarrying and is a reminder that descecrating the environment is something that the building industry has been indulging in for hundreds of years.

THINGS THAT GO WRONG WITH ROOF COVERINGS AND WHAT TO DO ABOUT THEM

CRACKING AND FLAKING

Weathering gradually erodes slates and clay tiles, but unless the roof is more than 200 years old it's unlikely that they'll be worn away to the point that replacement is necessary. (That's not to say that they won't need replacing for other reasons.) Minor cracks are nothing to worry about, either, unless they weaken the nail hole.

If you do need to replace slates and tiles, try to match new ones as closely as possible, using local materials, if available. In this case new really means new. Although this book advocates recycling throughout, this is one exception in which new can be better than second hand. The huge demand for old building materials keeps the rogue end of the architectural salvage industry going and encourages wholesale theft from, and damage to, many old buildings. Also, buying new helps keep small manufacturers in business. (There are, of course, many reputable architectural salvage companies and if you're confident that their materials are reputably sourced, then by all means buy reclaimed slates or tiles. Even so, reclaimed building materials are expensive, and it's usually cheaper to buy new. If you can't get an exact match, swap some slates round so the new ones are all positioned together on a less-visible area of the roof.

SLIPPED OR MISSING SLATES AND TILES

Minor slippage can be repaired with small strips of metal called tingles. The tingle is nailed to, or hooks over, the batten and is bent back round the bottom edge of the slate. If several slates are loose or have slipped, you should check the condition of the battens and the nails holding them in place. Traditionally iron nails were used, but these rust away. Replace them with galvanized steel or copper nails. The wind moves slates slightly, and over time this will wear the nail hole, which eventually becomes so big that it breaks through the slate. If all your slates are nearing this point, there's no alternative but to replace them. But before you resign yourself to a new roof, check to see how extensive the problem is. Slates on the east-and south-facing elevations tend to fare better (the strongest winds come from the west in the UK and Ireland).

OVERGROWN VEGETATION

Moss and ivy are the most common culprits, although a few vigorous garden climbers such as honeysuckle, wisteria, clematis and Virginia creeper can get out of hand too. The problem is that they hold in moisture. Some really boisterous climbers can even crack slates and tiles as well. Cut them off at the base first and let them die before you try and wrench them off. Ivy has particularly strong airborne roots. If you tug too hard when it's alive, it can bring tiles, render and goodness knows what else off with it. Moss lives only in damp conditions. Even in wettest west Wales a normal roof would be too dry, so the presence of moss indicates that something is preventing the water from flowing away. Sort out the problem rather than spraying herbicide over it.

LEAKING FLASHINGS

Flashings keep water out of the joints at the edge of roofs where the roof meets parapet walls, and the chimney (soakers are the bit of flashing below the chimney). They are usually made of lead, but sometimes cement fillets are used as a cheap alternative. Cement works, but in time it cracks and leaks. If you can, it's best to replace it all with lead.

LEAKING FLAT ROOFS

Most flat roofs in old buildings are covered in asphalt, but some will be covered in lead or zinc. A common problem in asphalt is blistering and splitting. Asphalt is a tar-based product and in warm weather it softens. Convection currents in the tar then cause the asphalt to bump up in places. If the asphalt was correctly laid in the first place, this shouldn't be a problem. It might look like a bad case of acne, but it shouldn't rupture. A way of minimizing the effect is to apply reflective paint or white stone chippings to reflect the heat. Most faults are caused either by poorly laid asphalt or by people walking on the roof and damaging it. If the roof is leaking, of course, it needs repair. If there is an obvious point of failure you can do a patch repair, but if the damage is more general the whole roof will need re-asphalting.

Part of the appeal of an old house is that natural materials often look better the older they get. Of course, there comes a point when 'weathered' becomes 'knackered'.

CASE STUDY_4 Maxwell's notes from the frontline

Mike and Catriona Ing have made a life-changing decision. The couple have already sold their house in Oxford and have decided to follow Catriona's parents, John and Sue, to Aberdeenshire.

While living in Oxford they owned a graphic illustration company, and propose to continue this business in Aberdeenshire.

Their Vision

The couple want to live in a rural property. There are a host of buildings in Aberdeenshire which could be perfect.

They have a total budget of £100,000, of which £20,000 is set aside for establishing the new business. By national UK standards £80,000 for a freehold property is unthinkably low, but the couple do have substantial do-it-yourself skills. Catriona's father works in a builders' merchants, which might provide handy discounts. They are confident that their friends will be happy to help. This 'sweat equity' is essential if they are going to achieve their dream.

The Front Runners
Letham Watermill

The village of Letham, north of Dundee, not far from Catriona's parents, was planned and laid out around 1788. The old mill buildings have a small garden running down to a fast-flowing stream, which at one time provided power for the now non-existent mill. There is a small cottage, of a type known locally as a 'butt and ben', with two rooms either side of an entrance hall. This cottage adjoins the two-storey stone-built mill building, which is currently in semi-derelict condition with a rusting corrugated-iron roof.

The area

The village of Letham has a unique form of local government. The village was established in 1788 by the Victorian philan-thropist George Dempster. The land had previously been farmland, and he created a new settlement around the mills. Once the idea had taken hold he also established an administrative committee, known as the Feuars, which held its first meeting on 26 April 1803. The Feuars were elected by the villagers and the committee exists to this day.

The Feuars (see 'The area') own the mill that Catriona and Mike are interested in and are happy to sell, though as a charity they are duty bound to take the highest offer. Scotland enjoys a unique legal process for buying and selling properties. All offers have to be deposited in a sealed envelope with the vendor's solicitors, and the owner can accept whichever one he wants with no explanation. For more on buying a house in Sotland, see pp. 58–61.

The Riggin

This is a most confusing house set at the end of a muddy, sloping drive above a small valley, whose lush green slopes are sprinkled with cotton-wool sheep and lambs.

The Riggin is a two-storey granite building with a pitched Aberdeenshire slate roof. There are three rotting caravans at the front of the property and what was once an established garden at the rear. There are signs that there was once a building abutting the house, which appears to have been vacant for some considerable time. This is a truly beautiful, isolated spot. There seems no obvious explanation why this house has been left abandoned.

Finding out about the home

The Riggin was built in 1756 and became a school for up to 120 pupils run by the strict presbyterian William Smith, who provided the only source of education for a large agricultural area. The strange little building behind one of the caravans was quite clearly once the boys' and girls' outside toilets. The mark of a gable on one wall of the house shows where the school building once stood. It was demolished in 1986, leaving just the house.

The Riggin evokes a marvellous piece of colonial history. Jessie Anne Smith, one of William Smith's daughters, was born in 1853. In 1884 she married her childhood sweetheart, who took her to British Columbia in Canada. Before they went, her father gave her some clippings from his beloved apple trees. Jessie Anne replanted these in Canada, grew prize-winning fruit and quite literally sowed the seeds of British Columbia's now-famous fruit-growing industry.

The Riggin has not been lived in for thirty years but was once a much-loved family home. Long after his family had left the house the owner would return to spend time in the garden in one of the caravans.

Now that he has died, his wife and family own the property, and they seem keen that it should pass into caring hands who would respect the memory of the husband and father.

Internally The Riggin is in surprisingly good condition. Once the debris and old furniture have been removed, the house will be ready for instant renovation. The wallpaper is readily peeling from damp walls, revealing good-quality plaster. The window frames only need repairing and redecorating, as do the doors. Some roaring fires in the fireplaces and some fresh air would soon bring this house back to life.

What Next?

Catriona and Mike loved both Letham Mill and The Riggin. However, the idea of being in an open commercial competition on the mill and the likely high price ruled it out.

The couple seemed confident that they could arrange a private contract direct with the owners of The Riggin, with whom they got on very well.

The property fits the bill in every way, is within their budget and is just what they are looking for.

CHIMNEYS

A chimney is a building's exhaust pipe. Until the 1950s, coal fires heated most houses in the UK and Ireland, and each room contained a fireplace and a flue discharging smoke and flue gases via one of the house's chimneys. We might get nostalgic about open fires now, but the combined effect of everybody heating their homes using coal was ghastly. When the weather was cold and still, the pollution lingered in the air and created a thick, mucky smog in many of our towns and cities. The Clean Air Acts of the 1950s and 1960s in the UK created smoke control areas and smokeless zones. (That legislation have been superseded by the Environmental Protection Act, but the requirements are still in place.) Because smokeless fuel costs more than cheap coal, open fires became more expensive to run and the arrival of cheap North Sea gas was the final nail in the poor old open fire's coffin.

Most chimneys, then, are redundant. There is an argument that you should get rid of them, but think before you do. Even if the house isn't listed or in a conservation area, without chimneys it might look rather odd; a bit like a person with no ears. Also, incorrectly sealed chimney openings are notorious for letting in moisture. If you're removing chimney breasts from the inside of the house to make more room, removing the external chimney can make sense. If not, it's best to learn to love and maintain your chimneys as an integral part of the structure.

Even if the house isn't listed or in a
conservation area, without chimneys
it might look rather odd; a bit like
a person with no ears.

THINGS THAT GO WRONG WITH CHIMNEYS
AND WHAT TO DO ABOUT THEM

LISTING

Sulphurous fumes in flue gases react with the lime in mortar to produce calcium sulphate. This chemical reaction causes the mortar to weaken and expand. Uneven expansion pushes the bricks apart and makes the chimney lean to one side. If nothing is done, eventually it will fall over. Burning gas produces more sulphur than burning coal, and the problem is common is houses where a gas fire has been installed without a flue liner. A chimney with a slight lean can probably be left alone, but if you want to put a gas fire in the fireplace you should also fit a flue liner in the chimney to prevent matters worsening. For a badly leaning chimney the only remedy is to dismantle and rebuild it. A disused chimney can be capped off, but make sure that it is ventilated in some way below.

WONKY POTS

Terracotta chimney pots are very resistant to weathering and can last for hundreds of years. They may look like overgrown flowerpots from the ground, but close up you'll see what big brutes they really are. The rapid descent of one from roof level would cause a good deal of damage on the way down and would pretty much destroy anything (or anyone) it landed on. Pots are held in place with a bed of mortar called a flaunching. In such a lofty and exposed situation, the flaunching takes a battering from the weather and after many years will begin to crack and crumble. Not only does this make the pot unstable, it also allows water into the brickwork and so the chimney stack's mortar will soon deteriorate too. Re-laying the flaunching is easy; just make sure that the pot doesn't get broken in the process.

WALLS

Despite the fact that many traditional and modern alternatives exist, the fact remains that few of us will ever live in anywhere with walls built of anything other than brick, and it is on this material that this section concentrates. Brick is an excellent building material; it's strong, relatively light, weather resistant and it comes in consistent sizes. It's also durable: the Guildhall in Blakeney, Norfolk, is one of the earliest surviving brick buildings in the British Isles – nearly 700 years old and still looking fantastic.

THINGS THAT GO WRONG WITH WALLS
AND WHAT TO DO ABOUT THEM

CRACKS AND BULGES

Cracked brickwork or cracks along mortar joints are a commonsight. Minor cracking is usually nothing to worry about, but watch out for signs of structural movement. Brick walls rarely just wear out, but the points at which they are supported by other building materials can weaken, and this is where cracks often occur.

Cracks above windows are often caused by failure in the brick arch or wooden lintel that holds up the window opening. This can normally be fixed by a fairly straightforward repair or rebuilding the arch. If the wooden lintel is intact it may not be necessary to do anything more than fill the crack.

Cracks up the side of bay windows or where an extension joins the main part of the house are quite common in Victorian houses where poor detailing meant that brickwork was often inadequately tied in. Effectively, the extension and the main house are two separate adjoining buildings and even a small amount of movement can lead to the few tied bricks snapping. If you're certain that the cracking isn't the result of major structural movement, you can repair it by re-stitching the brickwork together. If you're in any doubt, ask a surveyor or structural engineer to advise you.

Subsidence occurs when the ground below a building sinks (heave is when it rises). If this happens in a non-uniform way it can cause walls to crack. There are many causes of subsidence and heave, including cracked underground drains, but the commonest is when a heavy soil dries out. Houses built on river clay are particularly vulnerable. If you have cracks that look wider at one end than the other, you may have a

problem. Before you start to panic, remember that it's the width of the crack and the rate at which it's opening up that determine the severity of the problem. Small cracks that have stabilized are nothing to worry about. In fact, it would be remarkable if something as big as a house managed to last a hundred years or more without developing any cracks at all. With climate change altering our rainfall patterns, minor subsidence is a problem that is likely to become widespread. If you suspect you may have a problem, get a surveyor or a structural engineer's advice.

Bulging brickwork is quite common, particularly on side walls. It sounds pretty scary, but a mild case does not always necessitate remedial work. Don't be panicked into rebuilding the wall by a scaremongering builder. A structural engineer will charge a few hundred pounds to advise you what to do. This might sound expensive, but it's a lot cheaper than rebuilding a perfectly good wall.

DAMPNESS

Water may be the nectar of life, but in the wrong place it's the harbinger of doom for old buildings. Most building materials will happily hold a surprisingly large amount of moisture without complaint (a London yellow stock brick will hold a pint), but when the proportion of moisture reaches a certain level it will cause rapid chemical decomposition and physical deterioration by allowing fungi and insects to get a foothold. Wet bricks also transmit water to adjoining materials such as plaster and wood, which are far less resilient.

When bricks get wet they turn a darker colour. In the UK's climate they usually dry out within a few hours, but prolonged dampness allows algae to grow and stain the bricks green or brown. It can also wash out salts in the bricks and deposit them on the surface, leaving a white stain known as efflorescence.

There are three generally recognized causes of dampness in buildings: leaks, condensation and rising damp. In neglected buildings, leaks cause by far the most problems.

LEAKS

The individual causes of leaks in houses are covered elsewhere in this chapter, so rather than duplicate them here I'll simply list my top ten causes of leaks in neglected houses:

1. Overflowing uncleared gutters
2. Rotten window sills
3. Ill-fitting and broken guttering
4. Broken joints on rainwater downpipes
5. Weather-worn chimneys
6. Defective roof flashings
7. Worn-out wall pointing
(especially on parapet walls)
8. Badly made stone (concrete) window sills
with no drip bar
9. Badly fitting doors and windows
10. Seized ballcock valves on water tanks

Far from comprehensive and far from scientific, this list does illustrate the variety of problems that can cause leaks. If you find a damp patch on a wall, I'd suggest that you assume it's a leak and look for the cause. Only when you have eliminated that possibility should you consider condensation or rising damp.

Water may be the nectar of life, but in the wrong place it's the the harbinger of doom for old buildings.

CONDENSATION

Condensation occurs when water vapour in the air reaches its dew point and forms droplets on cold surfaces. Water vapour is almost always the result of human activity – cooking, bathing, breathing, heating; portable paraffin heaters are one of the worst culprits – so if the property has been unoccupied it's unlikely to have a condensation problem. Condensation is none the less important in old houses. Warm air holds more water than cold air, and as the air cools the gaseous water vapour gradually condenses to become liquid. This can happen when air in different parts of a house is at different temperatures. Some rooms are heated and some aren't, of course, but even within a room there can be large variations in temperature. The air close to a window on a cold day can be 10 °C colder than the rest of the room. As moisture-laden warm air hits cold areas, it drops in temperature and condenses on to the coldest surface. Often this is a windowpane, which is why windows become steamed up, but if other surfaces are cold enough for water to condense it can result in real problems. Condensation on walls can cause wallpaper to peel and paint to flake. Prolonged exposure to dampness can cause plaster to bulge and crumble. Really bad damp problems can affect timber, allowing wood-boring insects to gain a foothold and mould and rot to grow.

Fortunately, you don't have to stop cooking, bathing and breathing to avoid the problem. We're not designed to live in a crispy dry atmosphere and neither are our houses. In fact it doesn't matter how much water vapour you produce so long as your house is designed to cope with it all.

The three causes of condensation in houses are poor heating, poor insulation and poor ventilation. If you have more than one you're almost certain to have a condensation problem. Adequate heating keeps the air at a constant temperature so that it can hold water as vapour. It also heats surfaces so they don't attract condensation. Insulation helps keep the surfaces warm and ventilation takes water-laden air out of the house before it condenses.

Condensation problems occur most often in poorly heated rooms, particularly in areas where there is little air movement. Look behind wardrobes and in the corners of rooms at ceiling level. Damp will be obvious by yellowing and discolouration, often accompanied by black 'staining' which is, in fact, mould.

RISING DAMP

Rising damp is allegedly the result of water being drawn up from the ground into walls by capillary action in the same way that oil is drawn up a lamp wick. Many experts, however, claim that rising damp doesn't in fact exist. They might be right: laboratory experiments using brick walls in baths of water have failed to reproduce the phenomenon, and almost everybody who inspects buildings reports it as extremely rare or non-existent. So why is it that seemingly every mortgage survey of an old house recommends a new damp-proof course? Well, the huge damp-proofing industry isn't about to pack up its bags and go fishing on some boffin's say-so, is it? And, to be fair, there is opposing evidence that rising damp can occur in some circumstances. If you're of a cautious nature you might say that protecting a house against rising damp is a sensible precaution, but I'll leave you to make your own mind up. Just don't rely on the arguments of a dpc salesman to help you do so.

PEBBLEDASH RENDERING AND OTHER SURFACE COVERINGS

The scourge known as pebbledash, or roughcast rendering, to give it its proper name, first appeared in the early twentieth century. It was initially used as a decorative finish to small areas of wall surface, sometimes just the gable, but by the time of the First World War it had become fashionable to coat the outer surface of the upper floor, the main motivation being to save on the cost of expensive facing bricks. Then at some point during the 1960s people started to think that it would improve the look of their house if they covered the whole thing in the stuff. By the late 1970s when the nation came to its senses, tens of thousands of houses up and down the country were coated in a grey/brown porridge. In my view, to say that pebbledash has any aesthetic merit is like a cream-cake manufacturer pointing to the glacé cherry on an iced bun and saying, 'Look: fruit. This is health food!' There is perhaps an argument that pebbledash provides added protection against driving rain in very exposed areas, but really the only positive thing I can find to say about it is that it's less awful than stone cladding.

Stone cladding started life as an economy when constructing houses in areas where they were traditionally built from local stone. Stone-clad houses built using cheaper methods were more likely to obtain planning permission. Fair enough, I suppose. Then somebody came up with the idea of making the cladding out of concrete instead. This was cheaper still, but the finish faded over time and in a few years gave the appearance of an old concrete house rather than a new stone one. Worse still, manufacturers began to market cladding as an improved finish for existing weathered houses. Before long the stuff was defacing house fronts throughout the land. What could be a bigger eyesore than a stone-clad facade in the middle of a brick-built terrace?

REMOVING PEBBLEDASH AND STONE CLADDING

If your property has walls finished in either of these abominations, you might very reasonably think about getting it removed. But before you do, look to see if it was an original finish (i.e. was the house built like that?). How are similar properties in the street finished? If it's original, leave it. Removal will spoil the architecture of the house and may well expose an unattractive wall of cheap bricks underneath.

If a rendered finish sounds hollow when you tap it, the adhesion has gone. If a large proportion of the surface is like this, the render will be relatively easy to remove and the damage to the underlying brick surface won't be too great, although there will still be areas where the render is stuck hard and at least some damage is inevitable. Removing render isn't a specialist job, but it needs to be done slowly and with care. Repairing the resultant damage, however, will need some specialist input. Of course, you won't know exactly what needs to be done until you have removed the render. You might have to replace a proportion of the bricks or you might get away with brick slips (very thin bricks that can be stuck on to damaged brickwork to provide a new surface). If the damage is extensive you'll have to re-render the wall. On an old building a lime render will look best, but not necessarily much better than the pebbledash you've just removed. An easy and cheap alternative is to leave the pebbledash on and give it a couple of coats of paint. If you do, the advice below will prove useful.

PAINTED FINISHES

Whilst render is often painted, and usually looks better for it, most brick- and stone-walled houses were designed to be left unpainted. Weathering improves the look of most unpainted surfaces, especially those made from natural materials. Paint, on the other hand, tends to look worse the older it gets. Depending on the weather and the air quality, it'll need a recoat every five to twenty years. Painting can also damage walls. Modern polymer paint is impervious when it dries and will prevent a damp wall from drying out. True it should also stop a dry wall from getting wet, but there is bound to be some moisture in the wall when you paint it, and there will always be some unpainted areas where water can get in. An unpainted surface will dry out before you notice a problem but a painted one will just get wetter and wetter. If you do paint the walls, use something pervious such as a lime-wash paint that allows the wall to breathe.

If you're removing old paint applied before *c.* 1980, beware of the risk of lead, which was often used as an additive. Wear a mask and try to avoid creating dust by sanding old paint or scraping at it vigorously. If you do remove old paint, dispose of the waste carefully. Don't burn it – the fumes will be toxic.

DEFECTIVE POINTING

One of the commonest problems found in the brickwork of old houses is a bodged pointing repair (pointing is the term for the outer surface of the mortar applied between bricks). Pointing doesn't last for ever, and when it wears away it can create an access point for dampness. Builders and surveyors often say that the purpose of the mortar in a brick wall isn't to stick the bricks together but to hold them apart. They are right. Appreciating this point will help you understand what so often goes wrong with repairs. The mortar's job is to spread the load of the wall and to act as a cushion between the bricks.

Until the mid twentieth century most mortar was made from a mixture of lime and sand, not cement. Unlike cement, lime mortar is a relatively soft, porous material. It allows water to evaporate away from the wall and it also takes the brunt of any weathering. This means that over time the mortar erodes but leaves the bricks undamaged. Since the Second World War bricks have been made in a different way. They are baked hotter and longer and set harder and are tough enough to handle cement mortar. Consequently, builders have fallen into the habit of using cement and many of them don't know, or don't care about, the difference. If cement is used to repoint old walls, over time the combined effects of chemical action and weathering wear away the bricks, leaving the harder cement mortar standing proud.

Weathered lime mortar isn't a problem, it's simply doing its job. If it has not receded, leave it alone, even if all you can see on the surface is sand. If the mortar has receded further you should get it repointed. Match the type and colour of the mortar with the original, and bear in mind that the whiteness of the lime will tone down with time.

GRAFFITI

Abandoned houses soon fall prey to local artists carrying out what is now rather over-dramatically called environmental crime by the Home Office. The medium of choice is the aerosol spray. Solvent-based paints and those sprayed on porous surfaces are the hardest to get off. Although the surface paint can be removed relatively easily, a residue is often left in the pores, leaving a ghostly shadow. Cleaning buildings is a touchy subject. Some say you shouldn't do it because cleaning can destroy the outer surface (patina) of building materials, leaving them scarred for life, but if you've become the victim of a graffiti artist the only real choice is a chemical agent and a stiff brush. Experiment on a small inconspicuous area first and see how it looks. If the treated area looks so clean that it sticks out from the rest of the untreated surface you might need to clean the whole wall. Chemical removers are available

in most DIY shops and often come in the form of a gel that you apply, scrub in and later rinse off. You can alternatively employ specialist contractors to clean up for you. They will have access to more technological systems such as air-abrasion, laser cleaning and pressure washing. Selecting the right system is essential. Using the wrong one could push graffiti stains further into the masonry, making removal impossible, or permanently damage the patina of the wall.

Another option is to paint over the graffiti. If the surface has previously been painted this is the obvious solution, but don't rush into painting an otherwise original brick surface. Apart from the problems with impervious paints mentioned above, you could ruin the original character of the building. After all, you wouldn't paint an antique mahogany table, would you? For further advice on choosing paint see pp. 244–5.

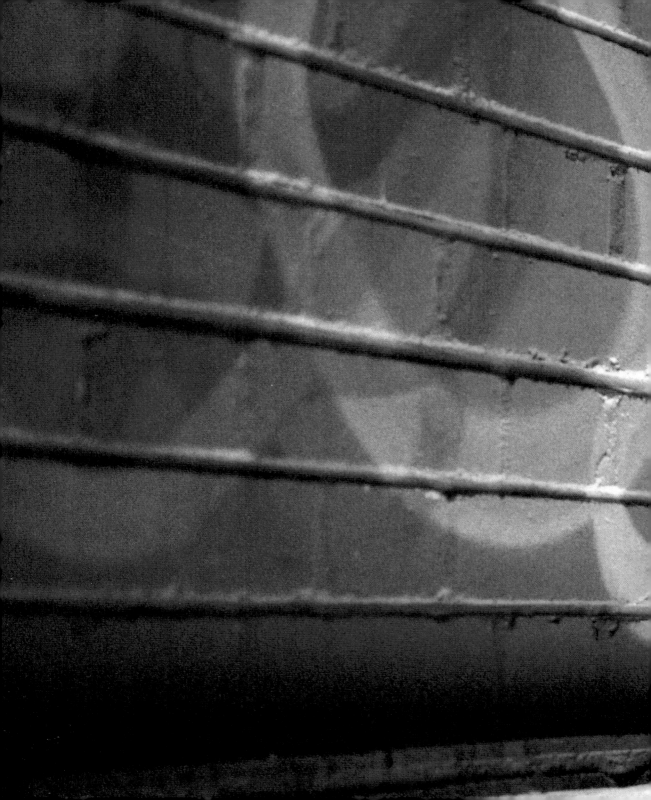

RAINWATER GOODS

Guttering and downpipes require regular maintenance. By definition, a neglected building won't have had much maintenance at all, so it's quite common for defects to arise here. In most old buildings rainwater goods would have been made from cast iron, but in some Georgian buildings they were made from lead. Today most are made from plastic. If cast iron isn't regularly repainted it will rust. It can also split and crack. Hopper heads and downpipes of whatever material are easily blocked by leaves and moss. Although uPVC doesn't rust, ultra violet light causes it to deteriorate and crack. Plastic pipework and guttering comes in standard sizes and colours and is fairly cheap, so if a small area has become damaged you should be able to replace it easily.

Don't patch up cast iron with sections of uPVC. It won't fit together well and will look horrible.

Leaking or blocked rainwater goods cause rainwater to overflow and run down the walls. You may see white staining, or, if it gets really wet, streaks of slimy green algae. Long-term problems can allow full-size plants to grow. (Buddleja has an amazing ability to grow into quite a large plant in the most inhospitable of locations. You quite often see it growing out of blocked gutters or through the pointing of walls soaked by leaking rainwater pipes. Its roots can cause brickwork to crack, and will certainly make blockages even worse.) Large plants need to be removed carefully. If you just yank them out brickwork and rainwater goods could be damaged or dislodged. If you have stained brickwork it's best to leave it to dry out, then brush the staining off.

Another common problem in empty buildings, especially in city centres, is pigeons. Rain hoppers and gutters are favourite nesting places and pigeons can breed in surprisingly large numbers in old houses. Their feathers and droppings quickly block rainwater pipes, causing them to overflow when it next rains. For more information on evicting pigeons and preventing their return see p. 158.

EXTERNAL WOODWORK

Timber is the oldest building material and one that has never really fallen out of use. Timber is used extensively for external doors, window frames and door cases. These parts of a building feel the full force of the weather and can deteriorate quickly if they aren't well maintained. On the plus side, well-maintained timber can last for ever.

WHAT GOES WRONG WITH EXTERNAL TIMBER AND WHAT TO DO ABOUT IT

The weakest points on timber-framed windows and doors are the joints. Peeling paint and missing putty allows water to enter, which can lead to warping and make the door or window stiff and difficult to open and close. Prolonged exposure to water will allow wet rot to start (see p. 128). External timberwork usually needs repainting every five to ten years. If it's left longer than this the paint will become dry and peel away from the timber. Once the sun gets to the wood it'll dry it out and cause it to crack, so creating new routes for the rain to get in. If your timber has reached this stage but has no rot you should fill the cracks before rubbing down the timber and repainting it. (For advice on choosing appropriate paints see pp. 244–5.) The warning on p. 144 regarding lead additives also applies here. Oil-based paint had particularly high amounts of lead in it, and woodwork is often covered in numerous layers of the stuff dating back many, many years.

When you find rotten timber you shouldn't automatically assume that you'll need to replace the whole window frame or door. If the rot isn't too extensive, the affected section can be cut out and new timber can be scarfed in. Repairs can be far cheaper than replacement, and once the woodwork has been rubbed down and repainted it'll look just as good.

The front door is a place where it really is worth making an effort. If you're lucky enough to have the original front door on the house, you should do whatever you can to retain it and revive it. Replacement doors nearly always look like replacements, and it's well-nigh impossible to find a replacement exactly the same as the original, anyway. If you have to replace doors and windows, try to have new ones made up to match the originals (but beware of the Building Regulations requirements on replacement windows – see pp. 246–9 for more details).

IRON RAILINGS, GATES AND BALCONIES

Two types of iron are used as a building material: cast and wrought. Cast iron, as its name suggests, is formed by casting molten iron into a mould. Wrought iron is shaped by beating or stretching strips to form a pattern. Like timber, iron will last almost indefinitely if it's properly cared for, and that means keeping it under a layer of paint. Iron left to the weather, as we all know, will go rusty. Ferrous oxide (or rust, as we commonly call it) is considerably weaker than iron so can easily erode or snap. Also it takes up more room, so where railings are mounted into stone, iron going rusty can cause the stone to shatter. As the chemical reaction isn't reversible all the rust has to be removed. Leave just a little bit behind and the rust problem will come back. Use a wire brush to remove surface rust. Very rusty iron can be cleaned up by sandblasting and wrought iron can be flame cleaned.

INTERNAL WALLS

Internal walls have two functions: they divide the property into rooms (partition walls) and support the upper floors and walls (load-bearing walls). Some do both. On the whole, an internal wall built of brick or stone will be load bearing. Most timber-framed (stud) walls, on the other hand, are non-load-bearing partition. If you're not sure, look at the floorboards. In most cases, if the floorboards run parallel to the internal wall then it's likely to be supporting the joists of the floor, but if they run at 90° it's likely that the wall isn't load bearing. If you're not sure and you intend to remove or replace internal walls, lift a couple of floorboards and stick your head underneath to see what's going on. If the wall continues down below the floor surface to the ground and if there are joists attached to it, the wall is load bearing. If the wall doesn't go below floor level it's a partition wall.

THINGS THAT GO WRONG WITH INTERNAL WALLS AND WHAT TO DO ABOUT THEM

DAMP

I have already covered in the section on external walls (pp. 140–41) the three causes of dampness in houses: leaks, condensation and rising damp, and the comments there also apply here. If the property has been recently occupied then water pipes and central heating pipes are another potential source of leaks. After resolving the cause the next problem is what to do about the plaster. Wall plaster can take a few soakings, but prolonged exposure to water changes the plaster chemically and makes it loose and crumbly.

Just because you have an area of defective plaster doesn't necessarily mean that the whole room needs to be replastered. (Many builders perpetuate this myth because it gives them more work to do and is easier than patch repairing.) Tap outwards from the defective area to determine the extent of the problem and carry out patch repairs instead, using the same kind of approach described below for repairing bulges. If you do this, the choice of plaster is important. You should use the same type of plaster as the original to make sure that the repair takes properly.

If a lath-and-plaster wall has suffered from a very long-standing damp problem it's possible for the wooden laths to rot. If this has happened you will need to demolish parts of the wall in order to investigate. It's possible for rot to spread beyond the area of defective plaster along the laths without affecting the surface plaster work.

CRACKS AND BULGES

Plaster moves and breathes and over time it can develop cracks and bulges. Fine cracks are caused by shrinking plaster. Indeed, you may notice that some cracks appear only in dry weather and disappear on damp days. Small cracks can be easily filled with patching plaster as part of your preparation for decoration.

Slightly bigger cracks are often a sign that the plaster has pulled away from the underlying wooden laths that support it. If the bulk of the plaster is sound, it's quite easy to do patch repairs. Remove completely any small bits of loose plaster around the crack or bulge, and reattach large loose sections by drilling into the plaster and screwing the piece back onto the lath using a washer. The whole area can be neatened up again by covering the holes with fibreglass tape and skimming over it with new plaster.

CEILINGS

Ceilings are there mainly for aesthetic reasons. (The underside of joists tend to look a bit ugly, especially when they have pipes and electric cables running along them.) Ceilings also provide a small amount of heat and sound insulation.

Most ceilings are made from plaster, and the traditional way of applying it was on laths. These are thin strips of wood that are tacked onto the underside of the joists at very close intervals. When the plaster is applied, it squeezes between the gaps, and as it dries forms a tight hold on the laths. Since the late 1960s plasterboard has taken over from lath and plaster as the most popular method for building ceilings. Plasterboard is simply a layer of set plaster between two sheets of paper. It's nailed onto the joists and a light coat of skim plaster is applied over it to even up the surface and provide a base for decoration.

THINGS THAT GO WRONG WITH CEILINGS AND WHAT TO DO ABOUT THEM

There is a building industry view that lath-and-plaster ceilings are unpredictable and can collapse without warning, so it's better to whip them out and replace them with plasterboard. This isn't really true, and old houses lose character when their ceilings are unnecessarily replaced. Ceilings don't collapse without warning, although you may need to look for the signs: damp patches, cracking and bulges.

CRACKS

Cracks can be a sign of a number of potential problems. Major cracks can indicate movement in the house. A poor loft conversion can lead to joists being overstressed or movement in an external wall caused by subsidence can cause a ceiling to stretch and split. Usually the ceiling cracks aren't the only sign, you'll find crack evidence elsewhere that contributes to an overall picture of a wider problem. Usually, however, ceiling cracks are small and signal a localized problem. A common one is damp. Plaster can absorb a large amount of water. When it does so the plaster becomes heavier and the laths and possibly even the joists can deteriorate. This can cause them to bulge and the plaster to pull away from the laths. Plaster that has been repeatedly wetted becomes crumbly and must be replaced. Laths that have been subjected to damp may warp or crack or even rot. If this has happend it's likely that you'll need to replace the whole ceiling.

Cracks in ceilings from less serious causes are common and usually can be repaired in much the same way as wall plaster (see p. 151).

SAGGING CEILINGS

Sometimes a ceiling seems to be sound and has no holes or cracks but still it's sagging. If it flexes when you push on it and it sounds hollow when tapped the plaster is in good condition but has become detached from the laths. Gently identify the area of plaster that's become detached by pushing and tapping. Surround it with screws and washers, and screw it back into the laths. For a large area you should screw in additional circles of screws inside the boundary of the area. For extra pulling and holding power, if needed, locate and anchor into the joists behind the plaster lath.

ARTEX

A legacy of the 1970s and 1980s is the decorative ceiling finish we call Artex. (Artex is, in fact, a trade name, but at the time most plaster companies produced a similar textured coat plaster.) Be very careful about how you deal with Artex. The temptation is to do the very thing you shouldn't: hack it off. Artex is plaster mixed with a binder, and up until about 1980 the binder was often asbestos. If it's in good condition, asbestos poses no risk until disturbed, when asbestos fibres can easily become airborne and breathed in. Just about the most dangerous thing you could do is to try and sand it down. The importance of this cannot be overstated. If you're in any doubt, don't touch it. One exposure to asbestos can be fatal.

If you want to get rid of Artex there are three safe alternatives. (1) Cover it up. For mild patterns a coat of a primer such as Unibond will give the adhesion for a new coat of smooth plaster to be applied over the top. (2) Under-draw the ceiling, i.e. create a new ceiling immediately underneath the existing one. You'll need to fix battens and attach a new ceiling on to these. Don't do this if there is any asbestos risk. Even screwing battens into it will cause some fibres to become airborne. (3) Replace the ceiling. If there is any chance that the ceiling may contain asbestos, don't do it yourself; contact an asbestos-removal company instead. They'll be able to test to see if the ceiling does contain asbestos and safely dispose of it if necessary. This won't be cheap, but don't be tempted to allow your builder to undertake the work if they aren't a licensed asbestos-removal company. (In the UK asbestos removal companies are registered with ARCA, the Asbestos Removal Contractors Association. See the directory for further details.) This really is an area where it's better to be safe than sorry.

INTERNAL DOORS

Badly fitting doors are one of those minor irritations that can make a house really annoying to live in. Individually they are insignificant, but if left unremedied they'll give the impression that the house is in much poorer condition than it really is. Doors should open and close easily without using any force. The most common reason for a bad fit is dropped hinges, where the weight of the door has pulled the hinges loose. Other possible reasons are loose door linings or warping of the door or frame. None of these should necessitate a new door. If the doors are original, or at least in keeping with the period of the property, you should make every effort to repair them. New doors are cheap to buy and it's tempting to replace a door that exhibits even the most minor fault, but in doing so you'll be losing a bit of the original character of the property. A good carpenter will be able to repair most faults: rotted and broken timber can be replaced by piecing in new wood and doorstops (the strips of wood that the door closes against, not the metal frog Aunt Nelly brought back from the seaside) can be adjusted to accommodate all but the most badly warped doors.

The one occasion when you may need to consider replacement is if you need to have fire doors, though even here it may be possible to upgrade doors using intumescent materials (see p. 97).

Badly fitting doors are one of those minor irritations that can make a house really annoying to live in.

FIREPLACES

Before central heating, open fires warmed most houses. There would normally be one in each room, from large decorative fireplaces in the main living rooms to small functional grates in the others. As older houses were modernized, fireplaces became redundant and were taken out or covered up. Initially, old fireplaces were seen as old-fashioned, worthless scrap and usually ended up in a skip. In the 1980s old became chic, and throwaway skip fodder became overpriced, must-have accessory. Ironically this led to more period fireplaces being ripped out by money-grabbing owners. In most neglected and empty houses, needless to say, the original fireplaces will have long gone.

Most fireplaces and fireplace grates are made from cast iron with a wooden or stone surround. Some eighteenth-century fireplaces were made of steel but these are rare. A common feature is tile inserts. Eighteenth-century fireplaces often had Dutch Delftware tiles with blue and white designs. In good condition these are highly collectable items and have often gone missing over the years. Nineteenth- and early twentieth-century tiles had more flamboyant designs, often forming a small frieze or picture. It's amazing how many reproduced designs are available, so it should be quite easy to replace missing or broken tiles. Even if your design isn't still in (re)production, specialist companies will make up new tiles to match old ones. One slight snag is that new tiles are generally thinner than old ones, so you'll need to pack out the back with dabs of plaster to make them fit flush.

Hidden fireplaces can be restored with a bit of work. Some flush-set fireplaces were covered over with a sheet of plasterboard to hide them. It's easy to take this off, but before you do you may want to drill a hole and have a poke round with a long straight bit of stiff wire to find out what is behind. If it's just a gaping hole you might decide you'd rather keep the plasterboard and be grateful that you didn't tear it all off in a burst of optimism. Bare cast iron was unfashionable for much of the twentieth century and so a lot of fireplaces were painted with oil-based paint to match the woodwork in the room. Paint can be stripped from cast iron using a proprietary paint stripper or a heat gun. You should use a plastic or wooden scraper to remove the old paint to avoid scratching the surface of the fireplace.

ELECTRICS

The electrical installation is one area where you shouldn't be nostalgic about preserving the original set-up. Old installations are a common cause of household fires. Wiring doesn't last for ever, and in any case, even if an old installation is in good condition it's unlikely to be able to cope with the sheer number of electrical appliances that we all have these days. Before the early 1960s electrical cables were insulated with vulcanized Indian rubber (VIR). It looks a bit like linoleum. Exposed cables such as light pendants were normally covered in a sheath of woven cotton. Over time VIR becomes crumbly, especially in damp conditions. This allows wires to become exposed, leading to a risk of short circuits, fires and electrocution. Even in the best conditions VIR has a limited useful life and can never be considered safe after forty years. In other words, if you find VIR cables your property needs rewiring.

From the 1960s onwards, electrical cables have been insulated with PVC. PVC is tough and durable, decomposing only if subjected to strong ultra violet light. As internal electric cables are rarely bathed in sunlight you can be fairly sure your PVC insulation won't decompose. That's not to say it won't be damaged. Rats, mice and the odd misguided squirrel find its texture very appealing to gnaw on, and many electrical installations have been ruined in this way. The first place to look for problems is the roof void. This is often where cables are most visible and most accessible to rodents.

Rats, mice and the odd misguided squirrel find PVC's texture very appealing to gnaw on, and many electrical installations have been ruined in this way.

PESTS AND OTHER UNWELCOME RESIDENTS

Nature has a wonderful way of claiming back what we don't want. Almost as soon as we humans abandon something, a creature or plant of some kind turns up to assess its potential as a home or as food. Houses are no exception and there are a number of species that are commonly found in and around neglected and empty properties that need to be evicted as part of any restoration programme and before we can move back in.

RATS AND MICE

These impressive little rodents have made a way of life out of our wastefulness. The house mouse and the brown rat are very common animals indeed, although you may rarely see them. Both are principally after food and where we're careless about disposing of it they'll come and investigate. Food doesn't just mean what we eat. Both these species have hugely varied diets and will happily munch through our rubbish if we don't store it properly.

Despite popular conception, rats and mice are relatively rare visitors to empty properties. They are seeking food and warmth and there is more of both in occupied property. The best indicator of their presence is droppings. Mouse droppings look like small black grains of rice while rat droppings are larger and look a bit like a small elongated rabbit dropping. Most rats live in sewers and if you have rats in your property, it's a fair bet that there is a breach in the sewage system that is giving them a route out. Sort out the problem and the rats will disappear. Both rats and mice are attracted to rubbish and if a house or garden has had rubbish dumped in it both may arrive in search of a meal. Clear up the rubbish and they should go away. If the problem persists, most local authorities offer a service for dealing with rodent infestation. This is normally offered free for occupied property, but if you haven't moved in you may have to pay.

PIGEONS

In large towns and cities pigeons are endemic and search out neglected properties with impressive efficiency. Once they find a property large numbers can appear and make the place their home. They are messy birds. Bits of nesting material, dead bodies (avian, usually!) and heaps of droppings soon litter the place.

They also carry a number of nasty diseases including salmonella, ornithosis and fowl pest. In fact you should consider pigeon droppings to be a hazardous material and either have it removed by professionals or make sure you're well wrapped up in protective clothing including gloves and a face mask before you touch the stuff.

Pest-control companies offer an impressive range of options for exterminating pigeons; from shooting and trapping to poisons, and even the contraceptive pill. However, you can kill pigeons all day long and not make any impact on their population. If your property is attractive, more will move in. A far better solution is to pigeon proof the building.

If pigeons are nesting and roosting on ledges on the outside of the building, a full-scale restoration will normally frighten them off. If they come back or you aren't planning repairs to the part of the building where they are roosting, you may need to apply some anti-perching devices. First of all, remove the nests and droppings and clean things up as much as you can. You can then either buy anti-perching products and install them yourself, or get a pest-control company in to do it. Anti-perching products include netting that stops the birds getting to the ledges, spikes, and spring wire systems that are attached to the horizontal surfaces. The spikes and wires make it very difficult for a pigeon to land. An interesting new product uses holographic images of owls' eyes to scare the pigeons off. Another anti-perching product is a transparent jelly-like substance known as 'Hot Foot' which again makes landing uncomfortable. This product is fine if it's applied correctly using a hardener compound, but often this isn't done. This not only reduces its effective life, but kills pigeons and other birds in an unnecessarily cruel way. Birds become trapped in it and sometimes lose a leg in their efforts to free themselves. Feathers may also become coated with it, preventing them from flying.

COCKROACHES

Despite (or perhaps because of) spending several years as an environmental health officer looking round houses alive with cockroach infestations, I've never overcome my phobia of these insects. Cockroaches run fast, breed fast and are difficult to kill. When conditions are right for them they can multiply into huge infestations. There are several species of cockroach in the British Isles and in typical xenophobic style we've named them German, Oriental and American cockroaches.

Cockroaches aren't native to northern Europe and can't live outdoors here. Their requirements are constant warmth, food (they'll eat anything) and somewhere to scuttle away to when humans appear. Their ideal des. res. is a large block of flats, especially one with a communal heating system. There is always somewhere warm for them and the ductwork for the heating gives them their own little concealed network of paths along which to roam the building out of sight.

Cockroaches are rarely found in individual houses and never in empty houses or ones that aren't heated in winter. If you do have them, don't bother spraying them with a domestic insecticide. They're tough as old boots and will probably survive whatever you throw at them. In any case, it's the whole army you want to kill, not a few footsoldiers. Professional pest-control companies have access to chemicals and treatments that work by disrupting the insects' hormones and preventing them from breeding. Sometimes this approach is combined with poisoning. (Cockroaches have surprisingly long lifespans and most people aren't prepared to wait for them to see out their natural life.) If you live in an infested flat, the only thing to do is treat the whole block together. This is expensive and will need a lot of organization from both tenants and landlord. Many managing agents and landlords take a very responsible attitude to this, but if yours doesn't you'll be stuck with an infestation problem that you may never be able to deal with entirely.

There are several species of cockroach in the British Isles and in typical xenophobic style we've named them German, Oriental and American cockroaches.

WASPS AND BEES

Wasps commonly make their nests in houses, usually in the roof void or between the floor—ceiling space. Less commonly you may get a bees' or hornets' nest. Unless you have an allergy to their venom, none of these species poses any great threat over and above the obvious discomfort of being stung. In fact they are beneficial if you have a garden. They feed on flies, greenfly and other pests and pollinate fruit trees. None will sting aggressively, though all will sting if threatened. You may have heard horror stories about African killer bees, but they won't trouble you here. The climate in the British Isles is too cold for them to survive.

Despite the generally benign nature of these insects, most people don't want a nest in their house. The best time to remove it is during the winter months. Most bees and wasps die with the onset of winter, leaving a small number of docile insects in the nest to keep things going for the next year. At this time it's quite safe to remove the nest by hand (wear a pair of gloves) and dispose of it. At other times of the year you'll need to kill or subdue the insects before you remove the nest, and there are a number of proprietary insecticides available to do this. An alternative method is to subdue them with smoke. You can buy smoke-generating tablets for this purpose. (Be careful, though, several people have set fire to their houses this way.) Pest-control companies are usually familiar with removing nests and can do the whole task for you.

Wasps' nests are beautifully constructed rounded structures covered in what looks like a series of papery scales. They can be anything from the size of grapefruit to elaborate structures several feet across. Admire it before you sling it in the dustbin.

FERAL CATS AND FOXES

These creatures are commonly found taking shelter in derelict buildings, but the merest hint of your presence will send them running. You don't need to tackle them. Indeed, don't try to corner a feral cat – if threatened, it may well attack you. Once there are people on site and you have secured the property, you'll see no more of them.

SQUIRRELS

The grey squirrel is probably the boldest and cockiest wild mammal you're likely to come across in an old house. They like the shelter that old roofs provide and have been known to make their nests in lofts. They don't gnaw through timber as they are sometimes accused of doing, but they can be quite boisterous when clambering about and chasing each other. This can dislodge slates and tiles, letting the weather in. It's pointless trying to frighten squirrels away – they won't be scared of you – and don't even think about trying to control their numbers. Grey squirrels are ubiquitous across most parts of the British Isles. Killing your local population will be effective for a day or two at most before their grateful neighbours move in and claim the territory as their own. The best defence is a well-maintained roof in good condition. This won't allow squirrels any opportunity to get in and they'll confine their antics to the trees or your neighbours' house instead.

OTHER CREATURES

Many other birds, mammals and insects are found in and around old houses, but if they don't affect the building or pose a risk to the inhabitants they are best left alone. There are a few protected species you may come across. It's a criminal offence to kill, injure or disturb these species and you may need to take special measures to ensure any work you do to the property doesn't endanger them. The protected species you're most likely to come across are bats, which are harmless and cause no damage to the building. For more on bats see p. 72 above.

JAPANESE KNOTWEED

Japanese knotweed is one of the most invasive plants you'll come across in Europe, and the hardest to get rid of. (The financial implications of its presence are discussed on p. 75.) It grows to a height of 2–3 m with bamboo-like stems, arching branches and clusters of white flowers appearing in the late summer. The dead woody stems stay throughout the winter and new shoots appear each spring. These grow at an incredible rate, producing impenetrable thickets within a few weeks. Once present, Japanese knotweed spreads very rapidly and soon takes over completely.

The plant regenerates vegetatively, so even tiny fragments of the root or the stem can grow and form new plants. You therefore need to be extremely careful when handling it. Causing its spread into the wild is a criminal offence in the UK under the 1981 Wildlife and Countryside Act, and carelessly disposing of it or chopping it down with a strimmer is likely to do just that. The plants are considered to be pollutants and require special permission for disposal. If you have it in your garden you need to take special precautions when you have building work carried out. The requirements are set out on the website of the Environment Agency and the Scottish Environmental Protection Agency.

Some horrendous herbicides are available for use, with permission, on Japanese knotweed, but recent research indicates that such treatment may be ineffective and may even exacerbate the problem by producing herbicide-resistant strains. The best method of eradication is physical removal. To do this you need to dispose of all the above-ground parts of the plant, then dig and remove all the soil that contains the roots (rhizomes). You'll need to remove several tons of soil, even in a small garden. A piece of rhizome weighing just 1 gram can form a new plant, so you can appreciate how meticulous you need to be. In reality, complete eradication is impossible and you'll need to deal with new plants as they appear each spring. You can remove these individually by digging out as much rhizome as you can find, or apply a herbicide. Effective herbicides include triclopyr, picloram and impazapyr but these are nasty chemicals and will poison the ground for quite some time. They are definitely not recommended if you have children or pets. So far as I know, there is no practical environmentally sensitive way to get rid of this plant. One positive thought though: despite its reputation, Japanese knotweed isn't poisonous; feel free to feed it to your rabbit, goat, or horse.

TREES

Trees are rarely true unwanted residents, but they seem to cause so much angst among surveyors and house purchasers that it's worth looking at them briefly here. The issue is whether trees close to a house pose a threat. A surveyor's report on a property will often warn about the dangers of tree roots causing structural damage, and will recommend the removal of trees that are nearer to the house than the height of the tree. The distance/height calculation is a very rough estimate of the potential risk and in many cases will lead to the removal of trees that pose no danger whatsoever.

Tree roots very rarely cause damage to properties by their physical presence alone. You'll often see garden boundary walls cracked and distorted by the roots of nearby trees, but this is unlikely to happen to a house wall. The soil under a building is dry and infertile and there is very little to tempt a tree into extending its roots there. What can cause damage, however, is a tree taking moisture from the soil around a house, causing the soil to shrink and leading to subsidence. It's the process of the soil shrinking that causes the damage. An old, well-established tree will be in equilibrium with the soil around it, any shrinkage will have occurred years ago so there is little risk. A young, fast-growing tree, on the other hand, will be taking increasing amounts of water from the soil each year, and this will make soil shrinkage more likely.

Trees suck moisture through their roots which then evaporates from the leaves (the process is known as transpiration). A large tree with lots of leaves will therefore suck more water out of the ground than a small one with few leaves. Trees with waxy leaves, such as laurel and holly, suck up less water than trees such as poplars, oaks and willows. Thus there are several factors that dictate whether a tree is likely to be a risk to the property or not: size, species, age, soil type and, of course, how near it is to the house. The table on p. 166 isn't definitive, but it should give you an idea of how close a tree can be to your house before you should think about dealing with it.

Safe planting distances for selected tree species

Tree species	Normal maximum mature height	Safe distance from property
Apple	10 m	5 m
Ash	23 m	18 m
Beech	20 m	10 m
Birch	14 m	7 m
Chestnut	20 m	16 m
Holly	12 m	6 m
Laurel	8 m	4 m
Leyland cypress	20 m	11 m
Oak	20 m	25 m
Pear	10 m	5 m
Pine and other conifers	20 m	7 m
Poplar	25 m	32 m
Silver birch	14 m	7 m
Weeping willow	16 m	20 m

If you have a tree that appears to be in the risk category, don't immediately chop it down. Doing so may well cause more damage than doing nothing. Soil that has been kept dry for years by a tree sucking water out of it will start to become wet again. This could cause the soil to swell and create the opposite problem of subsidence – heave. This can have just as damaging an effect on a building as subsidence.

In many cases a better solution is to keep the tree pruned. This will reduce the number of leaves and keep its transpiration rate down. One other possibility is to install a root barrier. This is, in effect, a wall built underground, normally to a depth of about a metre. This stops, or at least slows down, the growth of the tree roots and keeps them away from the building. You'll see that for most trees in the table the safe distance is about half the mature height of the tree. If you keep a tree well pruned at below its mature height, the safe distance would be correspondingly reduced. The table shows safe distances in clay soil types. Soils that are less prone to shrinkage would have lower safe distances.

Before you start chopping down or pruning trees you should check to see whether it is subject to a tree-preservation order. These orders are issued by local authorities in order to preserve ancient trees and retain the general greenness of an area. In conservation areas all trees are protected. You'll need permission to chop down or prune a tree with a preservation order on it, or any tree in a conservation area. Most local authorities have a tree officer who can advise you.

RADON

One other problem that affects some houses is radon. The risks, dangers and likelihood of radon are discussed on p. 75. This section provides a brief general guide on how to radon-proof your house. If you think you may have a problem with radon, however, don't rely solely on what follows but contact the BRE (Building Research Establishment) or the National Radiological Protection Board in the UK or the Radiological Protection Institute in Ireland for more advice. The contact details for all these organizations are in the directory.

FIND OUT WHAT THE RADON LEVEL IS

The solution you'll need to adopt will depend largely on how high the concentration of radon is in your house. If your house is in one of the risk areas listed on p. 75 it is sensible to carry out a radon test. The National Radiological Protection Board in the UK or the Radiological Protection Institute in Ireland can provide you with the necessary equipment and instructions for using it.

The soil under a building is dry and there is very little to tempt a tree into extending its root there.

HOW TO REDUCE RADON LEVELS, IN DECREASING ORDER OF EFFECTIVENESS

✚ Radon sump

Usually the most effective way of dealing with high levels of radon is to pump it out. A pipe goes under the ground floor and an electric air pump is fitted to it. This continuously pumps the air out and discharges it out at roof level. If you have timber floors you need to seal them by fitting a membrane between the floor and the ground. The pipe passes through the membrane and pumps the air out from below it. Be careful how you install the membrane. It must not be fixed too close to the floorboards or this will hamper ventilation and run the risk of rotting the floorboards.

✚ Sealing floors and walls

Seal the floor and all gaps between the floor and wall to prevent the radon entering. This is certainly a good idea if you are converting a basement into a room.

✚ Increase the under-floor ventilation

If you've got a suspended timber floor it's quite easy to increase the flow of air beneath the floor by fitting extra vents, or making existing vents bigger. Higher radon levels can be dealt with by increasing ventilation using a fan. If the house has a cellar or basement, improved natural or mechanical ventilation in these areas, where the highest radon levels are likely to be, can prove extremely effective and result in large radon reductions. Mechanical fans can be used to blow air into, or draw air out of, a cellar or basement.

✚ Positive pressurization or ventilation

You can pressurize the house using a fan which draws air from the loft space or from outside and blows it into the house. In practice this system works well only in newer houses that are reasonably airtight. It has the added benefit of alleviating condensation problems.

✚ Improving ventilation levels

For very low levels of radon, simply improving the ventilation in the house can sometimes be enough. In practice this will make a difference only if the ventilation levels were too low anyway. Installing trickle vents to sealed windows can help.

FIRE DAMAGE

Fire is a shockingly destructive force, and if you have never seen inside a burnt-out house it's difficult to imagine the effect that it has. Even a relatively small fire can be devastating, and heat and especially smoke can cause even more damage. Fortunately, fire is also relatively easy to prevent by following the guidance on fire safety on pp. 96–7.

If you're thinking of buying a fire-damaged house you will need to get a very thorough structural survey carried out before you decide whether to go ahead. Fire behaves in strange and unpredictable ways. Houses that look only slightly affected may have suffered great unseen damage, while the effects of an apparently devastating fire might be purely cosmetic. The deciding factor is likely to be the method of construction. Stone- and brick-built houses often fare well. (After all, they are built from the same material as fireplaces.) Modern houses are built to a high specification of fire resistance, but older wooden-framed houses can be more vulnerable.

After a house fire, however small, soot and smoke permeate everything. Often people end up losing all their possessions after a fire that directly affects only one room. The smell of smoke even gets into the wall plaster and black stains and the smells of burning can seep through redecorated walls. There are special paints on the market that claim to stop this happening. Most are oil based, so are viscous and difficult to apply as well as environmentally unpleasant. For a better alternative try to find a shellac-based product, which will be just as effective and sufficiently free flowing to apply using a roller or even a sprayer.

Fire behaves in strange and unpredictable ways. Houses that look only slightly affected may have suffered great unseen damage, while the effects of an apparently devastating fire might be purely cosmetic.

FLOOD DAMAGE

Flooding, unlike fire, is a problem that can come back year after year. Properties that are at risk of flooding are those near to rivers, streams and especially those close to the foot of a hill. If the widely predicted changes in our climate occur then rising sea levels, increased rainfall and more big storms are likely to make flooding a major problem in many areas of the UK and Ireland over the coming years. Water authorities and local authorities are working hard to prevent or at least reduce the risk of flooding, and if you feel suitably reassured you might consider buying a flood-damaged house. If you do, here is a list of potential problems:

➽ Look for any structural problems caused by the flood. Roofs are usually a good indicator of recent movement. Sagging or distorted roof pitches are a bad sign.

➽ Inspect the floors for signs of rot. Look at the wall plates and joists as well as floorboards and replace any that look less than perfect. Wood can take a soaking without damage, but if it remains wet for more than a few weeks the risk of decay becomes higher.

➽ The drying process may cause brickwork to shrink and crack. Wait until the walls have dried completely before you fill the cracks. As they dry you may see a white deposit forming on bricks and concrete. This is called efflorescence. It will cease to form once the wall is dry and can be brushed off fairly easily. Allow painted brickwork to dry fully before attempting to repaint; wet brickwork will stain through emulsion and cause oil-based paint to peel off.

➽ Some insulation materials will be destroyed by water and will need to be replaced, but natural ones such as wool and flax will dry out.

➽ Check door and window frames, not just for rot, but also to see if they are harbouring any trapped water or have become warped.

➽ Unless the flood was brief, some plaster will almost certainly be damaged. Gypsum-based plaster absorbs water and will be ruined by prolonged exposure. Water can become trapped behind studwork walls and dry-lining. Drill holes through the skirting board to let it escape and dry out.

➽ Kitchen units usually don't fare well in a flood. They are often made from chipboard carcasses which soak up water like blotting paper. Throw them in a skip.

➽ Modern electrical wiring can take a brief soaking, but prolonged exposure to water will ruin it. Don't be tempted to switch on the electricity to see if it works – you'll probably electrocute yourself or start a fire. Water can collect in junction boxes and switch covers so these must be checked, cleaned and dried out first. Ask an electrical engineer to conduct a full inspection before switching on.

➡ A mains water supply shouldn't be affected by flooding, but it's best to let the tap run for a few minutes just to be sure. A well or borehole supply is likely to have been contaminated and should to be left for a while before you try to use it. For advice, contact the drinking water inspectorate (details in the directory). It's a good idea to have the water tested before you proceed with the purchase of a flood-damaged property with a non-mains supply.

➡ There is a good chance that a flood will have silted up the house drains and sewers or septic tank. This is potentially very unpleasant. Not only will your sewage not flow away properly, it can lead to the problem of back-siphonage whereby sewage is sucked back up the drains and contaminates the drinking-water supply. In these situations you'll need to have the drains cleaned out with a high-pressure water jet.

If the house is still wet when you buy it, you'll need to dry it out before you do anything else.

➡ If there is standing water in the house hire a pump and pump it out into the rainwater drains.

➡ Brickwork dries out at a rate of about one vertical inch (25 mm) a month in dry weather, so a saturated house might take a year or more to dry without some artificial help.

➡ Take up all carpets and floor coverings. Take up a few floorboards in each affected room to let the air circulate.

➡ Turn on the heating (if it works) and hire some dehumidifiers. Don't light fires in the grates until the bricks are dry; the heat might cause the bricks to crack.

➡ Try to get things as dry as possible before winter. Wet bricks can be damaged if the water they contain freezes.

If the property is in a flood-prone area there are a few things you can do to minimize the damage when flooding occurs.

➡ Seal the house. Door and window guards are available that look something like shutters but provide a waterproof seal to doors and windows. uPVC doors may look awful but they do tend to fit well and this in itself offers a degree of protection from a flood. You can also buy airbrick guards that stop the underfloor space becoming flooded. Don't leave them on permanently, though, as this will result in ventilation problems.

➡ Fit drainage valves. Houses often flood because drains and sewers back up. Fitting one-way valves to the outlet pipes from your house will stop this happening.

➡ Rewire the house upside down. In most houses the ring main and junction boxes are sited under the floor with spurs rising up to the sockets. Putting the wiring in the ceiling void and running down to the sockets will minimizes damage to the electrics in a flood. You could also mount the sockets higher (the Building Regulations allow up to 1.2 m from the floor), which has the added benefit of making your home much more functional for wheelchair users.

➡ Choose building materials and fittings that are resistant to water or will dry out easily. Solid-wood kitchen units may sound extravagant but they'll withstand a brief flood much better than chipboard units. Rugs are much easier to rescue and move out of harm's way than fitted carpets.

PART THREE
GETTING TO
WORK

From the slums of Buenos Aires in the early 1970s emerged a precocious young man called Diego Armando Maradona. He was not very big, he was not even particularly handsome, but over the next ten years he grew and developed into arguably the most brilliant footballer the world has ever seen. At the peak of his career he led his country to World Cup glory and won the UEFA Cup, the Argentine, the Spanish, the Italian and the French league titles. There was simply nobody in the world to touch him. But when you get to the top there is only one way to go. His fall from grace was almost as dramatic as his rise. And as he neared the bottom, another character emerged from the same slums of Buenos Aires. He was the same age as Maradona and claimed to have been his best friend when they were children. He then made a rather more surprising claim; he said he was the better footballer. Maradona's reaction was interesting. He agreed they had been best friends and then amazingly concurred that the other man had been better at football. 'We both had talent,' he said. 'The difference was I actually did something with mine.'

Very few of us are blessed with the natural ability of Diego Maradona, but the lesson for me from this is that rewards in life don't come from talking, but from actually doing. It's easy for me to say – I was hopeless at football anyway. But this book isn't about football, it's about something else you can excel at: rescuing a house.

This third part deals with the practicalities of doing a house up. Obtaining planning permission and building control approval, appointing the right people, giving them the correct instructions, buying the most suitable materials and, lastly, getting your house properly heated and insulated. Suggesting that you use Maradona as an example to follow would be quite a heroic idea, given what happened to him in later years, but follow this part of the book and at least you won't end up like his boyhood friend – all talk and no action.

8 PERMISSIONS, APPROVALS AND CONSENTS TO DO

The British Isles aren't the Wild West. Nice as it would be to construct and alter buildings however and wherever we like, the problem of living in an established and densely populated country is that almost everything we do has an impact on somebody else. In the early 1990s an enthusiastic DIY-er in London decided to update his Victorian terraced house by digging out a basement and knocking the ground floor into a large open-plan space. Undeterred by the cracks that began to appear in the walls he carried on until he was stopped by the building control department of the local council who pointed out that he had caused his house to sink and the houses along the entire terrace on either side to lean into his like two sets of dominoes.

The clipboard-toting council official is to many people an annoying distraction from the business of developing a home. But the dominoes case above highlights the necessity of permissions and consents. This chapter describes the various consents you might need, when you'll need them and how to go about securing them.

CONSENTS YOU'LL NEED

There are two main types of approval: building control approval (by-law approval in Ireland) and planning permission. For some properties you may also need listed building consent. The first step is to ask your local authority if any previous applications have been made or consents granted to previous owners. It's possible that consents already exist that are still valid. It's also possible that previous applications have been refused. Understanding why may help when submitting a new one; obviously, if you submit an application identical to one that has previously been turned down, the new one is likely to be refused too.

The distinction between planning permission and building control approval is that, briefly, building control approval governs 'how' you build and planning permission 'what' and 'where'. Although both forms of consent are operated by your local authority, often by the same department, there are very few linkages between the two. You make separate applications for each, and gaining planning consent doesn't increase your likelihood of gaining building control approval or vice versa.

BUILDING CONTROL APPROVAL

Building control approval is necessary to ensure that all work you carry out meets the Building Regulations and is done in a manner that protects the health and safety of all concerned.

The Building Regulations are a set of legal regulations governing the standard and quality of new buildings and alterations. They are intended to ensure that buildings are suitably constructed and are safe for their occupants. They also govern energy efficiency in buildings and disabled access.

In the U K you can apply for approval in two ways: full plans or a building notice. Either way you will have to pay a set fee.

Starting building or even refurbishment works without the necessary permissions is a bad idea. You could be required to undo all the work you have carried out, sued for damage or even prosecuted. There are many cases in which people have been forced to demolish buildings they've just constructed and start again because they didn't get permission. It's wise to get consents early. In most cases, these are granted (or refused) by your local authority, usually your local district, city or metropolitan borough council. The system works slightly differently in Scotland, Northern Ireland and Ireland, and there is yet another system if your property is in a national park.

WHEN TO USE FULL PLANS

This is the route most people choose. You complete a Building Regulations application form available from your local authority and submit it with a full set of plans showing in detail what you want to do. The local authority checks them to see if they comply with the Regulations. If they consider the application satisfactory they issue an approval notice. If you're borrowing from a bank or building society to finance the work, your lender may ask to see an approval notice (or other evidence of Building Regulations approval) before advancing the money. Full plans may also help builders and quantity surveyors to give you a more accurate price for the work.

WHEN TO USE A BUILDING NOTICE

You may alternatively complete a building notice application form and provide a site plan only. The big advantage of this system is that you can apply very shortly before you want to start work, and the work is checked and approved as it's carried out. This is generally only a good idea if the project is small and you and your builders possess a good deal of previous experience. It places a greater burden on you and your builder to ensure that all work complies with the Building Regulations. If you're thinking of applying in this way it's best to speak to your building control officer first. Building notices have to be received by the local authority at least two clear days before work starts on site.

BUILDING WARRANTS IN SCOTLAND

In Scotland you need to apply for a building warrant rather than building approval. The most important difference is that some elements of the work can be self-certified by your agents provided they are suitably qualified. For example a structural engineer who is a full corporate member of the Institute of Structural Engineers or Institute of Civil Engineers can submit a structural design certificate stating that in his or her opinion the building meets Building Regulations requirements. This takes the place of a building control officer's visit and assessment.

BUILDING BY-LAWS IN IRELAND

The system in Ireland is quite similar to that in the UK, although there are fewer exemptions. Any alterations to a property will almost certainly require approval. Even erecting a garden shed requires approval in some parts of Ireland. As the name suggests, by-laws are local and vary from one part of the country to another, so you'll need to check the situation with your local authority and, if necessary, apply for building by-law approval from its building control section. This involves completing a form and submitting a small fee. The local authority is supposed to consider all applications within two months. You can go ahead as soon as approval is granted, but you must tell the local authority in advance when you're going to start work and notify them when you have finished.

Advice on UK Building Regulations and how to make sure you comply with them is provided in Ray Tricker's *Building Regulations in Brief*, details of which are in the directory.

PLANNING PERMISSION

Most land and buildings have a planning use class assigned to them. This is the use that the local authority considers appropriate for the building. Local authorities set out zones and, to prevent inappropriate development, restrict development to certain planning uses within each of them. This means, for example, that a developer can't build a factory in a residential street and also helps to preserve the character of an area, keeping shopping districts commercial and the countryside rural. The broad use classes for buildings are residential, commercial, agricultural and industrial. If you want to convert a building for a usage different from what it was or is, you'll almost certainly need planning permission for the change of use.

Planning permission also governs what buildings look like and their effect on neighbours and the surrounding area. In the UK, minor building projects such as the erection of a small fence or garden shed won't need planning permission. Neither is it usually required for internal alterations (though alterations to listed buildings may require listed building consent). For anything more extensive than this, however, planning permission should be sought.

Planning permission by its very nature is reactive. This can make it seem negative and sometimes pedantic.

WHEN YOU NEED PLANNING PERMISSION

Planning permission is required by law in the UK for all forms of 'development' – a broad term that may embrace even a change of use where no physical alterations are involved. The legal definition in the Town & Country Planning Act defines development as 'The carrying out of building, engineering, mining or other operations in, on, over or under land or the making of any material change in the use of any building or other land.' Sounds pretty all-encompassing to me! Unless you're a lawyer, it's best to assume that whatever you're planning is 'development' unless the planning department tells you that it isn't.

To discover whether you need permission you can check informally with your local planning officer. If you want a more definite answer you can apply to your local authority for a 'lawful development certificate'. You have to pay a fee for this and you'll have to wait for a few weeks, but it gives you a formal written decision as to whether you need planning permission.

There are several different types of planning permission and it's possible that you may need more than one. You can make just one application, sometimes called a full application, and apply for all the consents at once, or you can make them separately. The three usual permissions are:

✚ Outline planning permission

As its name implies, this means that the local authority has agreed in principle that a development can take place. It is usually applied for in order to obtain in-principle permission to erect a new building, although it can also be sought for the conversion of an existing building.

✚ Detailed planning permission

Also known as 'full permission', this is given only when the local authority has agreed exactly what development can be built using your detailed plans as their guide. Even the type of building materials can influence a decision at this point.

✚ Change of use

This permission will be required if you want to use the building for a new purpose. Converting a storage area above a shop into a flat is an example.

Making an application is an important and potentially expensive process, so it pays to get it right first time. Incidentally, you don't have to own the building to make an application, so if you know exactly what you want to do you can find out if you'll be allowed to do it before purchasing the property.

WHEN YOU NEED CHANGE OF USE PERMISSION

Change of use planning permission is usually required only if the proposed use of a premises falls within a different use class from the existing use, but there is the odd exception. One that crops up now and again is houses in multiple occupation (HMOs). Some UK local authorities apply a sub-division of the residential use class to HMOs to control the numbers of this type of development. You may therefore need planning permission to convert an HMO to single-household occupancy or vice versa. In rare cases it is possible to change the use class without permission, but this usually depends on a local interpretation of the law and varies from one council to another.

HOW TO GET PLANNING PERMISSION

First, of course, you need to apply for it. This is simply matter of form-filling, but mistakes and omissions could be expensive, so you should devote plenty of time and effort to getting it right. Telephone your local authority for an application form (some provide forms online), which will require you to provide such information as:

➡ Whether you own all, part or none of the property, and whether you're a leaseholder or freeholder. Remember, you can apply before you have completed the purchase of a property. If you aren't the sole owner, then the other owner(s) must be notified of your plans.

➡ The location of the property – if you can, include a location map, usually Ordnance Survey 1 : 2,500 or 1 : 1,250. The location plan from a land registry search will also suffice.

➡ A site plan with boundaries outlined in red, 1 : 500 scale.

➡ The nature and scale of the proposed development.

➡ Accompanying drawings and floor plans, 1 : 100 or 1 : 50 scale. If there are major exterior changes in your plans it can be a good idea to send isometric drawings (3-D views) or make up a model. Architectural design software can really help here. There are lots of CAD (computer aided design) packages available, one of the best of which is Arcon (details in the directory). However you display it, three-dimensional representation really helps the planners see what your project will actually look like.

➡ Details of materials to be used.

➡ Whether the development will involve a change of use.

➡ If your development is on a very large scale you may also need to provide, for example, an environmental impact assessment. It's unlikely that a single property development would require this, but if the property is very big, you should ask your planning officer.

In most cases the authority will advertise your application, both in the local paper and by placing a notice on the site boundary, so that interested parties have the opportunity to object if they wish. The format of these notices is very specific, and so dull and unfathomable that hardly anybody bothers to read them. In Ireland you need to produce your own notices and newspaper ad and submit copies of them with your application. Your application must be made within two weeks of the advertisement appearing.

If you're developing an empty property, your local authority's empty property officer (see p. 29) might be prepared to support your application with a letter of recommendation. In most cases you'll need to pay a fee, and you'll need to submit several complete sets of all the paperwork. Don't forget to keep a set for yourself.

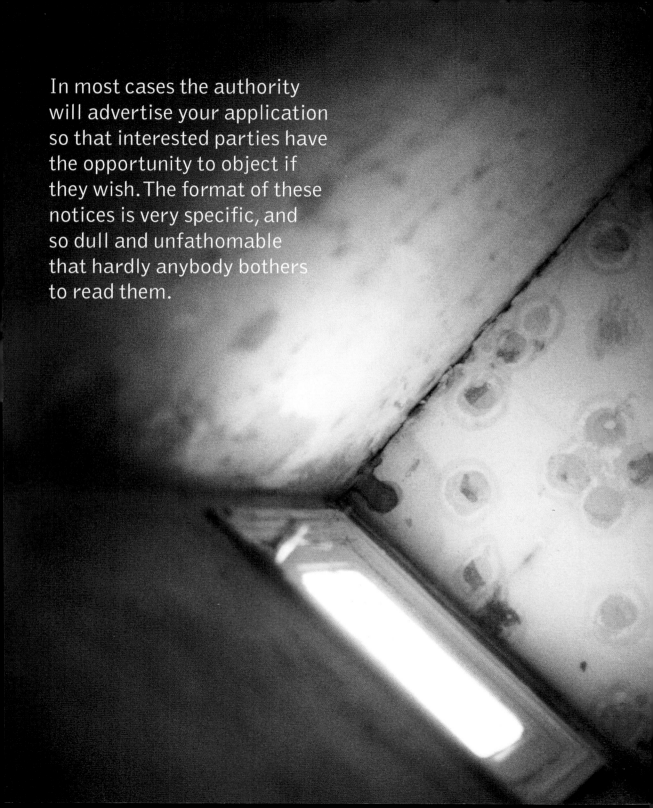

In most cases the authority will advertise your application so that interested parties have the opportunity to object if they wish. The format of these notices is very specific, and so dull and unfathomable that hardly anybody bothers to read them.

HOW TO INCREASE YOUR CHANCES OF SUCCESS

Submitting a poor application wastes everyone's time, so try to get it right at the first attempt. It's sensible to discuss your ideas with your local planning officer prior to submission. This will give you an insight into how favourably they might look on your application and how you might modify it to make it more acceptable. Take your architect or surveyor along with you. You should receive some feedback and have the opportunity to put your side of the argument, which will be a lot easier to win once you know what you're up against.

There is nothing wrong with a bit of canvassing to increase support for your application. A good place to start is with your future neighbours. If they are aware of your intentions, not only are they less likely to object to your planning application, they may even be prepared to write in and support it. Local backing is invaluable and can really make the difference to a marginal decision.

Your local councillor will be happy to welcome new people moving into the ward, especially if they think that could mean a few extra votes at the next election. Explain what you're proposing and request their support in the planning approval process. Even if your councillor isn't on the planning committee it's possible that he or she may have some influence. As long as you don't offer inducements you are doing nothing wrong; this is, in fact, how local democracy is meant to work.

THE DECISION PROCESS

In theory, the decision on whether to approve planning applications is made by the elected members of the council, and most councils have a planning committee comprising half a dozen or so councillors who meet monthly to consider all applications. In practice, most councils have planning departments that do most of the work and make recommendations to the committee on what should be approved or refused. Most of the time the committee follows their recommendations. Planning committees may delegate decisions on certain categories of application to senior officers in the planning department. In such cases it is the planning department rather than the committee that makes the decision. When planning officers speak of 'delegated decisions' or 'delegated matters', this is what they are referring to.

Once your application is submitted, it is formally logged. From this date the authority will be deemed to be considering it. The local authority target period within which planning applications should be assessed is eight weeks. More complex projects, particularly those involving change of use, often take longer – sometimes many months – hence the advice to apply as early as possible. (A late decision can be a ground for appeal, but more on that later. It's also a good idea to ask in your initial meeting with the planning officer how long the assessment of the application is expected to take.)

Once your proposals have been advertised, interested parties have a fixed period, usually twenty-one days, in which to make any objections known.

There are three possible responses to a planning application:

✚ Unconditional consent

This means you can go ahead with no further planning considerations. (In Ireland, interested parties have a month in which they can appeal against the approval. If there are no objections, official permission is granted a short time later.) In practice, unconditional consent is rare.

✚ Conditional consent

This means that the local authority will permit you to proceed only if you meet certain conditions. These may, for example, stipulate that the occupiers of the property own not more than one car, or require provision of a certain number of off-street parking spaces. In other cases you might be required to contribute to community facilities. These conditions might be referred to by the legal section under which they are made, such as section 106 or section 278 agreements. Such draconian measures are unlikely for a single house development; even so, in some cases the conditions may be so onerous that you cannot continue. If you consider them unreasonable you can appeal and apply for a relaxation of conditions. Both conditional and unconditional consent are time limited. Work must begin within five years of receiving consent for detailed planning permission or three years for outline permission. If it doesn't, you'll have to re-apply. For more on conditional consent see 'Planning gain' on p. 333.

✚ Refusal

This is the worst that can happen, but not necessarily a disaster. You'll be given a decision notice with the reasons permission was not granted, so you can either re-apply, addressing the points in the decision notice, or appeal. To appeal you must have valid grounds. Appeals are potentially costly and will substantially delay your work programme, which is why it's so important to get the right advice and submit a well-prepared application in the first place. A planning appeal must be submitted to the Planning Inspectorate within six months of the date of the decision notice. If no decision notice has been issued, the appeal must be submitted within six months of the end of the period when the decision should have been made. Forms for submitting an appeal can be obtained from the Inspectorate's offices in Bristol. In Ireland appeals are submitted to An Bord Pleanála. Contact details of both organizations are in the directory.

A word of encouragement. More than 80 per cent of planning applications are successful and many of the other 20 per cent fail simply because they are poorly prepared. If you do your homework there is every reason to be optimistic.

OTHER CONSENTS

LISTED BUILDING CONSENT

If the property is listed (grade 1, 2 or 2* – see p. 23) you'll need listed building consent before you can carry out almost any work on it. This consent is a separate entity to planning permission and building control approval, so even if you're applying for planning permission you'll need to apply for this as well. As with planning permission and building control approval, application is made to your local authority. The good news is that there is no fee to pay; the bad news is that the standards that must be met in order to obtain consent are much more stringent. You'll need to submit very detailed plans showing, for example, the type of windows you propose to install and how they are constructed.

CONSERVATION AREA APPROVAL

Conservation areas are those deemed by the local authority to be of special architectural or historic importance. Extra controls exist to try to preserve and (arguably) enhance them. Conservation area approval is not separate from planning permission, but your planning application will be judged against the these criteria in addition to the normal planning rules.

WILDLIFE

If your property is home to protected wildlife species you may need permission before you can start work. See p. 72 for details.

PARTY WALLS

Party walls are those that separate your property from adjoining ones. Although in most cases the boundary line officially runs through the middle of a party wall, the owners of both properties have legal rights to the whole of it because it supports both properties and protects them from fire. Consequently, any major work on a party wall requires permission from your neighbour. The Party Wall etc. Act of 1996 gives you the right to carry out work on a party wall, but requires that you notify all concerned neighbours at least two months in advance so that they have an opportunity to respond. If your neighbours agree then you can go ahead and do the works; if they object you need to reach agreement, either informally or through a party wall award (see below). Try to reach an informal agreement if you can. It's much quicker and cheaper.

Notice of proposed work on a party wall doesn't need to be on a prescribed form, but it must include your name and address, the name and address of your builder or agent and a description and timetable of the work you're proposing to do. It should also state that notification is being provided in accordance with The Party Wall etc. Act 1996 and that any objections should be raised within two weeks.

If the adjoining property is rented you'll need to notify both the tenant and the landlord. If the property is empty, you should try to find out who the owner is (you should be quite good at this by now) and notify them. If you can't trace the owner you should post a copy of the notice in a prominent place on the building (pinning it to the front door is best).

The Act covers any work that might affect the loading on the wall, for example installing a new beam or carrying out underpinning work. Excavation work outside the building is also subject to its provisions if it's close enough to another property to affect it (for more information see p. 119). Plastering or fitting electrical sockets, skirting boards or built-in cupboards are all classed as minor works so are exempt.

If you're unable to reach agreement with your neighbours you need to draw up a party wall award. This is a legal document detailing the proposed work and its schedule. The award records the existing condition of the wall on both sides, so if there are any problems later the extent of any damage can be assessed. You'll need to appoint a party wall surveyor to do all this for you. The surveyor should be appointed jointly by both parties, although of course you'll have to pay all the costs. If your neighbour refuses permission and won't agree to appoint a surveyor, you can appoint one on their behalf and go ahead anyway. If you do this you should appoint two independent surveyors – one for them and one for you.

If your neighbour objects to the award they must lodge their objection with the county court within fourteen days, and the matter will be resolved there. Although this system is quite new, it's based on a by-law that has operated in London since the 1930s and has a successful track record. The vast majority of party wall issues are resolved amicably and easily.

Pick the right people and you should
be able to get the job done more quickly,
better and ultimately more cheaply
than by doing it all yourself.

9 HIRING (AND FIRING)

I remember reading as a child a news report about a man in Brazil who
built a cathedral single handed. When I say single handed, I mean single
handed: he designed it, planned it, cut the timber, worked the stone, mixed
the mortar, operated the crane, erected the scaffolding and took it down
again. The project consumed his entire life, and I have a horrible feeling
he died before it was finished.

   I have come across one-person house-rescue projects, too. Whilst not
quite on the Brazilian cathedral scale, they still had a tendency to drag on
for ever and dominate the owner's life. The truth is that most house rescues
projects need to involve several people possessing different skills, different
contacts and different ideas. Pick the right people and you should be able
to get the job done more quickly, better and ultimately more cheaply than
by doing it all yourself. This chapter discusses the various professionals
you might need, what they do, how to choose them and how to get the
best out of them.

ARCHITECTS

You probably think of an architect as someone who designs buildings. This, of course, they do, but architects can do a lot more. They can manage the whole project for you, from helping you select the best property to start with right through to completion. They can also employ and manage all the other people you need.

All this comes (of course) at a price. An architect isn't a cheap person to hire. A qualified architect will have trained for at least seven years, just like a medical doctor, and the two professions charge similary for private consultations.

Traditionally architects charged a percentage fee basis which increased with the amount of responsibility you asked them to assume. So if you wanted only plans and specifications you might expect to pay around 5 per cent of the contract sum whereas the fee for employing contractors and managing the site might rise to 12.5 per cent. More and more often, however, architects are now working for fixed fees and it's become quite usual for developers to request quotations from architects in advance. The sum quoted will depend on the scope of the project, the architect's reputation and experience and, of course, how much they want the work, but fees in the low thousands are quite normal for typical house-rescue projects.

Architecture is part art and part science. All good architects understand the science of building but their artistic styles will be very different. A simple brief to design a building given to a hundred different architects would produce a hundred different results. Ask to see some examples of previous work so you can determine whether their idea of style matches yours. Trying to force an architect to design a house he or she doesn't like is hardly the best way to forge a harmonious relationship and get a good result. If you have no particular style in mind, look through some magazines and books to see what looks good to you and what doesn't. When you meet your architect, take with you some pictures of properties that appeal to you. This will convey your taste far better than hours of verbal description.

Books of house designs are also available. One of the best is Jan Prideaux's *1001 All Time Best-Selling Home Plans.*

FINDING AND APPOINTING AN ARCHITECT

You may know a local firm or have received recommendations from friends. These are good places to start, but you should also try to find a few other likely candidates and compile a shortlist. Most architects in the UK are members of the Royal Institution of British Architects (RIBA) and the RIBA website can help you locate members who may be suitable. A similar system operates in Ireland, where the relevant organization is the Royal Institute of the Architects of Ireland (RIAI).

Contact the architects on your shortlist by phone and briefly describe your requirements. Ask any who express an interest to send you literature showing their previous work, or whether they have a portfolio you could inspect. You might also be able to visit some finished buildings that they have designed.

Narrow your shortlist down to the one or two who meet all your requirements and with whom you feel comfortable (it's never a good idea to do business with somebody you don't like). Now is the time to discuss in detail your ideas, your budget and your timeframe, and the services you would like them to provide. Be honest about how much you're willing to spend on the whole project. Ask for a quotation, and if it seems a bit high don't be afraid to negotiate. Once you're happy, get everything confirmed in writing.

Architecture is part art and part science. All good architects understand the science of building but their artistic styles will be very different.

One slightly controversial point. Neither side will appreciate my saying so, but some architects can be rather snooty and some builders can be less than co-operative. Having the latter taking instructions from the former does not make for the smooth running of a project.

WRITING THE BRIEF

The brief is where you explain clearly what you want the finished building to be like and what you expect the architect to do to help you get there. A good-quality brief is crucial to the success of your project, and, if you have never employed an architect before, writing one can seem a bit daunting. Don't worry; a good architect should help you prepare it. (If they refuse, maybe they aren't a very good architect after all and you might do better to look elsewhere.)

The best way to write a good brief is to think about what information your architect will need. This will probably include the answers to the following questions, which should form the basis of the brief:

➡ What is the building for and how do you intend to use it?

➡ Are you looking for a design in keeping with the existing building or do you want a contemporary, funky or high-tech design?

➡ What authority will you have? Who decides on issues about the design, the costs, management?

➡ How important is it to you that the building has a sustainable/ecological design?

➡ How much do you want to spend in total?

➡ What do you expect the architect to do? Do you want them to employ contractors and/ or monitor the builder's work in terms of standards, schedule and cost, or do you simply want them to draw a plan?

To assist those embarking on a building project for the first time, RIBA Publications have produced 'Small works (SW99)', a standard form of agreement designed for use on projects where the cost of the building work isn't expected to exceed £100,000.

For more about appointing and using an architect, see Barbara Weiss ad Luis Hellman's saucily titled *Do It with an Architect*.

ARCHITECTURAL TECHNOLOGISTS AND OTHER DESIGNERS

Of course, you don't have to use a 'proper' architect. There are other people who design buildings. Architectural technologists are what were once called draftsmen. They used to work with architects (indeed, many still do) producing plans in the back office, but their profession has evolved and many now work independently. For many rescue projects they can provide exactly the same service as an architect and may charge you considerably less.

Architects and architectural technologists are both recognized professionals with their own qualifications but they are not the only people who can design buildings. Many building surveyors will be happy to carry out design work. You'll come across others with titles such as building designer or building design consultant. Many of these may well be very proficient, but unless they are members of a professional architectural organization the onus is on you to ensure they can deliver what you want. Whoever you use, the principles of selection and briefing should be the same as for architects.

DESIGN-AND-BUILD BUILDERS

Many builders can design, too, and some of them are very good at it. Most design-and-build companies are more interested in new build than a rescued house project, but you can ask. Although you could in theory ask a number of them to quote competitively against each other, this rather misses the point. Tendering is adversarial by nature, but this kind of project only really works in an atmosphere of mutual trust. If you use a design-and-build builder you'll have to employ hardly anyone else. If you choose this route it goes without saying that knowledge of your builder's past history is essential. Some small building companies, particularly in rural areas, have worked on this basis for generations and built up enviable local reputations. If you are lucky enough to find a company like this, you should expect a considerable wait before they are available. Nor will they come cheap. You should, however, find that the project runs much more smoothly and end up with a good quality finished article.

Architectural technologists have their own professional body, the British Institute of Architectural Technologists (BIAT). A list of independent architectural technologist practices subdivided by county is available on the BIAT website or by post.

BUILDING SURVEYORS

The term 'surveyor' is used quite broadly, and there are several occasions on which you might employ one. The first is right at the beginning of a development, when in all likelihood you'll employ a surveyor to help you assess the viability of your project, and again for your lender to decide whether to make a mortgage offer. But perhaps the two most useful surveyors you'll appoint are the quantity surveyor who helps you estimate the cost of your project and the project manager who makes it all happen.

Quantity surveyors calculate the costs and the quantities of materials required directly from the plans and drawings your designer has produced for you. Their skills mean that you don't over- or under-order materials, resulting in less waste and fewer delays. The role of the quantity surveyor is, however, under threat from rapidly improving computer software. Although lacking the intelligence and subtlety of a quantity surveyor, estimators and estimating packages are nearly as good and are a lot cheaper, although for large, expensive and complicated projects, employing a quantity surveyor is probably still a good investment.

Play to the strengths of those you employ: if your project involves a substantial amount of redesigning and remodelling an architect may be the best choice as a project manager; if it's largely a restoration, or at least renovation, project then a surveyor may be the better bet.

When selecting a surveyor you should follow the same sort of selection process as for an architect. Compile a shortlist from surveyors you have used before and from recommendations. If your shortlist is too short, the Royal Institute of Chartered Surveyors (RICS) holds a full member list that you can consult. Make your final selection by following the same procedure as on p. 189.

For more information on quantity surveyors and the alternatives see p. 310. Unlike 'archictect', the word 'surveyor' has no legal status (in theory, you could set yourself up and operate as one tomorrow), so it makes sense to limit yourself to members of the RICS.

Play to the strengths of those you employ: if your project involves a substantial amount of redesigning and remodelling an architect may be the best choice as a project manager; if it's largely a restoration, or at least renovation, project then a surveyor may be the better bet.

Eddie is 38 years old. At the age of 17 he moved to St Tropez and spent twelve heady summers there. During the winters, and in extreme climatic contrast, he travelled around Colorado, spending time at a large hippie commune.

More recently, Eddie has been renovating a Grade II listed Georgian house in Gloucester. The project has taken him eight years, and all the flats are now ready to sell. He cannot believe his luck: this hippie traveller now has a considerable amount of equity, and has decided to use it to completely change his life.

His Vision

Eddie currently lives in Gloucester, but his heart lies in Lincolnshire, where his daughter Polly lives. Eddie wants to renovate a derelict property, giving him and Polly a real adventure, plus a place where Eddie's friends in the travelling community will be welcomed.

The Front Runners
United Methodist Church, Creswell, Worksop

Most of the buildings in Creswell are owned by the Bentinck family's Welbeck Estate, as is the United Methodist church. One of the most striking buildings in the village, this is a complex of non-conformist chapel, school, hall and minister's house, crowned with some strange and inexplicable architectural detailing.

Most recently the chapel and adjoining schoolhouse have played host to an engine-oil blending business. The chapel and hall were crammed with large tanks of oil, some of which had over many years spilt oil on the floors and walls. The tanks have gone, but the smell and stains remain. The oil company's lease came to an end a few years ago and since then the buildings have stood empty, though they are in a fair condition.

They won Eddie and Polly's hearts from the start. Eddie saw the opportunity to live in the house, which needs no more than average refurbishment, and the chance to turn the chapel and adjoining buildings into a workshop and arts and community centre.

Former butcher's shop, Whitwell, Derbyshire

Whitwell is a pleasant little village near Worksop in south Derbyshire. The building is a single-storey brick building with a warm red clay-tiled roof, which proclaims its previous existence as a butcher's shop with a sticker in the window advertising the quality of its minced beef. Although the building is not completely derelict, the interior has been stripped of any recognizable shop features, apart from the glazed tiles on the walls.

This small, unassuming, single-storey building comes with a large plot of land at the rear, including a semi-derelict building, which may have previously been the butcher's abattoir.

The shop and land were bought by a property developer in 2004 for £70,000, who has consent for the conversion of the butcher's shop into a one-bedroomed bungalow. The developer is trying to get new planning consent to convert the shop into a double garage, demolish the abattoir building at the rear of the site and build a new bungalow.

What Next?

Father and daughter clearly liked both properties, despite the fact that the pair had originally envisaged a somewhat remote rural location.

They talked of buying the buther's shop and turning it into the strange but fascinating combination of an antique and sweet shop, while converting the building at the back to make a substantial family house. As the developer did not yet have consent, he was willing to sell the property to Eddie and Polly for around £100,000.

Eddie and Polly were also very keen on the United Methodist Church, which offered the space to build a workshop and arts and community centre.

Eddie put in firm bids for both properties, and finally opted for the chapel in Creswell. The Welbeck Estate now seems prepared to give Eddie a long lease at a modest or peppercorn rent to allow him to fulfil his dreams of a happy home for him and Polly and the creation of an arts and community building.

PROBLEMS WITH SURVEYORS AND HOW TO AVOID THEM

You may have heard the phrase 'A survey isn't worth the paper it's written on'. As a statement it's probably a bit harsh, but there is a serious point here. There is a wide gulf between what many people expect surveyors' reports to say and what they do say. Instead of providing helpful information, survey reports all too often contain a series of disclaimers such as, 'it was not possible to inspect the roof space, so we cannot verify the condition of same. We would recommend that you carry out a further survey of this area,' and 'There is no obvious evidence of dampness. However, we cannot verify that the property is free from damp and recommend that you employ a specialist damp and timber engineer to carry out a thorough survey.' Your lender then points to these sidesteps and you end up paying for half a dozen specialist surveys to discover what everyone knew in the first place – there is no damp/rot/infestation/ subsidence. (In case you think I'm making this up, the quotes are actual ones from the survey for my own house.)

The other contributing factor is that customers demand cheap and therefore quick surveys, so surveyors don't usually have the time to investigate thoroughly. After years of living in my house I can verify that it's free from dampness, but a surveyor would have only an hour at most to decide. It's difficult to prove a positive and most surveyors simply err on the side of caution.

Surveys of neglected and particularly empty properties are often more informative. The owner probably won't have attempted to disguise problems and if there is no occupier to consider it's much easier to lift carpets, poke holes in rotten wood and shove damp-meter pins into wall plaster. Here are a few tips on how to get more from survey:

INSIDE INFO
As in every profession there are a few incompetent surveyors out there, but what gives rise to the disclaimer problem isn't incompetence but insurance; public liability insurance, to be precise. If a surveyor reports that the roof is in very good condition and shortly afterwards it falls down, you could sue him or her for all your costs plus damages. Such claims would affect both a surveyor's reputation and insurance premium, so not unnaturally there has arisen a culture of minimizing risk. And the fewer risks taken, the less information appears in the survey report.

- Speak to the surveyor beforehand and state your main concerns. Ask how long they have allowed for the survey. If this sounds insufficient, ask for them to stay longer (but be prepared for a bigger bill).

- Meet the surveyor on site. You may need to do this anyway if the property is vacant.

- Discuss with the surveyor any areas of concern and ask for verbal opinions. Even if a surveyor isn't willing to commit an opinion to paper they may be prepared to give it face to face.

- If you can, clear furniture, clutter and rubbish out of the way before the surveyor arrives.

- If there is a loft space or cellar, make sure that there is safe and easy access. Bring along your own ladder if the existing one is unsound. Set it up before the surveyor arrives.

- Get hold of a couple of hard hats, a powerful torch and maybe a couple of pairs of overalls. The surveyor should have all this, anyway, but if not there will be no excuse not to inspect the loft or cellar.

- If you have any concerns about the roof, ask the surveyor to make a close inspection. Arrange this in advance and agree who is going to provide access and how.

There is a wide gulf between what many people expect surveyors' reports to say and what they do say. Instead of providing helpful information, survey reports all too often contain a series of disclaimers.

BUILDERS

You may have enjoyed the current rash of 'cowboy builders from hell' television programmes, but when you need a builder yourself it's no laughing matter. The reputation of the building industry is on a par with that of second-hand car dealers, time-share salesmen and politicians in the eyes of the public. And it's not without foundation. Some builders are incompetent, some don't care, and a few are just plain crooked. But there are many very able, trustworthy and conscientious builders trying to earn an honest living in a market that seems designed to bring out the worst in everybody, the client included. There is no easy solution, but a better understanding of that market and how it works might help you to avoid the bigger sharks out there.

First, you have two choices when hiring a builder. You can either hire one general contractor or separately hire each of the trades you want. Your decision will depend on how big and diverse the project is, how much experience you have in property development, how much time you can spend on it and how much money you've got.

Second, you can employ a project manager, an architect or a surveyor to do all this for you. They can hire, manage and pay your tradespeople, in which event there is no need for you to have any direct contact with builders at all. Read on, and this may begin to sound like an attractive proposition.

The reputation of the building industry is on a par with that of second-hand car dealers, time-share salesmen and politicians in the eyes of the public.

WHEN TO HIRE A GENERAL CONTRACTOR

A general builder will estimate or quote for and (hopefully) carry out all the physical work you need. (See p. 207 for the difference between a quotation and an estimate.) Most general builders directly employ a few general workers and then hire in other trades as subcontractors (subbies). There are still a few solo operators who hire in everything, but this is less common than it was owing to changes in tax law.

A general builder will organize or project manage the work on site. They will co-ordinate subcontractors, delivery of materials and the hiring of plant and equipment, and will also deal with building control inspections, meaning that you should have to visit the site less often. If there are any problems (there will be), you have one point of contact to get things sorted out. Perhaps the biggest advantage is that a general builder will have a much longer list of contacts than you, so can find individual tradespeople more quickly and easily than you could. If you are combining a rescue project with a day job and have a date by which the project must be finished, you need a general builder. A general builder will normally be the more expensive option – after all, you're paying for their project management skills and overheads – but don't let this lull you into thinking that this is an easy route to take. Many things can and frequently do go wrong, but more on that later.

WHEN TO HIRE TRADES PEOPLE OR SUBCONTRACTORS

Strictly speaking, you can't hire subcontractors directly. Well, you can, but if you do they cease to be subcontractors and are all main contractors. This may seem a pedantic point, but if they are hired as subcontractors, you become by definition the main contractor. This makes you responsible for administering your subcontractors' tax affairs; not something you probably want to be involved in.

Subcontractors – let's call them tradespeople instead – are usually individuals who specialize in a single trade, or even a single aspect of a trade. Some may work for small firms employing several people. They all have their own idiosyncrasies with which it's best to go along. Some will insist on supplying their own materials while others expect you to have everything ready and waiting for them.

If you have the time to spare, hiring trades separately can save you a lot of money, but don't underestimate the time you'll need to put in or the headaches you'll suffer. You'll have to be on site every day, and if you don't live near by this isn't a realistic option. You'll also need to be very well organized and able to revise your plans quickly when, inevitably, somebody lets you down. What will you do when the brickies you hired turn up but the brick delivery doesn't?

The trades you are likely to employ most often are listed below.

✚ Brickworkers (brickies)

They build the brick or block walls (obviously!), but if you're building an extension you'll need footings and foundations. You'll find this work needs another trade: groundworkers. Neither trade will expect to supply materials, so you'll need to order them yourself. Brickies will also carry out repair and repointing work.

✚ Roofers

Usually small firms or gangs who supply and fix or repair the roofing materials. Some specialize in flat roofs.

✚ Scaffolders

Supply, erect and dismantle scaffolding (some roofers can do this as well).

✚ Plasterers (spreads)

Usually individuals, they will plaster internal walls and ceilings and normally provide their own materials.

✚ Plumbers

Install central heating, bathroom fittings, water pipework and drainage, but not underground drainage or rainwater goods. Some plumbers dislike working on kitchens. (Kitchen fitting could almost be called a separate trade.) Plumbers prefer to supply their own materials, and not all are skilled at installing or repairing central heating systems. Central heating engineers are arguably a separate trade and often a better bet.

✚ Electricians (sparks)

Usually individuals who supply, repair and replace electrical installations, again supplying their own materials.

✚ Gas fitters

Install gas pipes, appliances and flues. They may be plumbers or central heating engineers but in order to operate legally they need to be registered with the Council for Registered Gas Installers (CORGI). Ask to see their registration card, which will list on the reverse side the types of work they are competent to undertake. If you have any doubts contact CORGI (see directory for contact details).

✚ Glaziers

Usually small firms who install windows, patio doors and glazed external doors.

✚ Decorators

You may prefer to do this yourself, but there are small firms and individuals who can decorate for you. Many specialize in internal or external work only, so you'll probably need two if you want to decorate inside and out.

✚ Carpenters (chippies or joiners)

Won't expect to supply materials; they'll deal with all timberwork except roof timbers, and will hang doors.

THINGS THAT CAN GO WRONG DURING BUILDING WORK AND HOW TO AVOID THEM

The cause of problems can be one of three things: the market, the builder or the client. Fortunately, you have control of one, perhaps two, of those.

HOW THE BUILDING MARKET CAUSES PROBLEMS

The economy has for the past thirty years or so followed a boom-and-bust cycle. When an economic boom comes along the building trade feels it more quickly and more strongly than other sectors of the economy. Very quickly demand outstrips supply, prices skyrocket and many builders, knowing that the good times can't last, take on more work than they can handle. Very quickly a skills gap opens up. Everybody who is any good is booked up for months ahead. There isn't time for new builders to gain adequate experience before the next slump, so a raft of new builders with poor skills enter the market. They charge the same expensive rates but often are ill equipped to deliver. Some experienced builders, on the other hand, having over-filled their order book, rush things, taking on subbies who aren't as proficient as they'd like and who take less care than is prudent.

When the next inevitable slump arrives the building trade is once again the first to feel it and is often hit the hardest. Supply now exceeds demand and builders find themselves struggling to survive in a cut-throat market. Large numbers of them go bust, many in the middle of jobs, leaving clients high and dry. In every recession thousands of experienced builders pack up their bags and go off and do something else, leaving the industry further deskilled. Just as equilibrium is reached and there are the right number of builders to do the amount of work available, it's boom time once more so off we go round again.

HOW BUILDERS CAUSE PROBLEMS

The way the market works explains to some degree how builders behave. The building industry can be a stressful one in which to work – subbies aren't much easier to manage if you're a general builder than if you're a lay member of the public – and if running your own project is a pain in the neck, think what it must be like running several at once. Experience and contacts do help, of course, and a reasonably competent general builder can manage three or four projects simultaneously without too much trouble. Unfortunately, bad debts and cashflow problems mean that they need to be running seven or eight sites at once to make a reasonable living.

There is a theory of employment called train driver syndrome. It works like this. Pat the train driver gets better and better at the job and becomes the best train driver in the rail network. In recognition of this, Pat is promoted to station manager, a job that requires none of the skills of a train driver and several new skills that Pat doesn't possess. Consequently, the railway company loses its best train driver and gains an inefficient station manager. General builders are often victims of this syndrome. A great bricklayer, after years of doing the same thing, feels ready to go it alone. Unfortunately, great bricklayers don't always make great project managers. Even the best struggle to manage eight sites. So things slip. In the end, most reasonably competent builders do deliver, but by the time they do so they are likely to be behind schedule, have cut corners and will probably have annoyed their client to near distraction.

Extras

Extras are additional work that the builder has not estimated for but which suddenly becomes essential once work is in progress. When they arise the client usually has no room for manoeuvre, and has little choice but to authorize the builder to continue at whatever price the builder quotes. Of course, there are many quite legitimate reasons for extras. Rotten wall plates may not be detectable until the floor is taken up. Plasterwork may look sound until the wallpaper comes off. Specification or plans are sometimes inadequate or inaccurate. The surveyor may have overlooked a problem, or ambiguous wording could mean that a builder misinterprets the surveyor's intention. And, of course, a survey of an old house can't be 100 per cent accurate.

Beware also of a non-VAT registered builder pretending that he is registered and charging you non-existent VAT. Most general builders are VAT registered – if their annual turnover were lower than the registration threshold they probably wouldn't survive – but legitimate exceptions would include new builders in their first year or two of trading and older builders who may be semi-retired. In any event, don't pay any VAT until you have received a proper VAT invoice containing the builder's name, address and VAT registration number. You will need this in order to reclaim VAT, if eligible.

Inside info

Such extras are what contingency sums are for. Most surveyors allow a sum of about 10 per cent for unforeseen work, although you will probably find that nearer to 20 per cent is more usual for a typical house rescue. This is perfectly legitimate. Not so legitimate is the way that some builders use extras as a way of increasing their profit margins once they are on site. Some builders charge more for extra works than they would have quoted at the tender stage. And here lies another danger: if an initial quote seems too good to be true, it probably is. Some builders who need the work submit unrealistically low quotes with the hope of bumping them up with extras once they are on site. Builders are adept at spotting a loosely worded specification. Some will try to clarify it with you and quote realistically, or even not quote at all to avoid a potentially troublesome job. Others will see an opportunity and exploit it.

Another set of builders' tricks that earn them an untrustworthy reputation are tax scams. Customs and Excise is the main victim of these, but sometimes clients can be caught too. It's not uncommon for a builder to offer a discount or to 'lose' the VAT in exchange for cash payments which in all likelihood won't be declared to the taxman. It's not illegal for you to pay by cash, but the discount you have received means that you have benefited from the scam and you could in theory be prosecuted with the builder for conspiracy to defraud. On many house-rescue projects you can reclaim the VAT anyway, so there's little point in taking the risk.

HOW CLIENTS CAUSE PROBLEMS

Surely the client is the innocent victim in all this? Well, victim, yes, but perhaps not always so innocent. The trouble is, the client's response to poor performance from the building industry often serves to make things worse.

Let's start with the selection process. Received wisdom dictates that the right thing to do is get estimates from several different builders to ensure you get the best price. But, think about it. To prepare a quotation properly takes a long time (and can be expensive if the builder entrusts it to a quantity surveyor).

Inside info

If clients ask two builders to quote, each has a 50 per cent chance of success, all else being equal. If clients ask for five quotes, that drops to 20 per cent. That's a whole lot of extra work for which the builder earns nothing, so the costs are passed on to existing clients and the builder has less time to manage ongoing projects. To avoid this scenario, builders commonly collude behind the client's back. Local builders all know each other (don't forget that freemasonry originated in the building industry), and they arrange things so that one does a proper quotation and the others all quote higher. Of course, this isn't always the case, but it happens more often than you'd imagine.

Payment is another bone of contention. Perhaps not unreasonably, clients have become wary of paying up-front. Cases of builders absconding with a client's money are very rare, but he who holds the purse strings calls the tune, and clients feel more in control if they hold back payment. This in effect means that the builder gives you interest-free credit. Most builders operate on fairly tight finances, so they in turn demand credit from their suppliers, and everything becomes balanced on a knife edge. One late payment and the whole thing collapses. Unpaid subbies refuse to come back on site, deliveries are cancelled, and the client gets fobbed off in the manner to which we have become accustomed.

Finally there are some really awkward clients who withhold thousands of pounds in payment over small snagging problems that cost only a few pounds to fix. Others throw contractors off site when a minor problem occurs without giving them an opportunity to rectify it. Clients can get into a financial mess too, and it's very easy to keep quiet about this and find an excuse not to pay the builder instead of coming clean. About one in twenty clients don't pay at all.

Those, then, are the problems. Now for some solutions.

In the end, most reasonably competent builders do deliver, but by the time they do so they are likely to be behind schedule, have cut corners and will probably have annoyed their client to near distraction.

HOW TO APPOINT A GOOD BUILDER

✚ Find out which builders operate in your area and which ones are competent.

If you have used a particular builder before and were happy with the result, this is obviously the best place to start. If not, ask people you know who have had building work done for their opinions. If you're using an architect or other building designer, ask for their recommendations. If all else fails, try some cold calling. Look around for recently refurbished houses or ones undergoing work and ask the owner for their views. Most people love to talk about improvements to their property and will be happy to talk to you.

✚ Put together a shortlist of builders capable of carrying out the work you want.

Try to include at least one large local builder in your list even if they weren't recommended to you. This can be useful for comparison with the smaller bidders. Keep your list short; three names is probably enough, and certainly no more than five. Sticking a pin in Yellow Pages (Golden Pages in Ireland) to compile your shortlist is a recipe for disaster. (By the way, bigger adverts don't necessarily mean bigger or better builders. It usually just means they are short of customers.) Many busy builders with full order books won't advertise at all.

✚ Phone or visit each of the builders on your list to find out if they are interested in doing the job.

Be honest about money. Tell them how much you have to spend and discuss with them how and when payments will be made. Very few will give you an outright refusal, but you should be able to get a good feeling of who is genuinely interested and who is just keeping their options open. Remove any in the latter category from your shortlist.

✚ Ask the builders for references and contact previous clients.

Ask about reliability, punctuality and how easily problems were resolved. You may also want to visit a site or two to check on the quality of the workmanship.

✚ Get your plans approved by building control before the builders quote.

Send your approved plans along with your specification (if you have one) to those builders who are left on your shortlist and ask for a quotation. When you do this, it's quite reasonable to ask them to inform you of their day rates and their mark-up on materials. This will avoid problems later if your plans change or extras arise. Give a closing date, allowing them at least three weeks to return quotations. If the job is a large one, and especially if you don't have a specification, you should allow longer.

✚ Give them the opportunity to inspect the property.

If the house is empty you'll need to either provide them with a set of keys or, preferably, arrange to meet them on site. This is another good test; if a builder misses this appointment or turns up very late, it's a bad sign. It means they are either very busy, disorganized or uninterested in your project, any of which could spell trouble later.

✚ Look for the logo.

You might be swayed by a builder's membership of a trade organization, but in many cases all this means is that the builder has paid a fee to use a logo. (Some builders even make up their own logos, so phone the organization to ensure that the membership is genuine.) The Federation of Master Builders has a dispute arbitration service and could perhaps help if things go horribly wrong. A logo worth looking out for is the UK government's quality mark scheme. Members must demonstrate technical competence, be in financial good standing and have adequate insurance cover. A similar system called Homebond operates in Ireland, run by the construction industry itself. In the event that something goes wrong Homebond provides guarantees against loss of deposit if the builder goes bust, water damage and smoke damage for two years after the building is completed.

✚ If everything has been done properly (on your side and the builders'), all the quotations should be similar.

In practice, this is rarely the case. If there is wide discrepencay and you can't see why, give the highest-priced builders a ring and try and find out. It may simply be they have too much else on, or they could have identified something expensive in the job that nobody else noticed. Alternatively, it could be an arranged pricing scam as mentioned on p. 202.

✚ When you have cleared up any anomalies, you should have a clear winner.

Don't award purely on price if the difference between quotations is just a few percentage points. Extras and other unforeseen works will probably negate this by the time you have paid the final invoice. If there is no clear winner you need to consider factors other than price. Who can start first? Who can complete the work in the fastest time? Who can be contacted most easily? If you still can't decide, pick the one you feel you can trust and get on with best.

A logo worth looking out for is the UK government's quality mark scheme. Members must demonstrate technical competence, be in financial good standing and have adequate insurance cover. A similar system called Homebond operates in Ireland, run by the construction industry itself. In the event that something goes wrong Homebond provides guarantees against loss of deposit if the builder goes bust, water damage and smoke damage for two years after the building is completed.

HOW TO WORK WITH BUILDERS

Better clients make better builders, but this doesn't mean you have be putty in their hands. Here are few useful tips:

✚ Be clear about your role.
You're in charge, and you know what you want, but the builder probably knows more about the detail of what's happening on-site. Respect the role of the builder and try to work in partnership with them. Avoid a 'them-and-us' relationship.

✚ Agree payment arrangements with the builder in advance.
Most will expect a deposit up-front, stage payments during the project and a final payment on completion. Whatever you agree, stick to it. Nothing will upset builders more than thinking you're a reluctant payer.

✚ If you employ a general builder, use them properly.
Instruct the project manager, not the subbies, otherwise the manager won't be able to manage the site properly. If you need something done quickly and you can't contact the manager, you may have to instruct subbies directly, but you should then contact the builder as soon as you can and say what instructions you have given. Make it clear that the only reason you have done so is because the builder couldn't be contacted.

✚ Be clear about what you want and stick to it.
Changing your mind every few days is a recipe for frayed relations and rocketing expense.

✚ Agree all extras with your builder.
Keep a duplicate book and document the price and nature of each one. Keep one copy yourself and give the other to the builder. (Your builder may well operate a similar system for such extras, also known as variation orders or VOs.)

✚ Communicate well and keep in touch.
Give your builder your mobile phone number. If you can always be contacted there is no excuse to do anything without your go-ahead. If you don't understand something, ask. Don't let the builder fob you off. Make it clear that you know the difference between excuses and explanations.

✚ Be honest about money.
If you have a cashflow problem discuss it early with the builder and try to reach a solution. Don't default on payments, and certainly never without warning the builder. Nothing will worry a builder more than a client who seems unlikely to pay, and a worried builder is a poorly performing builder.

✚ If things go wrong, don't start a war.
Everybody makes mistakes, and everybody should be given a chance to put them right. Try not to get angry, at least not over the first problem. If things are still not put right you can withhold payment, but don't do this lightly: it'll annoy the builder. If things reach this stage, make it clear how much you're withholding and why, and what the builder must do to trigger the payment.

✚ If it does go wrong ...
and it can't be resolved amicably, or at least civilly, consider arbitration; some of the trade bodies run arbitration services. It's a good idea to ask well in advance if your builder would be prepared to use them. This could even be one of the questions you ask at the time you select your builder.

In the worst case scenario, when all else has failed, you may need to fire your builder. Don't take this decision lightly; it will probably raise difficult contractual problems and you will have the devil's own job trying to find another builder to finish the job off. However, if you have reached this stage, try to put your emotions aside and sack your builder professionally. Relations may be frayed, but it's far preferable to reach an amicable separation than to fight it out in court. More often than not your builder will be keen to extricate himself from the job, too, and the only sticking point will be how much money you owe. If you can't resolve this you may need to resort to formal termination of the contract. Unless you understand contract law, don't attempt do this without professional advice. Good surveyors and architects are often very skilled at handling these sorts of problems and you may be able to hire one on an advisory basis, even if you haven't appointed one for the whole project. Alternatively, speak to a solicitor.

Nobody likes sorting out a mess created by somebody else, and builders are no exception. If and when you find another builder willing to finish off the job, expect to pay over the odds. Many builders are unwilling to take on this type of work, so you will not be in a strong negotiating position. Needless to say, it's far better to avoid getting into such a situation in the first place.

QUOTATIONS AND ESTIMATES

Although these two words are often used interchangeably, they mean very different things to a builder and it's important to appreciate the difference.

A quotation is a firm price; it means the builder agrees to do the specified work for that price no matter what. (This holds even if the builder adds VAT to the bill after omitting it from the quotation.) You're obliged to pay only the quoted amount. A quotation is a contract and, as such, is legally binding on both parties.

An estimate, on the other hand, is no more than an informed guess at how much the cost is likely to be. Even if the final bill is much higher than the original estimate you're still obliged to pay. It makes sense, then, to ask for a quotation rather than an estimate.

But accurately predicting the costs of restoration and conversion work on a rescued house project is notoriously difficult, so if you insist on a quotation it'll almost certainly be higher than if you asked for an estimate (although your final bill may be lower). A quotation doesn't include unforeseen work, so if extras arise it's quite reasonable that their cost should be added to the final bill.

CONTRACTS

A contract is simply an agreement to provide a specified service at an agreed price. Standard written contracts are simply a way of recording this agreement as clearly as possible. In theory, a written contract is unnecessary and much building work goes on without one, but when there are thousands of pounds of your money at stake it's as well to make sure that everybody is clear what you have agreed to spend it on. A contract allocates the risk in a project, specifying when the work should be finished, what the quality will be and how much it's all going to cost. Normally the contract puts the onus on the builder to satisfy those conditions, i.e. to take the risk, although different types of contract may allocate risk differently. The more risk you expect the builder to take, the more you should expect to pay.

For small jobs, and jobs where you're employing tradespeople directly, it's normal practice to enter into a verbal agreement rather than a written contract. Don't worry about this, a verbal agreement is still legally binding, and in any case, do you really want to be chasing every last plasterer on your site and getting them to sign reams of paperwork? When costs begin to approach the £10,000 mark, however, a written contract is advisable.

You can write whatever you like in a contract, but it's probably easier to use a prepared form. The most common are Joint Contracts Tribunal (JCT) contracts. Your architect or surveyor should know which one to use and how to obtain it. (Indeed, they should sort all this out for you.) If you're employing contractors directly, you can get copies of JCT contracts from the RICS and the RIBA bookshops.

**There are many different forms of standard contract available.
The main types you may need are listed below.**

✚ Design and build

Use this where the builder has responsibility
for design work as well as building work.
Different contracts can be used according
to whether the builder has sole responsibility
for design or for specific portions only.

✚ Minor works

Use this for minor works in non-residential
buildings, or buildings you don't intend to live
in yourself. You shouldn't need to use these
very often because in commercial residential
conversions you can use a home owner/occupier
contract provided you live in the property
when it's finished.

✚ Home owner/occupier

Use this for small-scale renovation works
where no architect or surveyor is involved.
A separate contract is normally used if you're
receiving a local authority grant to help fund
the works. There is another type of contract
if a surveyor or architect is managing the work,
but they should be able to advise you on this.

✚ Home repairs and maintenance

Use this where the works are very minor and can
be finished in less than four weeks. It allows only
for payment on completion in one lump sum.

A contract allocates risk; the more
risk you expect the builder to take,
the more you should expect to pay.

WHAT YOU COULD AND SHOULD INCLUDE IN A CONTRACT

SPECIFICATION

A specification is by far the most important thing to include in, or attach to, a contract. This is the part that states the work that you want the builder to do. Without it, the rest of the contract is virtually meaningless. The most common reason for building work going wrong is an inadequate or non-existent specification. A specification may not be necessary for a small project, but if the job is large enough to warrant a contract it definitely requires one. Detailed plans can be used as an alternative.

PAYMENT TERMS

For small jobs you can quite reasonably propose to pay everything on completion, although you are then passing all the risk to the builder and should expect to pay more. If a job is expected to last more than two or three weeks, weekly stage payments based on a valuation of works carried out are the norm. If you're borrowing or receiving a grant to pay for the work, it's quite possible that your lender or grant organization will release payment to you in stages, in which case you need to co-ordinate your payment terms with your builder to ensure you're not left short of funds. It's a good idea, although not essential, to tell the builder how you're funding the work, particularly if the money is coming from a reliable source such as a bank or building society.

INSURANCE

This is a potentially tricky area. If you are employing a general builder or project manager, you can quite reasonably expect them to have insurance cover in place and include the costs in their quotation, but there are certain risks you may need to cover yourself. Make sure you check that all the necessary insurance is in place and make sure the contract specifies who needs to cover what. If insurance is the builder's responsibility, ask to see a copy of their policy. There are three types of insurance essential to all projects:

➡ Public liability insurance covers risks to third parties, for example if your garden wall falls over and breaks a passer-by's ankle.

➡ Employer's liability insurance covers risks to people employed on site, for example if a roofer falls through your rotten timber roof and is injured. If you employ tradespeople directly you'll need to arrange this, because you are the employer. If you use a general builder or a project manager, they need to arrange cover.

➡ All Risks policies potentially cover any other calamity that might happen such as fire, or somebody making off with your stock of bricks.

Check the terms of your standard buildings insurance policy before you take out any additional cover. You may be surprised to find that this already provides much of the protection you need.

When arranging insurance cover, bear in mind that this is a specialist area. It's probably better to arrange it through an insurance broker rather than deal with the insurance companies directly.

PROVISIONAL AND PC SUMS

These are prices that are often included in contracts if there exists any doubt about the full extent of the work. The two terms are often used interchangeably, but they mean different things. Provisional sums are used where the amount of work isn't known at the time the quotation is written, for example the number of slates that will require replacement to repair an unsound roof. PC (prime cost) sums, on the other hand, allow the client to make a final decision about a particular item later. If you don't know which kitchen units you want, you can put a PC sum of £1,000 in the specification and you pay more or less according to the cost of the one you eventually choose. Provisional sums are all about risk. The fewer provisional sums a builder uses, the more risk he is taking, and the more he is likely to charge. It's incredibly difficult to estimate quantities accurately when renovating old buildings, and so most builders will prefer to include provisional sums. You must make sure that this doesn't become an opportunity for them to exploit you once the work is underway. You should at least agree labour rates and mark-up percentages at the outset so you can be sure that any additional work is carried out at the same rate as was originally quoted.

TIME PENALTIES

Time penalties are deductions you agree to make from what you owe the builder if the work is not completed within an agreed time limit. Normally these are used only where the client will suffer a financial loss if the project is delayed, such as a hotel opening late and being forced to cancel bookings. Of course, you as an individual could also suffer financial loss if the work overruns, such as additional mortgage or rental payments, but there are two good reasons not to include time penalties in the contract. First, time penalties aren't popular with builders and you will be starting your relationship on an adversarial footing. Second, most builders have sufficient experience of time penalty clauses to muddy the waters. If they are late delivering, you can be sure that it will be your fault rather than theirs and the smallest change of mind or specification on your part will excuse the longest delay. To be fair, there may also be delays owing to circumstances beyond everybody's control, such as bad weather or a materials shortage.

RETENTIONS

Retentions are sums you agree to withhold for a few weeks or months after completion (5 per cent is usual). This gives you a lever to make sure that the builder deals with any snags and should ensure that they will return to correct any faults that become apparent following completion. Retentions are quite common on larger jobs, but like time penalties they are unpopular with builders. A conscientious builder will act responsibly as a matter of course, and in this care a retention would probably be counter-productive. Others disappear into thin air the moment you pay the final invoice. You should ask previous clients about snagging and after-care when you take up your builder's references and make a decision based on the replies you receive.

It doesn't always follow that the best environmental options are the most expensive, or perform in an inferior way. In fact, the products with the best green credentials are often the most durable and of superior quality.

10 CHOOSING THE RIGHT MATERIALS

This book, although not as stridently environmental as some, unashamedly has green overtones. The very act of rescuing a house has good green credentials in itself. Reusing an old building means one less will be built on green fields as well as saving much of the material and other resources that would have been used in a new-build property. It would be a pity to negate all this good work by using environmentally inferior building materials. This chapter shows you how to buy good and sustainable building materials, lays out the choices you will be offered and examines the implications of those choices on your property, your health and the environment.

I hope this doesn't sound too sanctimonious. Every building material has a detrimental effect on the environment at some point in its production or use but, I hope to demonstrate that there exists a wide range of options for almost any building material you need to use.

WHY CHOOSING THE RIGHT BUILDING MATERIALS MATTERS

Cast your mind back to the introduction of this book for a moment. I talked then about how global environmental problems can seem too vast to be affected by the actions of an individual. Well, you'll be pleased to hear that the choices you make regarding building materials really can make a significant difference. Two-thirds of all the energy consumed in the UK, not to mention a good deal of the toxins and pollutants we generate, is accounted for by buildings and building construction.

In view of this, it's surprising that it has taken so long for sustainable building methods to become widespread. Whilst pioneering projects such as those produced by the Centre for Alternative Energy in Machynlleth and Robert and Brenda Vale (authors of *The New Autonomous House*) have been demonstrating the benefits of green building for decades, the bulk of the rather conservative building industry has had to be pushed greenwards by successive amendments to Building Regulations.

The primary reason for this change of heart is climate change. In the 1990s, perhaps too late, governments around the world woke up to the fact that our consumption of fossil fuels was creating so much carbon dioxide that it was actually changing the climate of the planet. A series of global summits, most notably those at Rio de Janeiro in 1992 and Kyoto in 1997, set international targets for the stabilization and reduction of carbon dioxide emissions. In order to meet these targets the British and Irish governments have introduced all sorts of regulations and incentives to encourage and/or force people to become more environmentally friendly.

The scientific community is still undecided about whether climate change will turn the British Isles into a desert, a glacier or Atlantis but, whatever the effects, they are unlikely to be beneficial. If we continue as we are, they may well be catastrophic.

This chapter examines the common building materials you need to rescue a house, and judges them against the four main impacts of housing on the environment:

➡ Energy used by houses once they are occupied.

➡ Pollution, both of the environment at large and internally. (Many products used in building construction and maintenance are potentially hazardous both to the people working on the property and the people who subsequently live in it.)

➡ The effect on biodiversity.

➡ Depletion of natural resources. An important invisible cost here is *embodied energy* – the amount of energy consumed in the production of any particular product. Some of this energy will be consumed locally (the petrol that powers the cement mixer, for example), while other energy will have been consumed elsewhere in the manufacture and transportation of materials. To calculate embodied energy is fiendishly difficult and there is no internationally agreed method of doing so. Consider a freighter with hundreds of different containers on board. What proportion of the ship's fuel should be included when calculating the embodied energy of some hardwood planks in one of the containers? Manufacturers and importers of building materials all provide embodied energy figures for their products, but there is little in the way of external verification. This is rough science, I'm afraid, but nevertheless important to take into account when making decisions about the building materials you're going to use.

In what follows I have tried to rank the various options environmentally and practically. This is a subjective judgement on my part and I claim no scientific rationale behind my ranking system other than that I have considered the four environmental impacts and the usefulness of each. The choices open to you may be limited, especially if the property is listed or in a conservation area. Some materials are simply unsuitable for use on certain properties, and, of course, your budget will often constrain your options. On this last point, try to take a long-term view whenever possible. An environmentally sound option may be expensive initially, but could well pay for itself in lower fuel costs, longer intervals between repair or replacement and an increased property value. These savings may even offset the higher repayment on a larger loan. Sustainability is long-term proposition.

BUYING MATERIALS

Before we examine the merits of the materials themselves it's worth looking at how you go about buying them. This may seem to require no explanation, but the building industry is a strange one to operate in, and nothing is quite what it seems at first. The business of supplying materials is a minefield of traditional practices and vested interests. This can make it difficult to buy the materials you want, as opposed to those that your builder would prefer you to buy. This section explains how it all works.

Builders buy almost all their building materials from general builders' merchants. Every major town has one or two builders' merchants, ranging from national chains such as Jewsons and Travis Perkins to small local companies. These outlets can supply just about everything you need to build or renovate a house, but often they have a limited choice of options for each product line; for example they'll all supply guttering, but perhaps not in the colour or profile you're looking for. A first visit to a builders' merchant can be quite daunting – and certainly confusing. There are no marked prices, or if there are, they're lower than the price you pay. Not much money changes hands because everyone seems to buy on credit. You have little opportunity to browse through the options. But most irritating of all is when the staff just ignore you in favour of regular customers. If you get the impression that they want builders' custom and not yours, you could be right. The national chains are becoming more customer friendly, but they are still a long way from the 'here-to-help' culture of the major retail outlets.

The reason for the pricing anomaly is that all prices in builders' merchants are quoted exclusive of VAT. The reason people buy on credit is that account customers usually pay less. If you, an ordinary member of the public, order a quantity of timber you may be quoted £150. A small builder with an account may be quoted £130 for the same timber, but a larger builder who is a valued regular customer may be quoted only £110. Account holders are usually invoiced for their purchases monthly, which explains why you see very little money changing hands.

If you employ a general builder, chances are they'll be a valued customer of one of the local merchants. The discount they receive on materials forms part of their profit from your job because they'll charge you the non-discounted price. If you specify a product that their favourite builders' merchant doesn't stock, they'll lose that hidden profit. Consequently, if your builder tries to steer you away from your preferred product and towards a 'better' one, the likely reason is that it's one better for the builder's bank balance rather than better for your project.

The building materials discussed in the following sections of this chapter are all available in the UK and Ireland, but some of the best ones are available only from specialist suppliers. This means it can be difficult to get your builder to use the materials you want.

There are a two ways round this:

✚ Specify at the tender stage exactly the materials you require.

Discuss with your builder precisely what it is that you want and leave no room for ambiguity. Builders can easily misread 'wool insulation' as 'mineral wool insulation', for example. They may also tell you that the product you want is unavailable. Contact details for all the suppliers mentioned in this chapter will be found in the directory at the end of the book. Include them or those of other suppliers of your choice in your specification.

✚ Buy the materials yourself.

I wouldn't necessarily recommend doing this if you're employing a general builder, but if you're employing trades people directly this is a good option. If you're buying direct, ask if it is possible to open accounts with each of your suppliers. This may help your cashflow and will help you negotiate better discounts.

ROOFING MATERIALS

If yours is a restoration project you'll probably want to follow the original design and materials, and if your property is listed or in a conservation area you'll probably have no choice but to do so. But in other cases, why not consider the alternatives? Most older houses have already had the original roof replaced at least once already, and if it needs replacing again you could give the whole roof a rethink. Also, if you're building an extension, don't feel obliged to match its roof to that of the main building. A contrast can work well in many situations.

BEST OPTIONS

PV (PHOTOVOLTAIC) ROOFS

Several manufacturers produce photovoltaic tiles that can be used as a roof covering. Improvements in design mean that some look quite inconspicuous, and can easily pass as slates, although they do have an oily sheen to them. If your house is listed or in a conservation area it's quite likely that the authorities won't be too keen on them, but if the roof can't be seen from the road you may have a good case to argue for them. The great environmental advantage of P V roofs is nothing to do with how they are manufactured, but the fact that the tiles generate electricity from daylight; in theory, a house can produce all the electricity it needs from a solar roof, but unfortunately it doesn't always produce it when you need it most – at night and in winter. Storage of electricity using a cellar full of car batteries is hardly practical, so the answer is a two-way meter, sometimes called a power gate. This enables you to draw electricity from the national grid when you need more than you're producing, but sell electricity back when you produce more than you need. In this manner, solar roofs can really begin to pay their way. At the moment installation costs are high and it will take many years to recoup your investment, but if you're replacing a roof or building a new one you really should consider this as one of your top options.

Photovoltaics in the UK is a small book that can help you calculate how much electricity an installation on your property is likely to produce. In the UK the Department of Trade and Industry offers grants that can defray a substantial portion of the cost of a PV roof. (See Chapter 13.) A list of suppliers and installers can be found on the British Photovoltaic Association's website.

WOODEN SHINGLES

Although a traditional roofing material in the English Home Counties, shingles are rare in the rest of the U K and Ireland. They are common in the U S A and have proved to be effective, durable and environmentally a good option. The best wood for shingles is cedar, but in the U K they are traditionally of chestnut. Both look fantastic in a rustic sort of way. For the first year they have a reddish tinge, but after that they mellow down to a slate-grey colour. Both cedar and chestnut are hardwearing and require no chemical preservatives. Shingles should occasionally be brushed down to ensure that dirt doesn't collect in them, but otherwise they are quite low maintenance (One occasional problem is woodpecker damage. The birds drill holes in shingles while seeking insects hiding in the crevices. The risk of this damage is reduced if they are brushed clean once a year.) The manufacturing process for shingles is simple and uses very little energy. The drawback, environmentally, is that the cedar is taken mainly from North American forests which aren't properly replanted. The good news is that this doesn't apply to chestnut shingles. If you can find them, recycled shingles are an even better environmental choice. You should be able to buy shingles through your local timber yard. If not, the U K's biggest supplier is John Brash & Co., who sell both imported cedar and home-produced chestnut shingles.

SECOND-BEST OPTION

RECYCLED MATERIALS

The most common recycled roofing materials are slates and terracotta tiles. Good-quality roof coverings can outlast the building so it's not uncommon to see these for sale. Recycled slates make the best sense environmentally, although they aren't much cheaper than new ones. Also, be careful who you buy them from; theft of roof slates and tiles is a problem on the rise.

THIRD-BEST OPTIONS

NEW SLATES

Slate, a sedimentary rock that splits easily into very thin sheets, is an excellent roofing material. Its thinness enables a whole roof to be covered in a natural stone that is light in weight and has a very even finish. Environmentally, though, it's not so good because a great deal of energy is used in quarrying and transporting it. Obviously, slate from local quarries will embody less transportation energy, and in most cases will be of better quality too. Welsh slate is arguably the best in the world. A good-quality slate will last a long time and will also have the potential of being recycled in the future. Unfortunately, most of our slate is now imported from Asia; the quality isn't great and the embodied energy costs are sufficiently high to give slate as a whole a low environmental ranking here.

NEW CLAY/TERRACOTTA TILES

Terracotta tiles have been popular for hundreds of years, and it's not hard to see why. They are watertight, hardwearing, light in weight, and they look great. They even improve with age, gradually taking on a softer, more natural colour. Terracotta is, of course, just fired clay. Clay is a very common soil type and reserves of clay suitable for making tiles are abundant. Very few clay tiles are imported into the U K or Ireland, and manufacturing plants are numerous enough that it should be possible to buy locally produced tiles wherever you are. Extraction of clay isn't highly damaging to the environment, even though the area surrounding a quarry usually looks rather messy. Most exhausted clay pits are returned to nature quite quickly after they have been used up and many become important wildlife habitats.

The reason clay tiles are only a third-best option is the firing process. Vast amounts of energy are used to heat the kilns and nitrous oxide, a greenhouse gas, and sulphur dioxide, which contributes to acid rain, are given off. The best tiles are fired at a higher temperature, which means more energy, and more nasties given off. However, as with slate, good-quality tiles will last for ages before they need replacing and have great potential for being recycled.

If you're a slate roof enthusiast, *The Slate Roof Bible* by Joseph Jenkins will tell you everything you need to know.

POOR OPTIONS

ARTIFICIAL SLATE

Artificial slate is made from aggregates of crushed slate and stone bound together with glass fibres and acrylic resin. They look similar to genuine slate, but you can spot the difference quite easily because the slates are just *too* perfect and lack the character of the real thing. Many planning authorities agree and it's quite common for their use to be banned in conservation areas and on listed buildings. The main advantage of artificial slates is that they are cheap, at least in comparison to the real things.

Older artificial slates contained asbestos as a binding material. Asbestos is, of course, highly dangerous and inhaling even a tiny quantity can be fatal. The effect is insidious; asbestosis and mesotheliomia (cancer of the diaphragm) take twenty years or more to become symptomatic. You should avoid moving any artificial slates unless you're sure that they contain no asbestos. Those made after 1980 should be asbestos free, though many roofs fitted in the early 1980s would, of course, have used pre-1980 stock. The manufacturing process uses up slate which would otherwise have gone to waste, although some slate and aggregate is quarried specifically for making artificial slate. Large amounts of energy in the form of heat and pressure are used in their production and the acrylic resin is produced by the petrochemical industry, which emits large quantities of toxins into the environment. One type of resin often used, Acrylonitrile, is a suspected carcinogen.

CONCRETE TILES

Concrete tiles are largely made of ordinary Portland cement with a covering of acrylic colouring and sand. Some of the thinner types of tile are bound together with fibres in the same way as in artificial slate. Concrete tiles are rapidly taking over from clay/terracotta as the standard material for new-build houses. Their design is much improved from the ugly interlocking tiles of the 1960s and 1970s, and it's quite difficult to tell the difference between some new concrete tiles and terracotta ones. The key word there is 'new'. Concrete doesn't improve with age and weathering will cause it to fade to a muddy brown colour.

The raw materials for cement are limestone or chalk and clay. These materials are abundant in the UK and Ireland, but the production of cement is something of an environmental nightmare. Cement production is pretty messy, and even the best-run plants discharge tons of cement dust, giving everything within a radius of a few hundred metres a grey tinge. The worst problem, however, is the huge quantities of carbon dioxide (CO_2) that are given off. This, of course, contributes to global warming. It is estimated that cement manufacture accounts for about 9 per cent of all the waste CO_2 produced on the planet.

Large amounts of energy are used in the production of the tiles, which involves high-pressure extrusion and high-temperature curing or firing. The firing process gives off a number of toxic substances including heavy metals, organic hydrocarbons and carbon monoxide.

ROOFING MATERIALS FOR FLAT ROOFS

BEST OPTION

PLANTED ROOFS

A few manufacturers produce flat-roof systems that can be covered with a layer of soil and planted. You can either go for the roof-garden approach (sometimes called intensive roofs – presumably because they need intensive work to maintain them), or use low-growing plants as a living roof covering (sometimes called an extensive roof, presumably because extensive is the opposite of intensive). This grass-roof approach can also work on a pitched roof. Soil and plants give quite effective insulation (although not as effective as a similar thickness of artificial insulation material), and if built properly require little maintenance. The roof will need to be sufficiently sturdy to cope with the substantial weight, which will increase considerably in wet weather. The environmental benefit of a planted roof is that it provides a fine, undisturbed habitat that encourages insects and birds. Don't underestimate the quantity of soil you'll need. Roof gardens will need 300 mm of soil depth. So-called 'grass roofs' don't have to have grass on them at all but are more commonly planted with low-growing sedums – tough alpine plants that will tolerate the difficult growing conditions on the top of your house. A tidy-up twice a year to clear out dead plants and occasional watering in the summer is all you need to do. You can also find lightweight systems that use artificial matting instead of soil. These weigh only a little more than a tiled roof and so are a quite practical alternative.

An innovative regeneration initiative in Deptford Creek, south-east London, is encouraging brownfield roofs (a variation on the planted-roof theme). The idea is to recreate the ecosystems of derelict land, a once-common habitat in south-east London that provided ideal conditions for the rare black redstart and other wildlife, but which earlier regeneration initiatives (oh, the irony!) have caused to be developed. Thanks to this latest initiative, the no doubt confused black redstart is making a comeback.

POOR OPTIONS

ZINC

Zinc roofs are in fact steel sheet galvanized with a layer of zinc to protect against corrosion. This is a relatively durable product, although it won't stand up to being walked on since the zinc layer scratches off easily, leaving the steel exposed. The thickness of the zinc varies according to the galvanizing method employed. Zinc isn't mined in the UK or Ireland and most is imported from distant countries such as Australia, Peru and the USA, meaning high embodied energy costs through transport. Smelting is highly energy intensive and results in several toxins being released into the environment. Zinc is often found in the same geological formations as arsenic and lead and these toxins often pollute the waste water resulting from zinc production. Some zinc is recycled. The recycling process itself is energy intensive, but environmentally far better than producing it from scratch.

LEAD

Lead is a commonly used material for flashings, but its cost means it has gone out of favour as a covering for entire flat roofs. Lead is found in the same geological formations as zinc, so the same environmental problems of extraction apply to both. The big problem with lead is its toxicity. It can cause damage to the nervous system and disrupt the body's production of red blood cells. Lead accumulates in our bones, from which it can emerge years later and poison us. It can be absorbed through inhalation of dust, ingestion and even directly though the skin. This means that rainwater collected from a lead roof should not be used for drinking or for watering plants. In lead's favour, it's easy to recycle owing to its low melting point, and its high price means that almost all of it does indeed get recycled.

ASPHALT

Asphalt is a product made from tar mixed with a fibrous binder. The tar is derived from thick oil that is produced by the petrochemical industry, one of the most polluting of all industries. The binder was traditionally an organic material such as hessian or wood fibre, but since the 1980s this has been supplanted by fibreglass. Asphalt is applied in situ or produced in sheets or tiles. Well laid in-situ asphalt can last a long time, although it does require maintenance and repair. Asphalt sheeting is now very cheap but has poor durability. Asphalt is rarely recycled; indeed, the presence of fibreglass makes recycling almost impossible.

Thanks to this latest initiative, the no doubt confused black redstart is making a comeback.

MASONRY

In a renovation project the choice of masonry is usually made for you.
Restoration work and extensions really need to be constructed in the same
materials as the original if they are going to look right. However, in some cases
a contrast can work, or if your renovation project is really extensive, you
might have an opportunity to rethink the masonry materials altogether.

BEST OPTION

RECYCLED BRICKS OR STONE

There is a thriving market in reclaimed bricks and
stone, and whilst the whole thrust of this book is
towards encouraging the reuse of buildings, there
will always be many more buildings that are
demolished. Recycling bricks and stone where
lime mortar has been used is easy; the lime comes
off readily and the bricks and stone are usually
left in good condition. Most recycled masonry
can be sourced locally, reducing transport energy.
There is really only one downside: cost. Recycled
bricks are usually more expensive than new ones.
Almost all brick suppliers sell recycled bricks and
stone, but some charge six times the price of the

cheapest new bricks for good second-hand ones.
A cheaper source is to try local waste-transfer
stations or recycling centres. They'll often sell
recycled bricks to you directly, although what
they have to sell will depend on what has been
demolished recently. Look in Yellow Pages
(Golden Pages in Ireland) under skips and phone
round to see what's on offer. If you're going to buy
recycled bricks by the pallet, a good tip is take a
few out and have a look at the inside of the stack
before you buy. Some suppliers have a tendency
to put all the good bricks around the edges and
fill up the middle with broken ones.

SECOND-BEST OPTIONS

LOCAL STONE
Both the U K and Ireland have plentiful supplies of limestone, sandstone and granite, but quarrying can create local environmental damage and often produces lots of waste. Energy is used in extraction and transport, so the more local your source, the better.

NEW BRICKS
There are many different types of bricks, all with slightly different manufacturing processes. Almost all British and Irish bricks are made by firing clay in hot kilns. This uses large amounts of energy. A number of toxic pollutants can be given off but the quantities and types depend on the impurities in the particular clay. Oxides of sulphur and nitrogen are commonly emitted and these contribute to acid rain. The best choice environmentally are perforated bricks. (These are the ones that have three or four holes through them instead of an indentation in the top, known in the trade as a frog, designed to hold the mortar during laying.) The materials they are made from are no different, but the holes mean less of it is used, which reduces firing times and energy consumed by transportation. An added benefit is that the air pockets give these bricks slightly better insulation properties.

Bricks are also made using sand-lime and concrete. These tend to be more expensive than clay and have rather a municipal-lavatatory-block look about them. They aren't very common and so I'll say here only that clay bricks are the better bet environmentally.

POOR OPTIONS

IMPORTED STONE
Considering we live on such a rocky set of islands, to import stone may seem like bringing coal to Newcastle. But the oddities of world economics mean that it's often cheaper to quarry rock in Asia or South America and ship it here than to quarry it in Yorkshire. The environmental issues for imported stone are much the same as for local stone (above), but embodied energy will be far higher. Carting stone around the globe is, as you can imagine, highly energy intensive.

ARTIFICIAL STONE OR FAIR-FACED BLOCKS
These are concrete blocks made with a mixture of cement and reconstituted stone or moulded to make them look presentable enough to be used as an exposed surface. The costs are much lower than for cut stone but the environmental, not to mention the visual, impact is as bad as for dense concrete blocks.

CONCRETE BLOCKS

Concrete blocks are cheaper, lighter and far quicker to build with than bricks. In the U K and Ireland they have been adopted as the norm for masonry that is hidden, such as the inner skin of a cavity wall or one that will be rendered. Some modern architecture employs them quite brazenly and exposed bare concrete-block walls are becoming rather chic in certain circles. It's unlikely that your planning officer will move in such circles, though, so for most people embarking on a rescued-house project the use of these will be limited to the internal skin of an extension.

BEST OPTION

AERATED BLOCKS

Aerated blocks are made from a slurry of lime and cement to which aluminium sulphate is added. The chemical reaction from this mixture gives off a great deal of hydrogen which causes the mixture to rise like proving bread. The mixture sets and is cut into blocks that are fired in steam. The detrimental environmental impacts of cement have already been mentioned on p. 221, but one unexpected advantage here is that the setting process causes the cement to carbonate. This means it reabsorbs some of the carbon dioxide given off when it was manufactured. Both aerated and lightweight aggregate blocks have excellent heat insulation properties and their light weight means that embodied energy costs through transportation are less than for other masonry materials. However, their low cost and fragility mean that there is practically no market for recycling any type of concrete block.

POOR OPTIONS

DENSE CONCRETE BLOCKS

These are similar to aerated blocks, but embody more transportation energy owing to their greater weight. Their production method means that the cement doesn't carbonate so the large amounts of carbon dioxide given off during manufacture aren't reabsorbed. They also have much poorer insulation properties than aerated blocks.

LIGHTWEIGHT AGGREGATE OR CLINKER BLOCKS

These blocks are made from a mixture of cement, sand and aggregate. Most aggregate is waste produced from other manufacturing processes: clay from brick manufacturing, slag from quarrying and mining, ash from furnaces. Clinker is a by-product of metal smelting. On the plus side, this is a method of disposal of waste products. There are even blocks that contain crushed bones and other delights that need to be disposed of from the meat industry. But there is some scientific evidence that blocks made with slag and fuel ash emit harmful radiation and increase the risk of lung cancer. This may all sound fairly horrible, but these waste products have to be disposed of somehow. Whether you want them built into your home or not is another matter.

Aerated blocks are manufactured by four manufacturers in the UK and Ireland: Celcon, Durox, Tarmac and Thermalite. All are widely available from building supply merchants.

MORTAR

Mortar not only sticks bricks and blocks together, it holds them apart and absorbs some of the load and thermal movement in the wall. In a restoration project, try to match what was originally used on the property. Otherwise, err on the side of lime mortar. The environmental impact of mortars concerns carbon dioxide emissions during production. Once in place, whichever mortar you choose will have little impact on the environment and pose no real health dangers to occupants.

BEST OPTION

PURE LIME

Pure lime is manufactured from chalk or limestone and is mixed with sand and water on site to produce mortar. It can be bought as bagged lime powder, quicklime or lime putty. The manufacturing process uses large amounts of heat energy (but not as much as for cement) and produces great quantities of carbon dioxide. However, much of this is reabsorbed when the mortar sets. Lime is strongly alkaline and is potentially hazardous in its raw state, so wear protective gloves when you handle it. There are no health implications from set lime mortar.

SECOND-BEST OPTION

HYDRAULIC LIME

This is lime either with clay impurities or with clay deliberately added to it. As its name suggests, it has resistance to water. It will set while wet, so can be used for structures that frequently take a soaking. The environmental implications are the same as for pure lime except that it doesn't reabsorb anything like as much carbon dioxide. There is no good reason to use it instead of pure lime mortar for above-ground work in any normal domestic building, although of course it's better environmentally than cement. Hydraulic lime is the best environmental choice as a mortar for footings and foundations.

Cement is arguably the most environmentally damaging product used in building construction.

THIRD-BEST OPTIONS

MASONRY CEMENT
This is simply a mixture of cement that includes a 15 to 20 per cent addition of lime. There is nothing special about this, but the lime content means less cement is used. The lime gives the mortar a more buttery consistency than pure cement, and is easier to work with. Masonry cement is commonly used for rendering. Some bricklayers mix their own masonry cement by adding lime to the cement mortar mix. It requires great skill when mixing several batches in this way to ensure a consistent mixture and colour from one batch to the next. The most common trade name for manufactured masonry cement is Wallcrete, and it is often referred to as such irrespective of the actual brand used.

ORDINARY PORTLAND BLAST-FURNACE CEMENT
Blast-furnace slag is a waste product of iron smelting and is added to cement for the same reasons it's added to lightweight aggregate blocks: it's a method of waste disposal and it's cheap. The same concerns about radiation exist, although the amounts of waste added are less than in the blocks so the risk is reduced. And at least the slag reduces the cement content.

POOR OPTION

ORDINARY PORTLAND CEMENT
Cement is arguably the most environmentally damaging product used in building construction (most of its environmental implications are discussed on p. 221). In addition to its high embodied energy, high carbon dioxide emissions and acid rain implications, cement mortar uses additional toxins as additives. Silicon dioxide can be inhaled while the cement is in powder form and exposure can cause silicosis. Chromate is linked to stomach cancer and calcium chloride can cause skin burns. A further problem with cement mortar is its inherent strength. In Chapter 7 I talked about the purpose of mortar. It doesn't actually need to stick the bricks together. In this respect, cement mortar over performs. It sticks like glue. This makes recycling of bricks at a later date all but impossible for anything other than hard-core.

TIMBER

Timber is a wonderfully versatile material. You can practically build a whole house out of it. From the walls to the roof, the floors to the doors . . . you can even buy teak baths and mahogany basins. Timber is unique in building in that it's a truly natural product that, if produced properly, can be genuinely sustainable. Timber grows using only the energy from the sun, minerals in the soil and water. As with all photosynthesizing plants, during their lives trees absorb more carbon dioxide than they emit. This makes timber seem something of a wonder product. Unfortunately, the reality is somewhat different.

It's true that all plants absorb CO_2, but plants also breathe. Respiration absorbs oxygen and gives off CO_2. Over its natural life a tree will indeed be a net consumer of CO_2, but most methods of commercial timber production mean that trees grown for timber don't live out their natural lives and are felled at a point where the balance between CO_2 absorbed and given off is marginal.

Other things that tend to occur in tandem with tree felling also produce CO_2 and other greenhouse gases. Timber production from old-growth forest is the most damaging. Tropical forests contain a huge diversity of plants, very few of which are suitable for timber production. The unwanted ones are often burnt, releasing all their absorbed CO_2 into the atmosphere. In temperate regions felling trees can cause soils to dry out, releasing methane and more CO_2. Far from being the answer to global CO_2 emissions, Greenpeace estimates that forestry is responsible for 30 per cent of them.

Many forestry plantations are dosed with artificial fertilizers, insecticides, fungicides and herbicides. Not only do many of these nasty toxins persist in the environment, the use of such poisons is devastating for biodiversity. Some forests have become almost monocultural as a result and harbour little more wildlife than might a field of wheat.

There are other serious issues, too, including loss of habitat and the displacement of indigenous peoples. Logging of tropical hardwoods continues at an alarming rate. Greenpeace estimates that at current production levels, the world's supply from commercially exploitable forests will run out by 2040. Although producers claim that they engage in selective logging, by building roads into forests they enable others to gain access to previously remote areas and fell trees for firewood or clear land for agriculture. All these activities have a devastating impact on biodiversity.

And on people, too. Many who for years have lived in and from old-growth forests find their livelihood and their homes disappear. Friends of the Earth report that in parts of Brazil the indigenous population has been hunted down and killed by logging companies in an attempt to eradicate them. Indigenous populations in Russia and Scandinavia are also reportedly under pressure from logging companies.

Although that's all rather depressing, the good news is that the environmental impacts of timber production vary enormously. By specifying the right timber you can avoid the worst of the problems and use a building material that not only has some of the best environmental credentials, but is one you can really feel good about.

There are so many different types of timber and so many potential uses that I can't possibly list them all here. On the premise that timber has to be considered in terms of where it came from and how it was produced (oak from one source may be a good environmental option but from another it could be a disaster), I have ranked the options by method of production rather than by type of timber.

Far from being the answer to global CO_2 emissions, Greenpeace estimates that forestry is responsible for 30 per cent of them.

BEST OPTIONS

RECYCLED TIMBER

Most timber used in buildings is capable of being recycled at least once, and many hardwoods could be used again and again. Unfortunately, getting hold of recycled timber isn't as easy as you might imagine. About 7 per cent of all rubbish sent to landfill sites in the UK and Ireland is timber, most of it from the building industry, through demolitions and domestic skips. Part of the problem is that timber is bulky and not particularly expensive. This means the economics of recycling aren't as good as for other building materials. Another problem is that demolition techniques don't lend themselves to reusing the timber. Timber is easily broken and, if reused at all, it's usually only fit for firewood.

There are some excellent recycling centres around that do sell timber directly to the public. Try contacting your local authority. One of the best is a privately run enterprise in Brighton, Community Wood Recycling. Another source is building/architectural salvage yards. These are good places to find timber windows, doors and floorboards, but not many sell boring old joists and purlins. Another source is Salvo. They run an excellent exchange, wants and offers website and publish news and information on building salvage.

CERTIFIED TIMBER

There are a number of certification schemes for producers of timber who abide by a code of good practice for forestry management and stewardship. In the UK the main scheme is run by the Soil Association. The best schemes (including the Soil Association's one) are monitored and approved by the Forest Stewardship Council (FSC). Many timber suppliers use the FSC logo, and you'll see it on packaging and promotional material to signify that the wood comes from a forest that is judged to have been responsibly managed and independently certified in accordance with the FSC's rules. The FSC also has other logos. There is, for example, a mixed-source label to indicate that the wood comes from certified forests or 'controlled sources'. This means none of it comes from forests where traditional or civil rights have been violated, where conservation is threatened, where illegal felling takes place, or where trees are felled in order to use the land for something other than forestry. It also means that no trees have been genetically modified.

To find suppliers selling FSC certified timber, use the search facility on the FSC website or try the free telephone advisory service they provide to help people looking for FSC-certified timber.

SECOND-BEST OPTION

BUY BRITISH OR IRISH

The UK and Irish timber industries are generally well managed, at least in comparison to some of those in South America and West Africa. Our forestry industries are all plantations and are reasonably sustainable. As a nation we no longer fell old-growth forest – we chopped it all down years ago to fuel the engines of the Industrial Revolution. The quality of timber produced here is excellent and something you could become quite patriotic about. Timber such as Scottish douglas fir and English oak really is some of the finest available.

Another advantage is that energy used in transport is far less than for imported timber. The major problem is actually getting hold of the stuff. Both the UK and Ireland are net importers of timber and much of our domestic production goes for wood pulp.

POOR OPTION

UNCERTIFIED TROPICAL HARDWOODS

All tropical hardwoods have made long journeys to these shores and therefore have high embodied energy costs. But for once embodied energy ought to be the least of your worries. The local impact of felling these trees is rarely anything but disastrous. The most commonly used tropical hardwood is Brazilian mahogany. It's very commonly specified for window sills as well as external doors and garden furniture. Brazilian mahogany doesn't grow in plantations and in the wild grows at a density of just one tree per hectare. In felling that one tree, most of the rest of the hectare of forest is usually laid waste and is given no opportunity to recover. This isn't a unique case. The use of most tropical hardwoods has similar environmental impacts.

For all its ills, trade in Brazilian mahogany is at least legal. You may be shocked to learn that much of the tropical hardwood traded on these islands is supposed to be protected by international law. For some reason it isn't perceived as a national scandal that many of our local and national building suppliers routinely sell the arboreal equivalents of Siberian tiger-skin rugs or gorilla-hand ashtrays.

The international law they are transgressing is CITES (Convention on International Trade in Endangered Species). This is a United Nations internationally agreed set of rules governing how

The quality of timber produced here is excellent and something you could become quite patriotic about.

wildlife and wildlife products are traded internationally. It applies to hundreds of species including rare birds, Siberian tigers, gorillas and many trees. In some ways it's been very successful; it's why you can't buy ivory any more, for example, and why if you want a pet tortoise you'll have to find one that was born here. CITES dates back to 1973 but its appendices are continually updated to take account of new risks and threats faced by the world's flora and fauna. The several tree species on the list are included for many reasons but a very common one is that people keep cutting them down for timber. Just like many animal species, these trees are all endangered and some are at risk of extinction. The CITES agreement means that importing timber or other products made from listed species is prohibited or allowed only under special circumstances.

Those species currently prohibited from trade, are:

Brazilian rosewood (*Dalbergia nigra*)
Chilean false larch, also known as Alerce
  (*Fitzroya cupressoides*)
Chilean pine (*Abuacaria arunacaria*)
Guatemalan fir (*Abies guatamalensis*)
Monteromro, also known as Paratores podocarp
  (*Podocarpus parlatorei*)
Pilgerodendron (*Pilgerodendron uviferum*)

Those that can be imported only with a special permit are:

African cherry, also known as Stinkwood
  (*Prunus africana*)
Afrormosia, also known as African teak
  (*Pericopsis elate*)
Ajillo (*Caryocar costaricense*)
Bigleaf mahogany (*Swietenia macrophylla*)
Black pine (*Podocarpus neriifolius*)
Caribbean mahogany (*Swietenia mahogoni*)
Central American mahogany (*Swietenia humilis*)
Cuban mahogany (*Swietenia mahogani*)
Gavilon blanco (*Oreomunnca pterocarpa*)
Pacific coast mahogany (*Swietenia humilis*)
Quira macawood (*Plastymiscium pleistachyum*)
Red sandalwood (*Pterocarpus santalinus*)
Spanish cedar (*Cedrela odorata*)

My advice is to avoid tropical hardwoods altogether. There is nothing in house renovation that absolutely requires their use and there are many better alternatives. If you're absolutely stuck and, for example, need some for a restoration project, try first of all to find some recycled timber. Failing that, buy new tropical hardwood only if it has FSC certification.

My advice is to avoid tropical hardwoods altogether. There is nothing in house renovation that absolutely requires their use and there are many better alternatives.

COMPOSITE BOARDS

Composite boards are an alternative to timber for many applications. A large number of them are made from wood or with wood as a major ingredient. They enable waste wood offcuts and chips to be used instead of being wasted, but they also provide a use for timber from undersize trees that should never have been felled in the first place. They provide adaptable, grain-free products with a multitude of uses. In fact the best choice/second choice rankings here may be debatable. Some types of board have specialist uses and may not be capable of substitution. Nevertheless, the production methods of these boards mean they vary greatly in their environmental impact. To avoid using the worst ones, look at the alternatives and see if you could use timber instead.

For some reason it isn't perceived as a national scandal that many of our local and national building suppliers routinely sell the arboreal equivalents of Siberian tiger-skin rugs or gorilla-hand ashtrays.

BEST OPTIONS

FIBREBOARDS

Fibreboards, including softboard, medium board and hardboard, but not MDF, are made almost entirely of wood. They are frequently used to cover uneven floorboards before carpet or other floor coverings are laid. They are also commonly used in the kitchen for the carcasses, worktops and sometimes the doors of kitchen units. Hardboard is also sometimes used for small partitions and built-in furniture. The disadvantage of fibreboards is that they can be ruined by even small quantities of water (hardboard is better in this respect but it's still unsuitable for outdoor use). Particles are compressed and heated to bind them together into a board. Embodied energy is used in breaking the wood into particles and in the binding process, but otherwise the production is relatively benign environmentally. A large proportion of the wood used is waste and so their production is in itself a form of recycling. The durability of these products isn't great, especially softboard, and their potential for recycling is limited.

STRAW PARTICLEBOARD; COMPRESSED AGRICULTURAL FIBREBOARD

A number of products are made from compressed straw to produce a composite board that arguably performs as well as composite timber board and can be used for the same purposes. The most widely available, STRAMIT (a trade name), is simply fibreboard made using straw instead of wood chips. All straw boards have the distinct environmental advantage that straw is a cheap and abundant waste product that has very little embodied energy.

OTHER RECYCLED PRODUCTS

There are many other products available that contain primarily waste, sometimes with small amounts of wood. Although these aren't strictly composite wood boards they are used in the same situations and so should be considered as an alternative. Tetrapak, a drinks-container company, makes a very funky looking board called Tectan which is made of compressed recycled drinks containers, and so consists of plastic, cardboard and aluminium. It has a multicoloured mosaic look and has become so fashionable in Germany that it's used as a decorative effect for kitchen-unit doors. Other products are made up of recycled plastic and wood mixtures. These products have very low embodied energy costs and are usually just as good as their timber counterparts in terms of performance. Whereas in choosing most building materials you're usually looking for the least bad option, these products really do have an environmental benefit. Not only are you avoiding using an environmentally damaging product, you're saving an equivalent volume of waste from an incinerator or a landfill site as well.

For a more detailed look at recycled composite boards see the Rematerialise website hosted by Kingston university: www.kingston.ac.uk/ rematerialise.

SECOND-BEST OPTIONS

CHIPBOARD

Chipboard uses a similar manufacturing process to fibreboards but the particles are bound together with synthetic resin. Chipboard is graded according to its moisture resistance. The higher the number, the more water resistant and the higher the resinous proportion of the product. The most common resins in use are formaldehydes. Free formaldehyde is given off as a gas during the first few months after production (although it can be emitted at a lesser rate for up to fourteen years) and so can be inhaled. The gas is a suspected carcinogen and has been linked to respiratory disease and nerve disorders.

A surprise solution to free formaldehyde may be a humble house plant. The spider plant (*Chlorophytum comosum*) has been shown to absorb formaldehyde from the air, though you'd probably need five or ten of them in a room to make much difference.

OSB (ORIENTATED STRAND BOARD) OR STERLING BOARD

OSB is a product very similar to chipboard; together they are sometimes known collectively as particleboard. OSB uses strips of wood to give it the appearance of grained timber. The production process and the environmental effects are as for chipboard, but in addition a different drying process causes emissions of VOCs (volatile organic compounds – see p. 244).

BLOCKBOARD

Blockboard is made up of a central core of small blocks of softwood sandwiched between layers of veneer. The blocks are in the main offcuts from timber used in manufacturing other types of composite board. The veneer is made using the same process as for plywood (see below).

All the components are stuck together with resin, and although the amounts used are less than for other composite boards, the most common type used, urea formaldehyde adhesive, is one of the worst, giving off large quantities of free formaldehyde. The one plus point for blockboard is that the veneer can act as a barrier and prevent free formaldehyde from escaping.

PLYWOOD

Plywood is manufactured from thin sheets of different timbers, bonded together with the grain of each layer lying at 90° to the grain of its neighbours. This makes a very strong board that suffers less from shrinkage problems than whole timber. It comes in a number of different grades and has various applications. It can be used to cover timber floors prior to laying floor tiles, linoleum or vinyl floor coverings, or as a backing for tiled shower enclosures. Unlike other composite boards, plywood is manufactured directly from whole timber and makes no use of timber waste. That said, most waste generated during its production is used in the manufacture of other composite boards.

Most plywood is imported from distant locations such as South-East Asia, so there are high embodied energy costs from transport. Much of the timber used is tropical hardwood taken from forests that aren't managed sustainably. The impact of deforestation in central Africa, South-East Asia and South America are environmentally horrendous, causing habitat loss and displacement of local people. The manufacturing process involving cutting, drying and pressing is also energy intensive. Boards are stuck together with synthetic resin adhesives but the quantity used is less than for other composite boards. The curing process tends to drive out most of the free formaldehyde, causing pollution problems at the production plant but reducing health risks in the home.

POOR OPTIONS

MDF (MEDIUM-DENSITY FIBREBOARD)

Like chipboard, MDF is a mixture of fine timber chippings bound together with synthetic resin. It is strong, reasonably water resistant, cheap and easy to work with and has consequently become very popular as a building material. It can be produced in moulds to any shape, so is often used for moulded skirting boards, architrave and kitchen unit doors. As with other composite boards, energy is used in cutting the timber into particles, pressing it and drying it. Only a small proportion of the timber used is waste wood, most being from undersize trees and forest thinnings. The manufacture of the resin itself is energy intensive and gives off toxic pollutants. MDF uses a higher proportion of synthetic resin than other composite boards and for that reason has to be considered slightly more hazardous. Some critics have suggested that MDF is the new asbestos – a health crisis waiting to happen. This is probably alarmist, and the product is probably not much worse than other composite boards in health terms. When working on MDF, you should always use a facemask. But ask yourself, could you use something less harmful to the environment?

WOOD CEMENT PARTICLEBOARD

This product uses mainly waste wood bound together with cement. It has a good resistance both to insect attack and to damp. Cement is no less damaging in this product than in any other. Most of the environmental problems here are associated with the cement content. Avoid using it if you can.

TIMBER PRESERVATIVES

Timber preservatives are designed to preserve wood by killing things that might damage it, such as fungi and wood-boring insects. By their very nature, then, preservatives are toxic and most are capable of killing a lot more than their intended victims.

There is a strong body of opinion asserting that timber preservatives are grossly over-used in the building industry. Indeed, it can be quite difficult even to find non-treated timber at some suppliers. The problem is exacerbated by an aggressive damp and timber-preservation industry that has a vested interest in the (over)use of such preservatives. Traditional links between such companies and estate agents and the cautious approach of surveyors and mortgage providers result in huge numbers of properties being unnecessarily treated with timber preservatives every time they are sold. See p. 321 for a number of mortgage companies that have a better track record in this respect.

In its favour, correctly applied preservation extends the life of timber, meaning less new wood has to be used, and can possibly make softwoods durable enough to be used in place of hardwoods for window sills etc. What is certainly true is that the timber industry now supplies poorer quality timber than it used to. Sapwood (the soft wood in the middle of the tree trunk) and low-durability wood that in the past would have gone for pulping are now supplied as building timber. Suppliers argue that preservatives help make this possible by extending its usable life.

A well-specified and well-constructed building shouldn't need timber preservation. In the UK, most fungi and insects will only attack damp timber. (The two exceptions are the powder-dust beetle and the house longhorn beetle, both rare and local to the south of England.) A well-built building is a dry building, so what's the point of preservation? The industry argues that preservation is a necessary safeguard, but just how effective are timber treatments, anyway? Most preservatives evaporate out of the timber in the first year or so (this explains why some are so dangerous: the evaporated preservative can be inhaled) and many preservatives stop working if the timber becomes wet and cannot dry out. Most product guarantees become invalid if the timber is damp, i.e. during the only circumstance when preservation is likely to be required. Some safeguard!

BEST OPTION

NOTHING

By now you shouldn't expect me to say anything else. A well-specified, well-built and well-maintained building needs no timber preservation. This means using correctly specified, well-seasoned timber, dealing with all damp problems prior to using it and maintaining adequate levels of ventilation.

SECOND-BEST OPTION

BORON

Boron is available under a number of different trade names. (Borax and Boracol are two of the most common and can be purchased through a number of outlets. For online purchases try The Green Building Store.) Boron is a water-soluble compound and is normally sold in solution, although it's also available in plugs that can be inserted into timber. Water-based preservatives have two advantages over spirit- or solvent-based products. First, they don't evaporate so quickly, so their effect lasts longer and they emit less toxic fumes. Second, water-soluble compounds tend to concentrate in the dampest parts of the timber, which is where rot and insect attack are most likely to arise. Boron is probably the timber preservative least harmful to people and the environment.

Most product guarantees become invalid if the timber is damp, i.e. during the only circumstance when preservation is likely to be required. Some safeguard!

THIRD-BEST OPTIONS

COPPER AND ZINC SALTS

Copper and zinc salts are highly toxic to fungi but are much less toxic to humans and other mammals than most timber preservatives. This isn't to say they are harmless, and there is a risk of poisoning, especially during application. This group of preservatives includes copper sulphate, copper naphlthenates, copper quatermium, acypetacs zinc and zinc naphlthenates.

FLUORIDES

Fluorides are used as the active ingredient in a number of timber preservatives. There are three compounds in this group: ammonium bifluorate, potassium bifluorate and sodium fluorate. All can give rise to unpleasant irritant effects during application.

PERMETHRIN

This powerful insecticide is used as the active ingredient in some garden insecticides as well timber preservatives. It is, in fact, a substance naturally produced by a member of the daisy family of plants, although any you buy will have been produced, artificially. Permethrin's environmental advantage is that its toxicity is targeted, it being highly poisonous to insects but far less so to humans and other mammals. The Nature Conservancy Council recommends it because it's less harmful to bats than other timber preservatives. This isn't to say that it's harmless. In large quantities it poses a danger to people and there have been suggestions that it might be carcinogenic.

POOR OPTIONS

ARSENIC

It'll hardly come as a shock to hear that arsenic is highly toxic. What might be surprising is that it's arguably the least bad of this poor bunch. Even so, just a tiny amount can be lethal. Mild exposure can cause skin and nerve problems and there may be a long-term cancer risk. The greatest hazards occur before and during application, although the toxic effect lasts for several weeks in the timber itself until it has dried out. After that it forms a stable compound with the timber and won't leach out. One of the commonest causes of poisoning is through splinters. The arsenic in a splinter can find its way into skin tissue or even into the bloodstream. Arsenic is normally sold as CCA (copper, chrome and arsenic).

CREOSOTE

Creosote is coal-tar oil, the residue of crude oil when the fuel oil has been drawn off. It varies widely in its composition owing to different distillation processes used by the industry. Its strong smell makes it unsuitable for internal use, but it is found widely as a preservative coating on wooden outbuildings and fences. Liquid creosote is an irritant and can cause damage to the skin and eyes. The vapour it gives off is largely made up of polynuclear aromatic hydrocarbons (PAH). It sounds horrible and it is. This group of compounds includes many carcinogens and genotoxins (toxins liable to cause genetic mutations). The wide availability and use of creosote has perhaps made it seem more acceptable than other preservatives, but this is a substance that has been banned in the USA for DIY use because of its health effects.

DIELDRIN

This is one that you shouldn't even come across, let alone use. Dieldrin, one of the most dangerous of all timber preservatives, is banned in the UK, Ireland and most other developed countries. It's reportedly no longer in production, but if you happen to come across an old stock of preservatives, read the label to make sure it doesn't contain this stuff. If it does, contact your local authority environmental health service to arrange disposal. Don't pour it away or leave it where it is.

PCP (PENTOCHLOROPHENOL)

PCP is another real nasty, and again one you should rarely encounter. Its use is severely restricted in the UK, but not yet banned outright.

PCP is readily absorbed through the skin and can cause severe skin complaints such as chloroacne. Long-term exposure can result in respiratory problems, kidney failure, immune system failure and neurone disease. It's a suspected carcinogen and is readily absorbed across the placenta, potentially causing damage to unborn children.

Another huge problem with PCP is its perniciousness. It doesn't break down readily, so once released into the environment it stays there. PCP residues have been found in Antarctic penguins thousands of miles away from the nearest point that timber preservatives would have been used or released into the environment. Most of the world's production of PCP now takes place in third-world countries and there are huge problems of dumped waste causing pollution. Its production causes the release of chlorine, a greenhouse gas damaging to the ozone layer. If you come across old preservatives, give the penguins a thought and make sure the ingredients don't include PCP.

LINDANE

Lindane is one of the oldest timber preservatives and its use was almost ubiquitous in the building industry in the 1950s and 1960s. This doesn't mean that it's in any way safe. Lindane is known to cause asplastic anaemia, central nervous system disorders, kidney disease, liver problems, brain tumours and blindness.

Like PCP, lindane can remain at lethal concentrations for years and residues have entered the environment causing chronic problems miles away from where they were released. Residues are found in fish all across the North Sea. Lindane is reckoned to be the main reason for the decimation of the bat population of the British Isles. Despite all this, lindane has still not been banned in the UK, although its use is now much restricted and it isn't available for DIY purposes.

TBTO (TRIBUTYL-TIN OXIDE)

TBTO is the active ingredient in a number of timber preservatives and paints. Its use is on the decline and it's now restricted to licensed contractors. Like PCP, TBTO has spilled out into the environment at large and is found in shellfish populations miles from where it would have been used. TBTO is toxic to wildlife in minute quantities; concentrations of 0.000000005 g per litre are enough to cause deformities and sterility in marine life. Its effects on people are almost as bad: blood conditions, neurological problems, liver and urinary tract damage and damaged eyesight are all linked to TBTO exposure.

PAINTS AND VARNISHES

Even the most devoted fan of exposed wood will end up covering most surfaces in a house with paint, or at least varnish. There is something very uplifting about decorating. After all the heavy work of renovating a property, it's the finishing touch that transforms the building site you've lived with for months into a home. The colour and textures you choose make it yours, and unless you're completely DIY phobic it's a job you can do at least some of yourself. Perhaps there is something in all of us stretching right back to our cave-painting ancestors that means we just love decorating our homes.

A quick trip to any DIY shop will reveal that there are hundreds of types and brands of paint to choose from. Too many to review individually, so this section simply gives you the information to choose the right paints for you.

Paints and varnishes both consist of a solid pigment dissolved in a liquid solvent (varnishes just have less pigment than paints). The solvent is there purely to enable the paint or varnish to be applied, after which it evaporates. Environmental problems exist with both the pigments and the solvents, but the real horror stories are solvent-based. Paint solvents have for many years been made from volatile organic compounds (VOCs). These are attractive in many ways because they evaporate quickly and predictably, giving quick drying times.

But there are many more ingredients in paint than just pigments and solvents. One that was a major cause for concern, lead, is no longer found in any commercially available paints, although great care should be taken when removing old paint that dates from the 1970s or earlier.

In recent years there has been a trend away from solvent-based to water-based paints. This sounds like a good thing, and on balance it probably is. Unfortunately, many paint pigments aren't readily soluble in water and so require the addition of various emulsifiers and other chemicals, many of which are unpleasant, in order to make the whole thing work.

VOCs are a major component of our polluted air. The United Nations Environment Programme said that their impact was comparable in size to the total emissions from motor vehicles. VOCs are highly dangerous to people, especially to the person doing the painting. Professional decorators are routinely exposed to highly dangerous quantities of them. Somebody working in a factory with the levels of VOCs experienced by the average decorator would be required to wear full-body protective clothing and breathing apparatus, and the room would be kitted out with a mechanical fume-extraction system. Most decorators have an open window, if they are lucky.

BEST OPTION

ORGANIC WATER-BASED PAINT

These have the lowest levels of VOCs and give off fewer emissions than other paints. Organic paint manufacturers tend to avoid some of the more harmful pigments such as titanium dioxide (brilliant white colour) and vermilion. There are only two drawbacks: they are unsuitable for use on timber and they are more expensive. Otherwise, a great choice.

SECOND-BEST OPTION

ORGANIC SOLVENT-BASED PAINT

These use plant-based solvents, and are ideal for painting timber. Plant-based sounds better than petrochemical-based, and probably is, but plant-based solvents such as turpentine are quite toxic too, and still give off VOCs (don't forget the O in VOC stands for organic). Alternatives such as linseed oil and citrus-peel oil are good, but make the paint more expensive.

THIRD-BEST OPTION

SYNTHETIC WATER-BASED PAINTS

These are often sold as low-odour paints because smelly solvents are substituted with water. This not only means less smell, but fewer VOCs. This is where the good news stops. Many of the other ingredients in synthetic paints are toxic and their production produces large amounts of pollutants including phenols and heavy metals. Many exterior-grade paints and those designed for use on timber contain fungicides such as the dreadful PCP.

POOR OPTION

SYNTHETIC SOLVENT-BASED PAINTS

These have the same impact as synthetic water-based paints but with the added problem of solvents. Most solvents are petrochemical based, produced by an industry that contributes over half of all toxic pollutants in the environment. Solvent-based paints give off the most VOCs on application.

There is something very uplifting about decorating. After all the heavy work of renovating a property, it's the finishing touch that transforms the building site you've lived with for months into a home.

For a good supply of organic paints try Auro Organic Paints or ecopaints.com.

WINDOW FRAMES

Window frames have just one job to do in the house: hold the windows in. It sounds so simple, but window frames seem to cause more upset than any other building component. Planners, builders and architects, to say nothing of the heritage and environmental lobbies, all have their own views about window frames, and not all of them agree.

The choice of materials is, in practice, between timber and uPVC. Over the years other materials, notably steel and aluminium, have been popular, but these are rarely sold today for residential use. Plastic window frames have become the pebbledash render of the 1980s and 1990s, a phenomenally popular building product that has scarred the face of many houses up and down the country. The success of uPVC is a result of its perceived durability, its low cost and, especially, its low maintenance needs.

Part of the problem is that people have lost confidence in timber window frames. Many timber-framed windows are poorly constructed and cannot dry out properly once they get wet. This allows the wood to rot. Another problem is maintenance. We live in a world where we expect things to be maintenance free, and repainting window frames every five years is no longer considered reasonable. But uPVC window frames aren't everlasting. They may never need painting, but after twenty-five years or so they'll probably need to be replaced altogether. Timber-framed windows, if well designed and well maintained, will last almost indefinitely. There is a church in the Essex village of Hadstock which has original and still serviceable wooden window frames dating from Saxon times.

BEST OPTION

TIMBER

Well, what else? There are many varieties of timber window frames, some better than others. Most are made from European softwoods. Although these have some natural durability they are usually soaked in timber preservatives (see pp. 240–43). If you're having windows made up yourself you should specify FSC-labelled, well-seasoned timber. If you must use a preservative, use an environmentally friendly one such as boron.

If you opt for hardwood frames then specify a European hardwood such as oak or chestnut. Hardwoods are naturally more durable than softwoods, and don't need preservatives applied to them, although they often have. Oak is so durable that it doesn't even need painting or varnishing.

The worst choice for a timber window frame is tropical hardwood. The only reliable source is timber that comes from FSC-accredited sources and carries their logo. The quality of tropical hardwood isn't always as good as you might think, since manufacturers are using sapwood for timber frames increasingly often. Sapwood is less durable than the outer wood and is treated with preservatives in an attempt to compensate.

An increasingly large sector of the market in timber windows is taken up by factory-made units. The requirements of Part L of the Building Regulations (Part J of the Building Standards in Scotland, Part F of the Building Standards in Northern Ireland and Part L of the Building Regulations in Ireland) has made it difficult for carpenters to make up widows on site that can meet Building Regulations requirements. In order to comply, windows now need to include such features as high-performance double glazing and be fitted with draught strips. In addition, consumers now demand extras such as friction hinges (which keep the window open at the point you want it) and espagnolette bolts (which improve security by locking the window at several points). These features are all included in factory-made units.

Timber-framed windows, if well designed and well maintained, will last almost indefinitely. There is a church in the Essex village of Hadstock which has original and still serviceable wooden window frames dating from Saxon times.

POOR OPTIONS

uPVC (UNPLASTICIZED POLYVINYL CHLORIDE)

uPVC is now the most popular material for window frames in house refurbishments. It's cheap and relatively durable, although it is affected by ultra violet light and some uPVC window frames installed in the early 1980s are beginning to decompose. Sunlight causes uPVC to lose its surface sheen (a process called chalking) and colour. White uPVC acquires a yellow tinge and can also become marked by grey patches if not regularly cleaned. Ultimately, it becomes brittle and breaks, leaving no alternative but to replace the entire window. Manufacturers claim that their products are now more resistant to decomposition, which may well be true.

An important quality in any material used for window frames is rigidity, since any significant flexing will cause the glass to crack. uPVC is a relatively flexible material and this is why the profile of uPVC window frames is often much wider than those of timber or metal frames. Early frames had profiles of more than 15 cm (6 in), making them look very different indeed from timber frames. Today manufacturers reinforce the frames with steel or aluminium (see opposite for the resulting environmental impact), allowing them to be made in profiles that (when new) are virtually indistinguishable from timber frames. Other aesthetic 'improvements' are textured finishes that look more like wood, and a choice of colours other than the usual brilliant white. Coloured uPVC has a reputation of fading quickly, however. You could always repaint them every few years, I suppose, but that rather removes the 'maintenance free' element – you may as well just buy timber frames to begin with.

The main ingredients of uPVC are crude oil and salt. Although the extraction of both has damaging environmental impacts, the high levels of salt mean the amount of oil used is less than for other plastics. Its light weight and production methods result in embodied-energy costs which are less than for other plastics.

On the downside, uPVC production is highly polluting. Things may have improved, but the production of all plastics still results in pollution. In the UK Her Majesty's Inspectorate of Pollution still rates uPVC production as the most damaging polluting production process to air, water and land. The most serious pollutants are dioxins, a group of chemicals amongst the most toxic known to man. They are proven to disrupt hormone production and are linked to a number of different types of cancers. Large amounts of dioxins have been found around uPVC production plants and trace amounts are found in the product itself (and are released in large quantities if it is burned).

A recent concern over uPVC production is its possible link to reduced human sperm counts. It's thought that pthalates, used as a softener in uPVC production, mimic the female hormone oestrogen. This is more serious than it sounds. Pthalate pollution disrupts the reproductive cycles of wild animals and is linked to breast and testicular cancer in humans. Because it's a rigid plastic, uPVC contains fewer pthalates than other types of PVC (remember, the u in uPVC stands for unplasticized) but they are still included in the finished product to reduce brittleness.

In their favour, uPVC window frames don't need painting (although, strangely, some paint manufacturers make paints specifically for the purpose) and so a whole set of potential environmental impacts are avoided.

METAL-FRAMED WINDOWS

From the 1930s to the 1980s metal-framed windows were a popular choice, first of steel and later of aluminium. Both are now rarely produced for the residential market, the most common remaining use being in patio doors.

Aluminium frames are moderately durable and are often left unpainted. After fifteen years or so the surface begins to show pitting from corrosion caused by the acidity of rainwater. To prolong its life you should either paint it or coat it in a preservative finish in a process called anodizing.

The production process of aluminium is just about as energy intensive as you can get. It is extracted from bauxite by heating, which consumes huge amounts of fossil fuels. Even where hydroelectric power is used, the fact remains that large amounts of CO_2 are given off during production, which also results in the release of heavy metals, hydrocarbons and fluoride.

Huge savings in embodied energy are possible if recycled aluminium is used instead. Recycling still uses a lot of energy, but the relatively low melting point of aluminium means that less energy is used than when recycling other metals.

Steel is a poor thermal insulator, and steel frames are particularly prone to condensation problems. Steel plus water equals rust. Repairing steel window frames is difficult and often not cost effective.

Steel is refined iron. The iron and steel industry is one of the most polluting of all industries. It uses huge amounts of energy and in the UK the raw materials are almost all imported, so embodied energy costs for both domestic and imported steel are very high. The smelting process of iron ore and the processing of steel give off large amounts of CO_2.

Whilst PVC production is the process most vilified for the production of dioxins (see opposite), recent research suggests that iron production is even worse. Steel production also causes the release of a cocktail of heavy metal and other pollutants.

A recent concern over uPVC production is its possible link to reduced human sperm counts.

INSULATION MATERIALS

Since by its mere presence insulation has a positive impact in saving energy, it could be argued that even those insulation materials with the worst environmental impacts are better than none at all. But, as with every other material, choosing the right products will help make your home an even better place to live. The best materials here not only minimize heat loss, they last longer and create less risk to the health of you and your household. And, of course, they have lower embodied energy costs.

Different insulation products have different potential uses, so not all the materials below are direct alternatives.

BEST OPTIONS

WOOL

Wool is a naturally renewable product that performs very well as an insulation material. Millions of years of evolution and thousands of years of animal breeding can't be wrong. If it's good enough for sheep and good enough for our winter clothes, wool is definitely good enough to keep our houses warm, too. Its u-value* is very similar to other top performing materials such as mineral wool. One big advantage of wool is that it can cope well with damp conditions and can absorb and release water without deteriorating. Indeed, suppliers claim that this quality means that it keeps buildings warm in winter and cool in summer. What is beyond doubt is that, despite appearances, wool has good resistance to fire, rot and insect attack.

Wool is sold in large flexible slabs and can be used in roof, floor and wall insulation.

Although there may be some issues about animal husbandry in sheep farming, this really is as good as it gets environmentally for building products. The only real drawback is cost. Although prices have come down in recent years as production is stepped up, wool remains an expensive insulator. The main supplier in the UK and Ireland for wool insulation is Thermafleece.

*u-values are a measure of the insulation properties of materials; for more details see pp. 285–7.

FLAX

Flax has been grown commercially in the UK and Ireland since the dawn of farming. The plant is naturalized here, so doesn't need to be sprayed with gallons of chemicals to help it grow. Its fibres have long been refined to make linen, but it's also starting to be used as an insulation product. Its qualities are very similar to wool and it has most of wool's advantages, one of which is that it can absorb even more water. This can prevent damp problems or potentially even wood rot from occurring. The only significant pollution is caused by whatever preservative is used. Boron is the most common, and although toxic it's arguably the least bad preservative environmentally (see p. 241).

Flax is a renewable and natural product and performs very well as an insulation material; it's u-value is one of the best of all insulation materials. It's sold in slabs that can be used for loft, wall or floor insulation, or in sheets that can be used as acoustic/thermal insulation under floor coverings.

CELLULOSE

Cellulose is the substance that gives all plants structure and rigidity. It's extracted from wood pulp to produce paper, which can then be recycled into cellulose fibre insulation by spinning it into a fluff. The finished product can be applied by hand, scattered between the ceiling joists in a loft, or it can be sprayed to form an insulating layer. As might be expected of a recycled paper product, it disintegrates if it gets wet.

Cellulose has reasonably low embodied energy costs and is normally sold pre-treated with boron (see p. 241) to give it resistance to insect attack and fire.

SECOND-BEST OPTION

FOAMED GLASS

This product, made from molten glass mixed with carbon, comes in lightweight slabs and is most commonly used in flat roofs, though it can also be used in floors. The reaction between the glass and the carbon causes thousands of tiny bubbles to form, producing a hard, foam-like block.

The embodied energy costs of making foamed glass are quite high, and a number of toxins are given off in the manufacturing process. Glass production itself creates sulphur dioxide, nitrogen dioxide and various chlorides and fluorides. The production of foamed glass generates large amounts of carbon dioxide, although much of this is trapped in the bubbles of the product.

The main supplier of both flax and cellulose insulation in the UK is Construction Resources.

POOR OPTIONS

GLASS WOOL

Glass wool is made from glass, which is spun like candyfloss to form a lightweight fibrous mass. It's inexpensive and commonly used in lofts. Glass wool production involves the addition of boron, sodium carbonate and sodium sulphate to the glass. The mixture is heated to a high temperature, meaning that glass wool has a high embodied energy cost.

The big worry surrounding glass wool is that its fibres may be carcinogenic if inhaled – another candidate for the new asbestos, along with MDF (see p. 239). Certainly glass wool is quite friable and tiny fragments of fibre are given off, some of which are a similar size to asbestos fibres. Scientists have pointed out that the body can deal with glass fibres in the lungs much more effectively than it can with asbestos, so the jury is still out. What is certain, however, is that inhaling glass fibres isn't good for you, so if you're working with it you should wear a breathing mask.

ROCK WOOL

Rock wool is made in much the same way as glass wool but volcanic rock is used instead of glass. This makes a denser product that is sold in slabs instead of rolls. It's used most commonly as insulation for roofs. The environmental impacts are much the same as for glass wool.

VERMICULITE

This mineral, when heated, expands into lightweight shell-like granules. The air trapped in and between granules gives it good insulating properties as loose fill insulation for lofts. The product has high embodied energy costs owing to the amount of heat used in its manufacture.

POLYSTYRENE

Polystyrene is a cheap and readily available material that is used in a number of different insulation products. Polystyrene beads are used in cavity wall and loft insulation, extruded polystyrene sheets are made into pipe insulation and can also be used in floor insulation. It's very light in weight, making it easy to work with, although the beads do tend to pick up static electricity and stick to you like leeches.

Polystyrene is made by heating a special type of plastic and forcing gas through it. Sadly, the best gases for the job are also the most environmentally damaging. Until the mid 1980s CFCs (chlorofluorocarbons) were used but these were phased out because of their devastating effect on the ozone layer and manufacturers started using HFCs (hydrofluorocarbons) instead. HFCs are just about the worst greenhouse gas imaginable, apart from CFCs, having an effect 3,200 times greater than that of carbon dioxide.

The manufacturing process involves the use of a lot of energy, which gives polystyrene a high embodied energy cost.

UREA-FORMALDEHYDE FOAM

This used to be a common insulation material for cavity walls and is still available even though its harmful effects are now fully recognized. Urea formaldehyde contains large amounts of formaldehyde, which I discussed in some detail on p. 238. Formaldehyde is a severe irritant and a carcinogen. If it sounded bad earlier, it's even worse here because there's far more of it. If you're having cavity wall insulation installed, check to see what material will be used and avoid this one like the plague.

PIPES AND PLUMBING

The average house has several hundred metres of pipework running through it to transport water, gas and fuel oil to where it's needed. In the past the choice was between lead and cast iron. Now the industry norm is copper, although PVC is an option for water-supply and central-heating pipework.

BETTER OPTION

COPPER

Copper is by far the most common material used for domestic pipework. It's hardly a green godsend, but it's the better option of the two available. Copper is a non-renewable resource, but those in the know think there are still plentiful reserves left. Copper production is highly energy intensive: about seven tonnes of CO_2 are given off per tonne of copper produced. Recycled copper is better, but copper's high melting point means that a lot of energy is used and a lot of CO_2 is given off. You're unlikely to see copper pipes advertised as being made from reused copper, but as about 70 per cent of all copper is salvaged it's quite likely that whatever you buy will have been recycled. Copper is very resistant to corrosion and, unlike steel, needs no special treatment to inhibit corrosion.

Fitting copper pipes is beyond the average DIY-er. It takes years of practice to be able to make a watertight joint and you won't know whether you've got it right until you cross your fingers and turn the water back on. Never try to fit gas pipes yourself.

WORSE OPTION

PVC

PVC has emerged as an alternative to copper in domestic hot water and central heating systems in recent years. It's cheap and easy to install, and the push-fit joints are easy to fit for the average DIY enthusiast. The durability of PVC systems has not been tested since the product is a fairly new one, and the production of PVC is an environmentalist's nightmare.

In most houses built before the Second World War lead was used for the mains water supply. Lead is a powerful toxin and in the right conditions can leach into the water supply and become a real health risk (see p.223 for more details). Your survey should identify whether you still have lead pipework (many old houses still do), but before you rip it all out, remember that lead in the concentrations found in domestic water is a risk only if you ingest it. So if your lead pipes carry non-drinking water (a supply to a bath, for example) it doesn't really matter. In a hard water area, calcium carbonate will settle out of the water in deposits we call limescale. If you have hard water, all your lead pipes will have a good internal covering. This acts as a protective layer and stops the lead leaching into the water. If you have lead pipes carrying drinking water and you live in a soft-water area, you should replace them.

RAINWATER GOODS

Rainwater goods – the collective term for gutters, hoppers and rainwater pipes – is another area where none of the options is environmentally satisfactory. The choice is between artificially produced materials and metals. The chemical and metal-producing industries are two of the most environmentally damaging on the planet, so, as none of the options are good, I've not ranked them environmentally. Cost, architectural suitability and durability are the real concerns.

CAST IRON

Cast iron is the traditional material for rainwater goods and was used in most properties through the Georgian, Victorian and Edwardian eras. On older houses cast iron usually looks right and in keeping with the property. Properly maintained it can last for very many years; indeed, many Victorian houses still have their original cast-iron rainwater pipes and gutters. In conservation areas and on listed buildings you'll probably need to use original materials, which in most cases will mean cast iron.

Cast iron is expensive and if your pipes or gutters are of a non-standard size or shape you'll need to have them specially cast, which is even more costly. Cast iron is heavy and awkward to work with. Fitting a cast-iron gutter is a much more difficult job than fitting a uPVC one and of course you'll need to paint it too. Cast iron is prone to rust and needs regular maintenance if it's going to last. Regular cleaning will stop water ponding in the gutters and painting prevents the iron from rusting.

STEEL

Almost as bad environmentally as cast iron, steel has better resistance to corrosion and is less brittle. Steel rainwater goods can thus be thinner than their cast-iron counterparts, and less metal produces less environmental damage. It's usually galvanized in zinc to improve its longevity.

uPVC

Rainwater goods made from uPVC are cheap to buy and lightweight, so much easier to handle and erect. It can be easily cut to length, it's strong enough to do its job but not strong enough to take the weight of a burglar so is a good choice from a security point of view, too. On the minus side it looks cheap and, unlike other materials, it looks worse the older it gets: smart black pipework will fade to a dull grey in a few years, although a coat of specialist paint for uPVC can freshen things up. The effects of ultra violet light (see p. 248) limit the useful life of uPVC to twenty-five years or so on a north-facing wall, but less in full sunlight on a south-facing elevation. Painting helps, but this of course increases both cost and inconvenience, which are two of the main selling points of uPVC in the first place.

GRP (GLASS REINFORCED POLYESTER)

GRP is a good compromise material for external pipework. It's light and quite easy to work with, and cheaper to buy than metal alternatives (although not as cheap as uPVC). GRP is made from layers of glass fibres bound together by polyester resin. Both component parts use large amounts of energy in their production and so GRP itself has high embodied energy costs.

Polyester is a plastic, but its manufacture is far less harmful than PVC production. The effects of glass-fibre manufacture are more or less the same as for glass wool, discussed on p. 252.

CARPETS AND FLOOR COVERINGS

Floor coverings are often one of the last materials to be chosen during a house-rescue project, so costs are often trimmed as the budget begins to run out. This is a shame; good-quality floor coverings nearly always look better and last longer than cheap ones. Synthetic materials dominate the cheap end of the market and it's these floor coverings where the environmental impact is greatest in high embodied energy costs and highly polluting production processes. The good news is that some attractive natural alternatives are becoming both cheaper and more widely available.

BEST OPTIONS

EXPOSED FLOORBOARDS

If the boards are in good enough condition, and weren't massacred when the central heating was installed, they can be an excellent floor covering. After sanding down (tool-hire companies supply specialist machines for doing this) they can be varnished or painted. Another advantage is that floorboards give little opportunity for the house dust mite to live and breed.

NATURAL FLOOR COVERINGS

In the 1990s carpets went out of fashion and a number of natural alternatives came on to the market in keeping with the decade's wholemeal-and-ethnic style. All these options are still available and they are all good environmental choices. Granted, they are all derived from plants that grow in tropical or subtropical zones and therefore have embodied energy costs from transport, but they are all new uses for old products, which keeps local industries going.

✚ Coir

Coir, a fibre that comes from coconuts (it's the hairy bit on the shell), can be woven into carpets and mats. Traditional doormats have been made out of coir for years, but the last decade or so has seen the emergence of a series of carpet replacement products. Coir would otherwise be a waste product, so its use in this manner avoids the need for its disposal. Coir is cheap to buy but can be expensive to lay, especially if you have the edges bound with fabric to stop it from fraying.

✚ Seagrass

Seagrass woven into a mat makes a smoother surfaced and slightly neater looking floor covering than coir. Seagrass is the common name for a plant that grows in abundance in shallow coastal waters in the tropics. It forms part of the ecosystem that includes mangrove swamps. Most of the seagrass for floor coverings comes from India and in some places excessive harvesting has caused damage to the natural ecosystem, although most production is now farmed in saltwater paddy fields.

✚ Sisal

Sisal is a fibre produced from the thick leaves of the sub-tropical agave plant. It has long been used for making ropes and nets because of its natural strength. Making floor coverings has kept production going at a time when the demand for sisal ropes has dropped. It has a softer texture than seagrass and coir.

✚ Jute

This fibre produced from the jute plant is also known as hessian. It's sometimes made into floor coverings, although it's more usually used as an underlay or carpet backing.

WOOL CARPET WITH FELT OR HESSIAN BACKING

Wool is the traditional material for making carpets, and for good reason. It's warm, soft and can be easily dyed to any colour in the spectrum. Wool is a plentiful and renewable resource and a well-husbanded flock has no detrimental effect on the environment. In fact, it could be argued that grazing sheep actually help to preserve the hilly grassland landscape of sheep-farming areas. The disadvantages are that large amounts of organophosphates are used in sheep dips, and all too often these end up in natural watercourses. On the positive side, wool needs less dye than synthetic carpets, and vegetable dyes can be used instead. Although they offer only a restricted range of colours, vegetable dyes create much less toxic waste.

LINOLEUM

Linoleum, or lino as we used to call it, is one of the few smooth floor-covering materials that isn't a complete environmental disaster. It's made from a mixture of cork, pulverized wood and lime set in a natural resin and linseed oil suspension. The mixture is rolled into sheets on a hessian backing. Basic linoleum is produced in a muddy brown colour, which may not be to everybody's taste, but it can also be made with pigments that give a wide range of colours. At the top of the range different coloured linoleums are joined together into a single sheet to form designs and patterns. There is no quick means of mass production for these designs, so every one is largely handmade. They are often very beautiful and nearly always very expensive.

CORK

Another smooth covering that you could consider is cork. Cheap and widely available, cork is produced from the bark of the evergreen cork oak, a tree that is widespread in southern Europe. Portugal, the world's biggest producer, has cork forests that are hundreds of years old and which form part of a unique and very beautiful landscape. The biggest customer for cork is the wine industry, but in recent years it has turned to synthetic cork, particularly for cheaper wines. Synthetic cork is probably better for the wine, but it's bad news for the cork forests, which are becoming uneconomic. Buying cork will in a small way help preserve this industry. (Alternatively, you could just buy lots of expensive wine!) Cork flooring is normally supplied in tiles and is produced in a manner similar to fibreboard. The cork is chopped up, boiled, baked and pressed into shape to make a product that is reasonably hardwearing and resistant to water and decay.

Portugal, the world's biggest producer, has cork forests that are hundreds of years old and which form part of a unique and very beautiful landscape.

SECOND-BEST OPTIONS

STONE

Stone is an expensive but very hardwearing floor surface. The stones most commonly used for floors are limestone, sandstone, slate and marble. For information on the merits of and problems with stone, see pp. 224–5.

CERAMIC TILES

Ceramic tiles are made largely of glass. The embodied energy costs of making glass are quite high, and a number of toxins are given off in the manufacturing process including sulphur dioxide and nitrogen dioxide and various chlorides and fluorides. Some ceramic tiles are made from recycled glass, which are a far better choice as their manufacture results in much less pollution.

LATEX

Latex is most frequently used as an underlay, although in the past it was used as a floor covering as well. Latex is natural rubber and is derived from the sap of the rubber tree. The production of latex involves tapping it from living trees without cutting them down, so it's a good, sustainable production process.

Latex is made into solid tiles or sheets or is blown into a foam. Foam is more damaging environmentally because of the gases that are pumped into it to aerate it. Until recently, the most commonly used gases were HFCs and CFCs, both of which are highly damaging to the ozone layer and are devastating greenhouse gases. Carbon dioxide and ammonia are used more frequently now, which are also greenhouse gases, though less damaging to the ozone layer.

LAMINATE

Laminate flooring is an artificial product which is normally designed to look like wood block flooring. It can be surprisingly realistic. This, along with its hardwearing properties, cheapness and ease of laying, make it an attractive and popular choice. It's supplied as tongue and groove interlocking planks or squares which consist of four layers sandwiched together. The top layer is a wearing layer made from melamine resins with aluminium oxide additive. Beneath this is a decorative print layer, in effect a photograph of some wood. This is glued to a middle core layer made from a composite wood board, usually medium fibreboard or MDF. Behind this is a backing layer that is stuck to the floor. If laid properly, laminate is very durable. The most common reason for it failing is that it has been laid on a damp floor, which causes the composite wood base to deteriorate. The production processes are quite energy intensive and some of the various component parts create pollutants during manufacture. Melamine is a type of plastic that has been in production for many years and its production process is much less environmentally damaging than that of PVC and many other modern plastics.

POOR OPTIONS

POLYPROPYLENE CARPET

Polypropylene is the most popular artificial carpet material. It's a type of plastic and, like all plastics, has high embodied energy costs. The raw material for it is oil, a non-renewable resource, and its manufacture into plastic is a highly polluting process. The petrochemical industry is responsible for over half of all emissions of toxic pollution and emits particularly large amounts of nitrous oxides and sulphur dioxide that contribute to acid rain and climate change. Polypropylene carpets give off large amounts of harmful VOCs (see p. 000), and not just from the carpet fibres. The backing and underlay give off even more, but the worst culprits are the styrene butadiene latex adhesives used to bind the carpet to its backing. VOCs tend to be given off quite quickly and within a few weeks of being laid. In a well-ventilated house newly laid carpets shouldn't pose a serious health risk, but in a poorly ventilated draught-proofed house, especially if it has also been decorated recently with solvent-based paints, VOC levels can reach alarming heights. Avoid them if you can; definitely not a good choice for a child's bedroom.

NYLON CARPET

Nylon is rarely sold as a complete alternative to wool these days, but it's commonly found mixed with other synthetic materials to make hardwearing, cheap carpets. Its production poses much the same problems as polypropylene, but VOC levels are lower.

ACRYLIC, POLYESTER AND POLYURETHANE CARPET

These are three more materials that are used to make synthetic carpets. Polyurethane is used in underlay as an artificial alternative to latex. All three are made from types of plastic and the environmental implications are more or less the same as for polypropylene.

VINYL FLOORING

Vinyl flooring is waterproof, cheap and comes in hundreds of different styles and colours. It isn't very hard wearing in comparison to other floor coverings, but should give you five years or so of life depending on the amount of foot traffic it gets. It's made from polyvinyl chloride (PVC). Most of the environmental implications of polypropylene also apply here. In addition, the two main ingredients, ethyl dichloride and vinyl chloride monomer, are both highly toxic and are known carcinogens. The other ingredients including pigments and plasticizers aren't much better with pthalates (see p. 248) contributing to hormone disruption and various cancers. All these chemicals contribute to the high levels of pollution found around production plants. In fact, PVC manufacture is arguably the most polluting production process of any product used in the building industry. In the home, PVC gives off small quantities of vinyl chloride monomer and benzene chlorides from the plasticizers. These are known or suspected carcinogens and can also cause skin and eye irritation.

11 HEATING AND INSULATION

Before you get carried away, remember that the sole object of the exercise is for your appliances to work and for the temperature to be maintained at a comfortable level. In other words, what we want is not energy as such, but what that energy can do for us. This is sometimes overlooked in the macho world of big boilers, funky heating systems and electric everything. If you're replacing the system, the choices you need to make concern fuels, type of boiler, radiators and heating controls. I'm afraid there is no perfect system, just a series of decisions and compromises which, if thought through properly, will give you the best heating arrangement for your needs and your property.

FUELS

Deciding which fuel to use is usually quite easy since usually there is little choice. The location of the property is often a governing factor: in towns and cities the usual choice is either mains gas or electricity and in rural locations it's either oil, L P G or electricity (mains gas is available to only about 70 per cent of U K homes, less in Ireland). The other considerations are environmental impact and cost. This isn't simply a straight comparison of unit costs. You need to consider installation costs, too, which can be very high for some fuels. How much would it cost to install an oil-storage tank in your garden, for example?

ELECTRICITY

The environmental impacts of electricity depend almost entirely on how it's generated. Electricity isn't really a fuel at all but a means of conveying energy, and to be honest it's not very efficient. A great deal of energy is lost in transmission and unused production. The best thing about electricity is that, because nearly all homes are connected to the national grid, its installation cost is zero. Against that, electricity is expensive on a cost per unit basis. So your decision will depend largely on how much heating you use and how much time you intend to spend in the property. Low usage and a short period of residence will make mains electricity a more cost effective option.

Since the electricity industry was privatized in the U K, production and supply have been deregulated. You can now buy electricity from just about anybody, and it's worth shopping around. There are some good savings to be made, particularly on so-called 'dual fuel' tariffs whereby you purchase gas and electricity from the same supplier. You can also buy electricity from green producers. This may appear to be a slightly weird concept, considering that all electricity at the consumer's end is taken from the national grid, but the idea is that a green producer guarantees to produce by sustainable methods as much electricity as their customers demand and feed it into the grid. The more customers who use this sort of tariff, the greater proportion of our electricity generation will be green. Of course, most green electricity is produced by inland wind farms, which carry their own set of environmental baggage.

Another way to reduce electricity costs is by installing an off-peak meter. In the UK Economy 7 enables you to buy electricity at about 40 per cent of the standard rate for seven hours during the night. You pay a bit more for your standing charge but if you manage things well you can easily trim 10 to 20 per cent from your bill. Storage heaters are well suited to this arrangement. They draw power during the night when electricity is cheap and discharge it during the day. Appliances such as washing machines and dishwashers can also be timed to make use of the cheap-rate period. Storage heaters are probably the cheapest way of heating your home with electricity, but they are both inflexible and unsightly. If your lifestyle doesn't fit into a regular routine, they aren't for you. There are several other off-peak tariffs apart from Economy 7. Economy 10, for example, allows a small amount of discounted peak-time use. A similar system in Ireland, Nightsaver, gives nine hours of discounted electricity during the night.

A directory of green electricity suppliers is available at www.fetch.co.uk.

GAS

Gas is the most popular fuel for heating in both the UK and Ireland. It's a non-sustainable fossil fuel, so it's going to run out one day. Most of our supply comes from the North Sea, where production has already peaked. On the plus side, gas is the cleanest fossil fuel, it produces very little sulphur dioxide or nitrous oxide and CO_2 production is much lower than for some other fossil fuels.

Its other great attraction is its price. Gas is cheap, at least it is at the moment, and in all urban centres and some villages in the UK and Ireland it can easily be piped straight to your house. As the North Sea supply declines we will need to find alternative sources of gas. Pipelines from other parts of the world or even shipping it in frozen are possibilities for the future. This will inevitably make gas more expensive.

OIL

Oil is the most popular fuel where gas isn't available. Since there is no mains system, it requires both regular deliveries and a storage tank in which to put them. These look ugly if they are sited above ground and are very expensive to install below ground. Many people opt for a tank with sufficient capacity to hold a year's supply of oil (about 2,000 litres). This reduces ongoing costs because (a) better discounts are available when buying in bulk and (b) oil can be purchased when it is at its cheapest – in the summer. Oil boilers are more expensive than gas ones and need more maintenance, but are slightly more efficient. Most oil boilers are, in fact, adapted versions of gas models and are produced by almost all boiler companies. They look the same and come in a similar, albeit smaller, range to their gas-powered cousins. Plant-produced oil is commonly known as biofuel and is now marketed by BP and a number of other oil companies. As fossil fuel supplies dry up biofuels are bound to become more cost effective to produce and use. This could be a really important fuel for the future.

If you want to get ahead of the game, Brian Horne's book *Power Plants* gives a good overview.

LIQUID PETROLEUM GAS (LPG)

LPG is known to most people as Calor gas. (Calor is in fact a trade name of the UK and Ireland's largest supplier.) A domestic LPG storage tank requires a specially built enclosure owing to the potentially explosive nature of its contents. Suppliers will normally build the enclosure for you, but you do need to be able to site it at least 3 m from any building and 3 m from the boundary of your property. This means you need quite a big garden even to be able to consider LPG, and unless your garden is very large indeed, the enclosure could end up dominating it. LPG boilers are mechanically very similar to other gas-powered boilers, so it's very easy for manufacturers to make LPG versions of their mains-gas models. This means that there is a wider range and they cost less than oil boilers. LPG can also be used as a cooking fuel, either as a stand-alone system fuelled by gas in bottles or canisters, or as part of an LPG-fuelled property. Environmentally, LPG is very similar to oil.

BIOGAS

When organic material decomposes it gives off methane. This is practically the same gas that we buy as natural gas from the North Sea. If you're living off the land and have lots of manure available it may be worth investing in a biogas plant. This collects the methane and safely stores it for you to use as a heating and cooking fuel. The idea of cooking your food on what amounts to bottled animal flatulence may not sound terribly appetizing, but what smell there is is no worse than natural gas, and there is no risk of disease. The plant can be expensive but the savings in fuel costs and waste disposal mean that the costs can be recouped in as little as six or seven years. To make such a scheme worthwhile requires a relatively large number of animals – six cows or pigs would be a minimum number to fuel an average family house. Methane contributes to global warming, so although burning it gives off CO_2 the net environmental effect is minimal. In effect you turn one greenhouse gas that was going to be emitted anyway into another.

WOOD

Wood is a fuel worthy of consideration if you live near a ready supply. The best supply, of course, is from your own land, if you have sufficient. An average sized home using wood as a primary fuel needs about a hectare of woodland to provide a sustainable supply. The most productive method is to grow native deciduous trees and coppice them on a short-rotation basis. This means dividing your land into seven equal areas and coppicing one area a year. This way you'll be harvesting seven-year-old wood, which maximizes the growth potential of the trees and gives a regular supply of manageable-sized logs. Don't underestimate the hard work that this will involve. Trees are big and heavy and chopping them up requires lots of muscle and time. You'll probably also need a suitable vehicle, or at least a trailer to move it about. Chopped logs need to be stacked in a dry store until you need them. Ideally, wood should be chopped a year before it's used to give it time to dry out properly, but four- or five-month-old wood is fine too if it's well dried. This means you need to prepare for winter early and stock up on your supply of wood in early summer. Well-dried wood burns relatively well and modern wood-burning stoves can burn at 65 per cent efficiency.

On an environmental point, there are two different theories on the effects of sooty fires on the environment. One view is that soot from wood burning may be deposited many miles away from its source, turning glaciers ice-grey in colour causing then to absorb more heat from the sun. This, if true, may be accelerating glacial melting, and exacerbating the effects of global warming. The other theory is that soot particles in the air prevent so much of the sun's power getting through that they actually help cool the earth and offset global warming.

PEAT

Peat, more commonly known as turf in Ireland, is a fossil fuel formed from partially decomposed vegetable matter, an early form of coal, in fact. It's a traditional fuel that has been harvested and burned for centuries in much of the UK and especially in Ireland, where it still provides about a fifth of the country's energy. In Ireland peat is still a cheap and plentiful fuel and is burned in stoves in much the same way as wood. The two drawbacks to peat are both environmental. First, burning it gives off a lot of CO_2, although arguably not much more than wood. There is a programme in Ireland of replanting with trees those areas from which peat has been extracted. The argument is that the trees absorb CO_2, making peat a carbon-neutral fuel. The second argument is that peat is non-renewable. Peat bogs are hugely important ecosystems, supporting rarities such as the sundew (our only carnivorous plant) and a wonderfully named yellow fly called the hairy canary. Peat was traditionally cut by hand. This slow method allowed some moss vegetation to regenerate, but faster modern methods of mechanical extraction give the bog no chance to recover.

COMBINED HEAT AND POWER

Combined heat and power (CHP) is a new concept for generating electricity from waste. It uses a mini generator to generate power from the energy in waste gases given off by gas and oil boilers. CHP units have been used successfully for many years in large district heating schemes, but the technology has been miniaturized and small domestic units are now available. These replace the traditional domestic boiler, producing all your hot water and heating. When the unit produces heat, it also generates electricity which can either be used in the home or fed back to the electricity grid through a two-way meter.

Another variation on this theme is the Microgen system pioneered by British Gas and Powergen. This in effect is a large Stirling engine powered by gas. The engine also produces electric power that can either be used directly in the home or sold back to the national grid. It also creates heat for hot water and heating as a by-product.

Photo: WINDSAVE

WIND POWER

Until recently, generating your own power from wind wasn't really an
option for the individual householder. Wind turbines were expensive, noisy
and generated electricity at the wrong voltage for domestic electricity
consumption. However, a new development called ROCS (renewable
obligation charges system) is set to change all that and make tiny roof-
mounted wind turbines cost effective. The system essentially allows
electricity supply companies to buy electricity from you by claiming a
subsidy from the government according to how much your turbine has
generated and reducing your electricity bill by the same amount. At least
one company, Windsave, already makes roof-mounted turbines costing
about the same as a standard boiler installation. They are small enough
to be mounted on a chimney like a television aerial and are no more
visually intrusive than a satellite dish. An average system should pay
for itself within three years.

***Windpower Workshop* by
Hugh Piggot tells you how
to build your own wind
generator. An easier option
is to buy wind-generated
power directly from green
electricity suppliers.**

SOLAR POWER

Solar panels have been available for domestic houses for many years. Following a brief spurt of popularity after the oil crisis in the early 1970s they faded back to a minority interest product with payback periods too long to interest the mainstream, but recent technological advances have made them once again a serious choice. It's a common fallacy that the British Isles are just too cloudy for solar panels to be worthwhile. In fact, we receive about two-thirds of the amount of solar radiation that southern Spain gets and more than half the level in Kenya. Of course, there are regional differences – northern Scotland receives about 30 per cent less solar energy than southern England – but, on average, well-designed solar panels that are installed properly can produce enough power for between 80 and 90 per cent of our hot water in summer, 40 to 50 per cent in spring and autumn and about 10 to 15 per cent in winter. A south-facing pitched roof is the best location on which to site them. On east-or west-facing elevations they will suffer a 10 to 15 per cent drop in efficiency. There are two different types of panel available: solar panels that heat water and PV (photovoltaic) cells that generate electricity.

Hot-water solar panels come in two types. The traditional system has a circuit of water flowing through the panel and into the hot water cylinder. Because they absorb heat from the sun, they work best when the weather is hot, which also tends to be when you need hot water the least. In windy weather they are prone to wind chill, and work less well. Vacuum tube solar panels are a modern development; they are more efficient because they absorb energy from sunlight rather than the sun's heat. They work on the same principle as a thermos flask. Radiant heat passes through the glass outer coating and through the vacuum to be absorbed by the water pipes; the vacuum insulates the pipes and stops the heat being lost through convection. This means they work well on bright but cold winter days.

The drawback to both systems is their cost. The cost of heating hot water is surprisingly low (less than a fifth of the total fuel bill for most houses), so it takes a very long time to recoup the cost of solar panels. (At current prices it would take at around thirty years, although fuel prices are expected to rise, so this figure could fall down.) Finally, I should mention PV cells, full details of which will be found on p. 219. These create electricity (rather than hot water) directly from the sun. They are more expensive than hot water solar panel systems, but government grants can offset the cost considerably (see pp. 342–45 for more on grants).

A couple of books for further reading on solar panels are the excellent *The Return of the Solar Cat* by Jim Augustyn and, if you're feeling really green, *Solar Water Heating: A DIY Guide* by Paul Trimby, which contains instructions for making your own solar panels from waste materials.

HYDROPOWER

Hydropower is generated from water movement and, like solar and wind power, is a completely renewable and non-polluting source of energy. It is, of course, only any use to you if your house is built near a stream or river that is running at a fast rate. If your property is in such a location, hydropower is worth investigating. It's more likely to produce a constant supply of energy than wind or solar power, and is also likely to produce more power in the winter when watercourses are fuller, and when you need power the most.

You can connect a hydropower system to the national grid via a two-way meter and use it to subsidize your electricity bills in the same way as for solar-and wind-generated power. You can also, in theory, use it as your principal power source. This may make the difference when assessing the feasibility of rescuing a property that is remote from mains electricity. This is quite possible in some parts of the country, although you'd probably not be able to generate enough electricity to use it as your main heating source as well. A small turbine on a hill stream, with a flow of say 20 litres per second, should generate 1 or 2 kw. This is enough to power lights and a few appliances. Domestic hydropower generators aren't easy to come by, although they are produced for sale in countries such as China and India where hydropower is more widely used than in the UK and Ireland. Scotland's landscape and climate mean that it probably has the best potential for hydropower in the British Isles.

Try the Scottish Community Renewables Initiative or the British Hydropower Association for more information.

GEOTHERMAL POWER

There is one other renewable source of power that you can use directly, and that is heat from the ground. It helps if you live in an area of hot thermal springs and geysers (in Iceland 85 per cent of homes are heated by geothermal power) but, we don't have many of those here. However, there is still energy stored in the ground beneath your feet right now. A few feet below the surface, the earth maintains a remarkably constant temperature throughout the year of between 10 and 15 °C (50 and 60 °F). This mightn't sound very impressive as a source of heat, but with the right equipment it can be extracted and used to heat your home. A heat exchanger can extract and magnify the earth's heat. It can also draw heat away from your home to keep it cool during hot weather.

If you own a fridge, you own a heat exchanger (that's what all those pipes on the back of it are). An outdoor system works in the same way. A network of pipes is buried in the ground near to the house and a fluid, usually a mixture of water and antifreeze, circulates through them to absorb or release heat. In the winter, the system removes heat from the pipes and pumps it into the house. In the summer, the process can be reversed and the heat pump moves heat from indoors to the heat exchanger. The heat removed from the indoor air during the summer can also be used to heat up your water (for free). You do need a large garden to make it worthwhile and you'll have to dig it all up to a depth of several feet. This isn't a cheap system to install, but once it's up and running your heating costs will be tiny. A good installation can recoup your investment in less than ten years.

There are several suppliers of geothermal power systems, but only a few manufacturers. The leading one is probably the Swedish company Thermia Varne AB, whose products are often sold under the brand Eco Heat Pumps in the UK.

BOILERS

Other than fuel type, there are two main choices in deciding which boiler to go for. First, whether to opt for one that heats a tank of hot water or one that provides a supply of instant hot water; second, whether to have a conventional boiler or a more efficient condensing boiler.

TRADITIONAL BOILERS

First, the hot-water issue. Traditionally designed boilers heat up water both in a hot water tank and for the central heating system using the same heat exchanger. The fuel is burned in jets, which blast their heat on to cast-iron blocks. The blocks take a bit of heating up, but when they are up to temperature they hold the heat well. Pipework passes through the blocks and water running through these pipes is heated up in turn. There are two pipes running through the blocks – one for the central heating water and the other for the hot tap water. The central heating water is said to be heated up directly because the water in the central heating pipes and radiators passes directly through the boiler. The hot tap water, on the other hand, is heated up indirectly. The hot water that flows out of the taps won't actually have passed through the boiler at all. The tap water is stored in a cylinder or tank, usually sited in an airing cupboard. A sealed pipework loop runs through it and to the boiler, where it's heated up. The loop runs back to the tank and passes on its heat to the water within. This system has been used for years and works very well. It's normally reliable, plumbers understand it and it's easy to fix if things go wrong. The main drawback is that it isn't very efficient (about 30 per cent of the energy in the fuel is wasted in the process of heating the water; in other words, they are about 70 per cent efficient). Those iron blocks use a load of energy in heating up, and all that pipework radiates heat on its route to and from the water tank. The water tank itself takes up a lot of space, and although many people like having an airing cupboard, having 100 litres of hot water sitting round going cold is an expensive way of keeping your laundry dry.

COMBINATION BOILERS

The alternative is a combination boiler (often called a combi). This does away with the water tank altogether and heats up tap water directly and instantaneously as you need it. It does this by having two heat exchangers, in effect two boilers in one box. Combis are more efficient (about 85 per cent), but also more temperamental. They need to be set up properly in the first place, serviced more regularly and need a corrosion inhibitor in the central heating water to stop the heat exchanger corroding. A drawback with combi boilers is that they don't work very well with mixer showers. They just can't heat up the water quickly enough, so your shower becomes more of a dribble. Combi boilers are more expensive to buy than traditional boilers, but if you're installing a complete system the extra cost will be more than offset by not having to buy a water tank.

CONDENSING BOILERS

These boilers are the most efficient of all, extracting up to 95 per cent of available heat energy from the burning fuel by having extra-large heat exchangers which transfer more of the heat to the water. Flue gases from condensing boilers are given off at about 50 °C compared with 250 °C from a conventional boiler. At this relatively low temperature, water in the flue gas condenses and a cloud of white steam called a plume is emitted from the flue, hence the name condensing boiler. Condensing boilers are manufactured either as combis or for traditional indirect systems, and are available for all common fuels. Many plumbers and central heating engineers dislike condensing boilers, and may tell you that they are prone to corrosion, unreliable and high maintenance. These criticisms may have been valid in the very early days, but such teething problems have long since been ironed out. It's more likely that the installer doesn't know how to fit one and can't be bothered to learn. It is true that condensing boilers are more expensive to buy, but the payback in lower fuel bills will cover this cost in a few years. You may also be eligible for a grant to cover the additional outlay (see Chapter 13). If your property is in England or Wales, the Building Regulations (if applicable – see p. 299 for conditions) will allow you to fit a conventional boiler only if there is no practical alternative, so the discussion is rather academic. And if you need a new boiler, common sense dictates that it should be a condensing one, anyway.

HEAT TRANSMISSION SYSTEMS

RADIATORS

Most houses are heated with white pressed-steel radiators. They are quite ugly, but so familiar that most people don't really notice tham. Generally speaking, the bigger the radiator, the higher the heat output. The smallest radiators (300 mm x 400 mm) give out 0.25 kw and the largest (700 mm x 3000 mm) give out 4 kw. A double radiator emits a little less than double the output of similarly sized single. Fins on the back increase the surface area and enable a bit more heat to be squeezed out.

If you prefer a different look there is an increasingly wide range of radiators designed for style. A number of manufacturers produce chrome-plated radiators that, far from being ignored, are there to be noticed. They are expensive, but style always costs. If you're a retro fan, traditional Victorian radiators are grand-looking things. Made from cast iron columns, sitting on four feet and decorated with mouldings, they look more like a piece of furniture than a plumbing component. Reconditioned Victorian radiators are available from salvage companies, but you should have them pressure tested to make sure they don't leak and, ideally, shot-blasted to remove old layers of paint. One drawback is that the pipework diameters are different from today's standard sizes. Conversion rings are available, but you'll probably end up with a cone shape of several rings sitting on the end of your radiator to achieve an exact match. A number of specialist manufacturers make reproduction Victorian radiators with pipework in standard metric sizes. Cast-iron radiators are slow to heat up and you need the circulating water to be at a high temperature in order for them to be effective.

UNDERFLOOR AND CONCEALED HEATING

Some radiators can be hidden from view completely. Skirting radiators, as you might imagine, take the place of skirting boards. They aren't invisible, and it's obvious that they aren't normal skirting boards if you look at them carefully, but they are very unobtrusive none the less.

An increasingly popular option is underfloor heating. In effect, the whole floor becomes a huge radiator and if you're carrying out a major refurbishment that involves both a new heating system and new floors, this is an option you could consider. Flexible pipework is looped back and forth across the whole floor and a cement screed is laid on top. The effect is very comfortable; the temperature gradient keeps your feet nice and warm and your head pleasantly cool. This is both more comfortable and more efficient than traditional systems which heat the air above your head and allow cold draughts to whip round your feet. The water temperature in an underfloor system is much lower than in a traditional system (imagine if your floor were as hot as a radiator on a high setting), so underfloor heating is in theory more economical than a radiator system. Whether you benefit from this, however, depends on how you use it. Like storage heaters, the cement screed takes a long time to heat up and cool down, so underfloor heating works best for those with predictable lifestyles. Underfloor heating can be laid under wooden floors, too, although wood is a good insulator and so doesn't conduct the heat so efficiently. For more on night storage heaters see p. 265.

HEAT-RECOVERY SYSTEMS

Mechanical heat-recovery systems aren't an alternative to radiators, but properly installed they can mean that you use less energy for heating. As a concept, they're great. They extract stale air from the house, recover the heat from it and use that same heat to warm up fresh air drawn in from outdoors. They give constant ventilation without draughts and they're excellent if your house is on a noisy road because you can ventilate it without letting in the traffic noise. They aren't cheap, though, and although they recover energy they also use it. An electric fan runs continuously, so the overall net energy saving can be quite small. They tend to work most efficiently if the airflow is turned down. A system operating at more than one air change per hour will use more energy than it saves.

Large systems can be installed to run throughout the house, replenishing the air in every room. These systems can become noisy with age and are quite expensive to install. The amount of ductwork they need makes them a viable option only if you are undertaking a major refurbishment and are lifting all the floors anyway. There are, however, mini systems that can serve one room which are small enough to fit into the gap left by an airbrick.

HEATING CONTROLS

A tyre manufacturer once used the slogan 'Power is nothing without control'. The same could be applied to heating systems. It's not just a matter of making a house hot; a good heating system will maintain a suitable temperature in every room according to its use and whatever the temperature outside. Controls on heating systems both improve the comfort level of your home and reduce the amount of fuel you use.

Most modern central heating systems have three different types of controls: programmers, thermostats and thermostatic radiator valves (TRVs). If you have an old central heating system, you can add these controls to it.

PROGRAMMERS

These are what we used to call timers. In fact, they still are timers but have become more sophisticated and do lots of other things too. You can use them to programme when the heating and hot water are turned on and off, of course, but modern programmers also have separate controls for heating and hot water and will allow you to set them differently for different days of the week, or different settings for weekdays and weekends. Some systems are also zoned, allowing you to have the heating on in one part of the house only, (though in order to work this also requires changes to the plumbing with new motorized valves installed. Zoning is useful if you have a granny flat or a lodger.) Basic programmers are surprisingly cheap and can pay for themselves in reduced fuel costs in a few months.

THERMOSTATS

There are several thermostats you should have on a central heating system to maximize its efficiency. The one you might be most familiar with is a room thermostat (plumbers call them room stats). This is a box with a small dial marked with temperatures from 10 °C to 30 °C. It's often located in the hall and controls the heating for the whole house, switching it off when the temperature it's set at is reached and switching it on again when the temperature falls. Most people set them at between 18 °C and 21 °C. Find what is comfortable for you and then reduce it by 1 °C. This isn't a hair-shirt punishment. The body doesn't register a difference in air temperature of 1 °C and this small reduction can save you £50 a year in fuel costs. In my opinion, you should fit both a room stat and TRVs (see below). Think of the room stat as the main control and TRVs as precision adjustments for each room. However, if you do have both and you set the room stat too low, or site it in the wrong place, it'll make your heating system difficult to control. You should take care not to site the room stat where it could get too hot (for example near to a radiator) or too cold (for example near to a draughty front door).

Another useful but usually non-essential thermostat is a frost thermostat. This activates the heating if there is a danger that the water in the system will freeze, overriding the programmer to do so. These are useful if you often go away during the winter, and are essential if the boiler is sited in an unsuitable location such as a garage, where it could well freeze.

Cylinder thermostats control the temperature of the water in a hot water cylinder (you won't have a cylinder if you have a combi boiler). They are normally about the size of a matchbox and allow you to set the temperature at anything between 40 °C and 80 °C. They are a good addition to a conventional system, allowing you to maximize its efficiency. Set it at 60 °C and turn it down a degree or two at a time until you reach optimum efficiency. The best temperature is the minimum that meets your needs. Hot water is usually mixed with cold when it's used so the ideal temperature for you is determined by how much hot water you use rather than how hot you like it. Once you find the optimum, leave it set at this temperature.

All these thermostats are very cheap to buy and cost little to install. The outlay will be recovered in a matter of months at most. Fitting them is probably the most cost effective improvement you can make to a heating system.

TRVs

Thermostatic radiator valves replace the old manual valves on the flow side of each radiator. They open and close to maintain the air temperature at whatever setting you select. Most new radiators have them fitted already, but they can be easily and cheaply added to existing radiators. Some plumbers will tell you not to bother with TRVs because they don't work. They do work. The real problem is that some people just don't understand them. The setting measures the air temperature and not the temperature of the water in the system. Increasing the setting won't necessarily turn the radiator on if the room is already warm, and turning it up high won't make the room heat up any faster. It's best to adjust the setting until you feel comfortable and then leave it alone.

Some plumbers will tell you not to bother with TRVs because they don't work. They do work. The real problem is that some people just don't understand them.

UPGRADING OR REPLACING A CENTRAL HEATING SYSTEM

If your property already has a central heating system, you have to decide whether to upgrade it with new or additional components or replace it altogether. There is a general consensus that a central heating system lasts for about thirty years, although the life expectancy of individual components may be shorter or longer. A boiler will last between ten and twenty years, a pump or a motorized valve perhaps ten years. Radiators can last much longer (don't forget those Victorian ones that are still going strong), and copper pipes don't deteriorate under normal usage so provided they go to the right places there is no real reason to replace them. One problem that does occur in old systems is sludge resulting from a mixture of oxidized metal from the radiators and other parts of the system and impurities in the water. Over many years this can build up in pipes, and especially in radiators, reducing their efficiency and in extreme cases causing a blockage. Introducing proprietary additives into the central heating water can prevent sludge from building up, but if it's already present you need to get rid of it. You can flush out the system by opening a valve at the lowest point and tying up the ball valve in the header tank. This will push the sludge around the system a bit and get rid of any that is in suspension in the water. It may even remove a blockage, but will still leave most of the sludge in the system. A more effective method is to add a proprietary flushing agent to the water first. This causes more of the sludge to become suspended in the water and so be flushed out. For badly sludged systems, use a power flush. (Some central heating engineers will provide this service.) As the name implies, a power flush increases the water pressure in the system and blasts it out along with a large amount of the sludge – useful if you're replacing the boiler but not the radiators.

A large proportion of the cost of replacing pipework lies in taking up and replacing floorboards. If you're planning a major refurbishment and lifting all the floors anyway, you may find that replacing the pipework is only marginally more expensive than a power flush. In these cases a complete replacement may make more sense.

INSULATION

A good insulating material is a poor conductor of heat. If you have two saucepans on the stove, one with a metal handle and one with a wooden handle, you know which handle is going to feel hotter. The reason is that metal is a good conductor of heat and wood is a good insulator. Wood is thus a better material than metal for saucepan handles, and similar decisions need to be made about materials used for building houses. In the British Isles the outside temperature is such that we need to heat our homes for six to seven months a year. We feel comfortable in temperatures of 18 °C to 21 °C and nature rarely provides such a degree of warmth outside the summer months. An adequate heating system can raise the temperature inside a house to this level quite easily, but in a poorly insulated house the heat energy quickly dissipates as building materials conduct the heat away and air circulation sucks the warm air outside. This means the heating system has to work much harder to maintain a comfortable temperature. A well-insulated house cools much more slowly, so its heating system works less hard, uses less fuel, will probably not need to be so highly specified, will last longer and all in all is going to be a darn site cheaper. Literally as well as environmentally, it pays to insulate your home. In practice, you have little choice but to do so because the Building Regulations specify quite extensive insulation for refurbished homes.

A well-insulated house cools much more slowly, so its heating system works less hard and uses less fuel.

u-VALUES AND R-VALUES

The way we measure how good a material is as an insulator is by its u-value, which is a measurement of the flow of heat energy through a material. If you are unfamiliar with them, u-valves and R-values may seem a little daunting, but once you understand them you'll be much better equipped to make decisions about how to heat and insulate your home.

A u-value is calculated from the amount of heat energy in watts that can pass through a square metre of the material in an hour. A good insulator will allow only a little heat through whereas a poor insulator will allow a lot through. The higher its u-value, the poorer are a material's insulation properties.

A related unit of measurement you'll hear about is a material's R-value. R stands for resistance, and R-values are in inverse proportion to u-values, i.e. an R value is simply 1 divided by the u-value.

For R-values higher is better.

Scientists have calculated u-values for a huge range of potential building materials, so it's possible to work out the insulation value of a wall, a room or even a whole house. This is where R-values become important. All the u-values of the various materials are converted into R-values, added together and then inverted to find their combined u-values. For an accurate calculation, figures for surface resistance must be added. This is because air adheres to the surface of most materials and gives a very small insulating effect.

R-values of common building materials

Material	Typical thickness (mm)	R-value
Clay bricks	102	0.13
Dense concrete blocks	100	0.05
Aerated concrete blocks	100	0.90
Plasterboard	12.5	0.05
Plywood	18	0.14
Chipboard	18	0.14
Timber	50	0.37
Unventilated cavity	25	0.18
Plaster/render	2.5	0.03
Fibre glass/rock wool	150	3.80
Wool/flax	150	3.90
Unventilated wall cavity	–	0.18
Loft space	–	0.20
Surface resistance external	–	0.05
Surface resistance internal	–	0.10

u-values of walls and roofs

Material	u-value
Solid brick wall (225 mm)	2.2
Brick and concrete block cavity wall	1.0
Brick and concrete block insulated cavity wall	0.5
Tiled roof with no felt	1.9
Tiled roof with felt	0.9
Tiled roof with felt and 150 mm insulation	0.3

The difference in thermal performance between apparently similar products can be dramatic, which is why knowing their R- and u-values is so important. For example, 100 mm dense concrete blocks have an R-value of 0.05 whereas aerated concrete blocks have an R-value of 0.9. A wall built of normal dense concrete blocks could lose ten times as much heat as a wall built of aerated blocks, depending on the construction method, potentially costing you hundreds of pounds in wasted fuel.

How typical u-values of components of a building can vary

u-value in an	u-value required to meet		u-value to
	average house	2000 Building Regulations	aim for
External walls	0.46 to 2	0.45	0.3 or less
Windows, doors, skylights	3 to 5	3.30	2 or less
Roof	0.5 to 2	0.35	0.2 or less
Insulation in unconverted loft with a pitched roof	0.37 to 1.6	0.25	0.2 or less
Ground floors	0.35 to 0.7	0.35	0.25 or less

HOW HOUSES LOSE HEAT

The amount of heat that a house loses depends largely on the materials of which it is made, their u-values and the size of each component. In an average unmodernized house the main sources of heat loss are as listed below (see also the table above):

➡ walls: 30 per cent
➡ draughts through doors, windows and chimneys: 25 per cent
➡ windows: 20 per cent
➡ roof 15 per cent
➡ floors: 10 per cent

These figures are, of course, approximate and will vary according to the particular property. A detached house, for example, has more external walls to lose heat through than a terraced one.

DRAUGHT-PROOFING

If you do nothing else, you should draught-proof your house. Reducing draughts is cheap and easy to do, and the payback time is usually less than a year. Outside doors and windows are the place to start; you can buy brushes, foam strips and rubber blades that fit around them to fill in the gaps. You can also get insulated letterboxes and covers (escutcheons) for keyholes. These are all available from DIY shops and builders' merchants.

This would all be delightfully simple if it weren't for the issue of ventilation. Houses need good ventilation and this appears to contradict the need for them to be draught-proofed. Good ventilation helps prevent condensation by moving wet air out of the house. It prevents the air becoming stuffy and smelly and gets rid of nasty gases such as formaldehyde and VOCs. Just what is a good level of ventilation is a matter of some debate; the level required by the current Building Regulations for new houses is 0.5 air changes per hour (this means that half of the air is renewed with fresh air every hour), but an uninsulated Victorian house may have four air changes an hour. If you have a brand-new house this may be cause for concern, but most old houses are so leaky that whatever amount of draught-proofing you put in you're unlikely to suffocate yourself.

If you'll be heating only part of your house or if you intend to heat different rooms to different temperatures it makes sense to draught-proof internal doors too. Be careful, however, in any room containing a gas fire, especially a coal-effect model. These use up oxygen as they burn. If you seal the room up too tightly the reduced oxygen levels will cause the fire to give off deadly carbon monoxide instead of carbon dioxide. You must in any event install an external airbrick in any room containing a large-capacity gas fires (7 kilowatts or greater).

Fireplaces are another major source of draughts; an average open-flue fire will admit 20 litres of cold air per second when not in use. Some fireplaces have flaps in the chimney to allow you to close them. (If you convert an old fireplace into a gas fire you'll need to remove this flap to reduce the risk of carbon monoxide poisoning.) These only mitigate the problem and you'll still get a draught. There is no simple answer. We all like the look of open fires, but if you want a warm, well-insulated house you'd be better off blocking up your fireplaces and relying on the central heating.

INSULATING WALLS

The sheer quantity of heat that is lost through a house's external walls means that it is always worth investigating to see what you can do. There are three main types of external wall: cavity walls, solid masonry walls and timber-framed walls. Insulating cavity walls is nearly always cost effective, but the other types can be more problematic. Most timber-framed walls will already be well insulated (at least in modern houses) and should need little or no extra insulation. Solid masonry walls can be insulated, too, but the payback period is much longer and the process much more difficult.

HOW TO FIND OUT WHAT TYPE OF WALL YOU HAVE

A cavity wall is, in effect, two walls built parallel to each other with a small air gap between. The outer wall is usually built of bricks and the inner wall of concrete blocks. Most houses built since the 1930s have cavity walls, although some coastal properties dating back to the beginning of the twentieth century had them too. Before the 1930s most houses were built with solid walls that are normally the thickness of the length of a brick (225 mm).

Cavity walls are laid in a pattern known as garden-wall bond (see photos, p. 290), in which all the bricks are laid lengthways. If you measure the thickness of the wall it should be about 300 mm. Solid masonry walls were built in a number of different bonds, but in all of them you'll be able to see that about half of the bricks are laid end-on and half lengthways Such walls are usually about the same thickness as the length of a brick. Timber-framed walls usually have an outer skin of bricks and are indistinguishable externally from an all-brick built house. The bricks will follow the same pattern as a cavity wall, but in most cases the wall will be less thick (usually no more than 250 mm). If you tap the inside of a timber frame wall it should sound hollow.

CAVITY WALL INSULATION

Most cavity walls can be filled quite easily and cheaply, but there will the odd property where it's not suitable. The coastal properties mentioned earlier were built with cavity walls not for thermal insulation but to keep out driving rain. Houses in exceptionally exposed positions might need cavity walls for the same reason. In these cases filling the cavity could create a bridge across which rainwater could pass into the house. Very few properties are built in such exposed positions, but if you think yours might be one take advice from your energy advice centre.

Walls with cavities of less than 50 mm might not be suitable either, because the insulation won't disperse properly when it's installed. Measure the thickness of the wall; if it's less than 250 mm, the cavity is too small to insulate.

On occasion, wall cavities have been used as passageways for electrical cables. If this has been done in your house you shouldn't insulate the cavity unless you rewire the property, removing all the live cables from the cavity. If you don't, the insulation could cause the cables to overheat and catch fire. The only way to find out whether your house has been wired like this is to lift some floorboards and trace the cable routes.

Insulation is blown into the cavity on a stream

of air through holes drilled through the mortar of the outer skin wall. The holes are then repaired with mortar and, if it's done well, should be virtually invisible afterwards. If you don't want to risk damaging a pristine outer wall surface you could drill holes from the inside of the house instead. This, of course, would entail replastering several rooms afterwards. The three most commonly used insulation materials are mineral fibre, polystyrene beads and urea formaldehyde foam. All of these materials have environmental costs to them, especially urea formaldehyde foam, which really is one to avoid.

SOLID WALL INSULATION

Insulating solid walls is more expensive and more problematic than insulating a cavity wall. The two approaches are to insulate the inside of the wall in a process called dry lining, or insulate the outside by cladding it. Both approaches have their advantages and drawbacks. The type of property and the type of refurbishment will usually make the decision for you and rule out one or even both these options.

Dry lining involves attaching a layer of insulation to the wall and covering it with a layer of plasterboard. This sounds simple enough, but don't forget that radiators, skirting boards, door architraves, kitchen units and bathroom fittings will all need to be removed and refixed over the plasterboard layer. All this makes good sense if

you're ripping everything out anyway, but if not it's very disruptive. Another drawback is that the rooms end up smaller. You can add as much or as little insulation as you want, but there seems little point going to all this trouble for a marginal benefit. I'd recommend at least 50 mm of insulation, resulting in a reduction of about 6 cm in the room's width and length.

Thermal boards, a composite product incorporating the insulation, the plasterboard and a vapour barrier, make installation easier and quicker but exclude the possibility of using some of the best insulation materials such as wool or flax (thermal-board insulation is usually polystyrene, mineral wool or polyurethane). A conventional installation involves fixing timber battens to the wall and fitting the insulation between them. Over this goes a vapour barrier, traditionally a polythene sheet, and on top of this goes the plasterboard. Any gaps around pipes must be well sealed to prevent water vapour entering and causing condensation problems.

The second alternative, **external cladding**, also has many drawbacks. It's expensive, it changes the look of the house substantially and you might have problems obtaining planning permission to use it. However, there are a number of well-proven systems, and some houses are so ugly anyway that any change is for the better. If internal dry lining isn't appropriate, cladding may be better than nothing.

The sheer quantity of heat that is lost through a house's external walls means that it is always worth investigating to see what you can do.

The External Wall Insulation Association is a trade body that maintains a list of installers and can provide information on different systems.

ROOF INSULATION

Hot air rises, and any that hasn't already escaped through the doors, windows, floor or walls will make a beeline for the roof. It makes sense to insulate your roof and some forms of roof insulation are among the most cost effective around. There are three different types of roof from an insulation point of view: loft roofs, attic rooms and flat roofs. Loft roofs (i.e. lofts in pitched roofs that haven't been boarded or converted) are the easiest and cheapest to insulate. Attic rooms and flat roofs are best insulated as part of a refurbishment.

FLAT ROOFS

There are two methods of insulating flat roofs. The **sandwich method** is probably the best, but it requires that the roof is opened up so once again is only cost effective if the roof is being replaced or substantially repaired. It involves sandwiching insulation between the roof deck and the weatherproof covering.

The **inverted method** works well on flat roofs that are in good condition, as there is no need to strip off the roof covering. An insulation layer is simply fitted on top of the weatherproof covering and held in place with a layer of ballast (normally paving slabs).

LOFT ROOFS

Installing insulation in a loft is a piece of cake; it's simply placed in position. This is best done in two stages. First, the gaps between the joists are filled either with quilts of materials such as wool or mineral fibre or with loose material such as blown cellulose. On top of this another layer of quilted insulation is placed at 90° to the joists. You should aim for a minimum of 250 mm in depth. Don't forget to insulate the loft hatch and put draught excluder round it.

An insulated loft will be much colder than an uninsulated one, so water tanks and pipes need to be protected against the risk of freezing in winter. To prevent this from happening you should fit insulation around and over the tanks, but not underneath. This will allow warm air from the house to keep it from freezing. The opposite problem can be caused to electric cables clipped to the joists. The insulation can lead to them overheating, so it's best to reroute cables above the insulation. Make sure that the roof is ventilated properly; moisture in the cold air is more likely to condense on roof timbers and the inside of the roof surface, making them prone to wood rot and insect attack. If the roof is unventilated you should install ridge-tile ventilators.

Hot air rises, and any that hasn't already escaped through the doors, windows, floor or walls will make a beeline for the roof.

ATTIC ROOMS

Attic rooms, including loft conversions, are the most exposed rooms in a house and will experience extremes of temperature in summer and winter. A poorly insulated attic room won't only waste large amounts of heat, it'll be very uncomfortable to inhabit for much of the year.

There are two methods of insulating attic rooms: the ventilated-roof method and sarking insulation. **The ventilated-roof method** is the best for insulating an existing attic room. Insulation is fitted between the rafters leaving a ventilated gap of at least 50 mm between the insulation material and the underside of the roofing felt across the whole roof. This allows air to circulate from under the eaves to keep the roof dry. If the pitch of the roof is too steep the air won't circulate properly and you'll need to fit some ventilated ridge tiles. A vapour barrier (usually a polythene sheet) must be fixed across the underside of the insulation before covering with plasterboard to form the wall and ceiling surfaces.

Water tanks in attic rooms should be treated in the same way as in loft roofs.

The second method is **sarking insulation**. This uses rigid insulation boards fitted on top of the rafters and necessitates removal of the roof covering. If you're doing this anyway, then sarking is fairly easy and cheap, but it wouldn't be cost effective otherwise. An advantage of this system is that it requires no ventilation and there is no need for a vapour barrier because the rafters are on the warm side of the insulation, so are less prone to condensation.

FLOOR INSULATION

Everybody knows that if you sit still the first part of your body to feel cold is your feet. People feel most comfortable when their heads are slightly cooler than their feet, but poorly insulated floors create the opposite conditions. Floor insulation may be fairly low down on the ladder of cost effectiveness, but you may consider it worthwhile because of its contribution to your comfort. Heat tends to be lost from floors abutting an external wall, so it's a bigger problem in a detached house.

The methods used to insulate floors depend on floor type. The two main floor types are solid concrete and suspended timber.

SOLID CONCRETE FLOORS

Fitting insulation on solid concrete floors is the more difficult of the two. If you're laying a new floor you can install it underneath the concrete using an insulation material such as foamed glass that is dense enough to take the weight. Alternatively you can install insulation above an existing concrete floor. The usual method is to build a second floor suspended over the concrete one, filling the void with insulation on top of a vapour barrier. This, of course, will raise the floor height and reduce headroom. You'll also need to trim doors and re-hang them, refix skirting boards and kitchen units and adjust the foot of the staircase.

SUSPENDED TIMBER FLOORS

Suspended timber floors are an easier proposition. Floorboards can be lifted quite easily, and in a refurbishment project you may well have them up for other reasons anyway. You can choose from a wide variety of insulation materials. Stiff materials can be held in place with battens and loose materials hung in suspended mesh between the joists. You need to be careful not to block any air vents in the walls, as this can lead to condensation and encourage wood rot. To increase thermal comfort you should also fill any gaps between the floorboards. If you're fitting a carpet, a layer of hardboard does the trick. If you're intending to have a stripped wooden floor you can fill the gaps between the boards with a mixture of wood glue and sawdust (you can use the sawdust created when you sand the floor or buy some from a pet shop, where it will be on sale as a bedding material for hamsters). When it has dried, lightly re-sand the whole floor to create a smooth, draught-free surface.

WINDOWS

However you design them and whatever you do to them, a significant amount of heat loss through your windows is unavoidable. You can, in theory, apply as much insulation as you want to a wall, but there's no point in filling a double-glazed window cavity with wool. That being said, manufacturers have improved the technology to a point where the very best windows now have insulation properties equal to an uninsulated solid brick wall.

FRAMES

The first thing to consider is the frame. A surprisingly large amount of heat can be lost through the frame itself and the material it's made out of is critical. Wooden and uP V C window frames have similar u-values and are the best materials. Steel and aluminium aren't so good.

DOUBLE AND TRIPLE GLAZING

Glass itself does have some thermal insulating properties, but a single sheet is so thin and has such a large surface area that it leaks heat like a sieve. Air is a much better insulator, so by trapping a layer of it between two sheets of glass double-glazing manages to achieve much better thermal efficiency than a single-glazed window.

Modern windows take the principles further; some inert gases have better insulating properties than air, so in most modern designs the gap between the panes is sealed and filled with argon or something similar (the best gas for this purpose is xenon, but it's more expensive and only marginally better than argon). Another development is low-emisivity coating. This is a layer applied to the glass that reflects long-wave heat energy but lets through short-wave heat energy. Heat from the sun is short wave, so it passes through the glass, but heat generated in the home is long wave, so is reflected back in.

Tripled-glazed units are also starting to become more popular. If you make the gap between the panes of glass any bigger than 20 mm the air or gas will begin to move around because the gap is wide enough for convection currents to occur. So with a large gap the thermal efficiency of windows will actually be less. The way round this is to divide a larger gap in two by inserting another a pane of glass. This gives you triple glazing. There are two main types; thermal triple glazing is made simply for improved thermal efficiency; but there is also thermal/acoustic glazing, discussed on p. 86–7. This has one small and one large gap, so helps to insulate the house from external noise as well as internal heat loss.

SECONDARY GLAZING

An alternative to replacing your existing windows is to install secondary glazing. This means leaving your existing windows in place and installing a second layer of glass inside the window. Secondary glazing can be either made up to fit or purchased ready made. It isn't as effective as double-glazing but it certainly reduces draughts and will help prevent condensation. Secondary glazing works properly only if the inside panes (i.e. the new secondary glazing panes) have draught stripping applied to them. Ready-made units will already have such strips fitted. Don't draught strip the original window or condensation will form between the panes.

CURTAINS

Curtains make surprisingly little difference to the thermal efficiency of windows. There is, perhaps, a cosy feel about them which makes us think they are keeping in more heat than they really are, but look at the u-values of curtain material and you'll see it's small beer. This is not so surprising. Tents are made of similar material, and how warm do they keep you on a chilly night? There are such things as thermal curtains but these are made of thick, quilted material with a heat-reflective coating. They may not be quite ready for the domestic market yet, unless you want your house to look like a set from *Doctor Who*.

HOT WATER SYSTEMS

PIPES

There is a theory that hot water pipes don't need insulating; after all, they give off heat into the house which is detected by thermostats and compensated for by reduced heat output from the radiators. This plausible argument ignores two important points. First, houses don't need heating for half the year so heat emitted from the pipes in the summer is wasted. Second, when heating *is* needed, different rooms are heated to different temperatures, and heat lost from pipes on the landing won't keep your living room warm. Well-insulated pipes, on the other hand, can save you 5 per cent of your fuel bills.

Traditionally pipework was insulated by wrapping with hessian. Although this isn't the best insulator in world, it's better than nothing. These days, however, most people use readily available custom-made pipework insulation, which appears to be made only from polyurethane foam and comes either in lengths of tube which are slit down one side, enabling you to push them in place, or as a roll of adhesive-backed strip which can be wound round the pipes. The two most important lengths of pipework to insulate are the primary pipework between the boiler and the hot water cylinder and any hot water pipework in the loft space.

CYLINDERS

Probably the cheapest and most cost effective insulation measure you can take is to insulate your hot water cylinder. All cylinders made since the mid 1980s should have factory-fitted foam insulation. To be effective this needs to be at least 50 mm thick, but even so it is far from a complete solution. You can supplement it with an insulating jacket available from most DIY shops for a few pounds or euros. Make sure you buy one that is at least 80 mm thick and your investment should be repaid in reduced fuel bills in less than a year. A cheap DIY alternative is to cut up an old hollow-fibre duvet and make your own jacket.

There are such things as thermal curtains but these are made of thick, quilted material with a heat-reflective coating. They may not be quite ready for the domestic market yet, unless you want your house to look like a set from *Doctor Who*.

ENERGY REQUIREMENTS OF THE BUILDING REGULATIONS

The Building Regulations apply to alterations to properties in England and Wales with a floor area of more than 50 square metres, which includes everything except small studio and one-bedroom flats. It covers all extensions with a floor area of more than 6 square metres, which excludes porches but not much else. The only possibly grey area is, what exactly does 'alteration' mean? It certainly includes a project involving any of the following: new heating system, new windows, replacing the majority of a roof, replacing or re-covering a substantial area of external wall, replacing the majority of a floor, replacing or replastering a majority of internal walls.

The regulations specify maximum u-values that must be achieved on completion. This can pose something of a challenge. If you're working on a modern house the u-values will already be quite low, but old houses present more of a problem. To make this easier, the Regulations do allow some leeway provided that the total overall u-value of the house is equal to or lower than that which would have been achieved had all the individual targets been met. For example, an underperforming wall might be offset by a roof insulated to a standard higher than required.

In addition to this the Regulations set minimum efficiency standards for new and replacement boilers. The minimum efficiencies are fairly easy to achieve with modern boilers and will usually be exceeded by some margin by a condensing boiler. Here again you can trade off efficiencies and so circumvent seemingly unachievable insulation targets, such as when planning permission is granted only for inefficient single-glazed replacement windows to match the originals in a listed building.

Although the minimum ratings aren't too challenging, don't assume every new boiler will pass muster. Most will, but some won't, and you shouldn't rely on the manufacturer's claims. Your building inspector will be referring to a publication called the *Little Blue Book* published by the Energy Saving Trust which gives independent efficiency figures based on tests conducted by the British Research Establishment. These figures are generally lower than those provided by the manufacturer, whose tests always seem to be carried out in ideal conditions rather than real-world circumstances. Like your car's claimed fuel consumption, such figures are rarely achieved in everyday use.

You can get hold of a free copy of the *Little Blue Book* by calling the EST's Energy Efficiency Hotline.

The Regulations' minimum boiler efficiencies are:

➡ mains gas: 78 per cent,
➡ L P G : 80 per cent,
➡ oil: 85 per cent,
➡ oil combination boiler: 82 per cent.

In addition to the efficiency rating, the Regulations require that you incorporate the following controls into a system with a new or replacement boiler:

➡ a programmer that independently controls heating and hot water;
➡ a room thermostat with a boiler interlock (this switches the boiler off when the selected thermostat temperature is reached).

If a whole central heating system is being replaced you must also divide it into at least two independently controlled temperature zones, either by installing a zoned heating system or using a room thermostat and fitting thermostatically controlled valves to each radiator.

The bulk of the rather conservative building industry has been dragged kicking and screaming into environmentally sustainable construction by successive sets of Building Regulations.

MAKING EFFICIENT USE OF WATER

(Yes, I know water isn't heating or insulation, but where else am I supposed to put this bit?) Water is a resource that most of us take for granted. After all it's cheap (even free in Ireland), and if you pay for your water through water rates or service charges you don't save any money by using less. Water isn't likely to run out; not here, anyway. We use it, flush it away, treat it, let it flow into rivers and seas for it to evaporate and fall as rain ready for us to use again – a pattern known as the water cycle. True, in many parts of the world it simply doesn't rain enough to provide the water people need, but putting less water in our baths won't change that.

Well, it's certainly the case that the UK and Ireland are big on rain. Trouble is, we're big on people, too. The population of the British Isles is growing and each of us is using more water.

So it's a good idea simply to use less water. If your home is one of the ever-increasing number that has a water meter, you'll save money into the bargain. If you still pay water rates and carry out a few of the recommendations below it'll probably be worth while to ask your water company to fit a meter because you will then almost certainly pay less as a low user. (Most water companies encourage the installation of meters and fit them free of charge.) Many water-saving measures are quite expensive, and I wouldn't expect you to rush out and replace your perfectly good WC with a water-saving model. But rescuing a house provides an opportunity to ensure that any new appliances you have to buy will use as little water as possible without spending much more than you would have done otherwise. The financial argument doesn't really apply at all in Ireland, because most people still pay nothing for their water, so I can only appeal to the conscience of anyone rescuing a property there.

There are three main approaches you can take to saving water.
➡ Use less.
➡ Reuse more.
➡ Collect your own.

USING LESS WATER

About a third of the water we use literally goes straight down the toilet. Its pretty odd, when you consider it, to spend money treating water to bring it up to drinking quality, then dump it into a sewer, but every week each of us does just that with 100 litres of the stuff. Traditional WCs use about 9 litres a flush, but 4 litres will easily do the job, if you'll pardon the expression. Modern low flush WCs use between 4 and 5 litres. Their cisterns are small and can be easily concealed if you want an uncluttered look. An easy and cheap alternative way to improve the efficiency of a traditional WC is simply to put a brick or a filled plastic bottle in the cistern.

Insulating your hot water pipes is a good way to reduce your fuel bills (see p. 297), but it will also mean that when you run the hot tap it will take less time before the hot water starts coming through.

When you buy a washing machine or a dishwasher, choose one that has a low water usage. The sales blurb will usually mention it. Low-water-usage models are usually more expensive, but they're often the better models as well.

Spray taps use less water by mixing the flowing water with air. This isn't much help if you want to fill up a basin with water, but if you only want to wash your hands they're just as effective as conventional taps. Use them on washbasins in cloakrooms. (Screw-on aerators are available that do the same job and fit on to existing taps.)

These are the conventional water-saving methods, but there are also some slightly cranky options that you could go for if you really want to embrace the sustainable lifestyle. Compost toilets, for example, don't use any water at all, but if you want to keep your friends they are really suitable only for outside use.

RECYCLING MORE WATER

Much of the water we use can be used again. Water used for washing the dishes, for example, is fine for watering the garden or flushing the loo. Collectively, such options are known as grey water systems. (Black water is the polite way of describing waste from the toilet. All other wastewater from the house is rather less unpleasant, hence the designation 'grey'.) Grey water tends to be produced at a quite predictable and steady rate. This means you don't need to store very much of it, or store it for very long, since there will always be a fresh supply. This sounds great in theory, but there are problems. First of all, grey water soon becomes stagnant. It mightn't be too bad at first, but store it for a day or two and it'll positively stink. It can also breed germs and become a health hazard. Grey water also contains scraps of food, grease, body hair – all sorts of things that, after having flushed them down the sink, you have no wish to be reunited with a day or so later.

Such problems are the reason grey water systems are still quite rare, but with a little ingenuity they can all be overcome. Companies such as Aquaco make water-treatment and filtering systems that clean out the gunk and eradicate the smells. Most suppliers can provide a complete grey water system for about the same cost as an installed boiler. A cheaper DIY approach is to build your own filter using a straw trap. Straw is great for cleaning up water. If you have a garden pond, adding a bale of barley straw to it will keep the water clean and clear. Ordinary straw will do the same for wastewater. Simply divert your waste-water pipe into a basket filled with straw (about a quarter of a bale) before it goes into a storage tank and most of the grot will be taken out. Every few weeks replace the straw and put the old stuff on the compost heap. However, even straw-filtered grey water should be used as soon as possible. The most practical use for grey water is to water the garden, so such a system is more useful in the summer. In winter it's probably better to divert your grey water back into the drain.

COLLECTING YOUR OWN WATER

The amount of rain that flows off your roof and down the drain is almost certainly enough to provide about half your annual requirements. In the west of Ireland that figure is nearer to 100 per cent. The problems are similar to those of solar panels: nature is unpredictable and the time we need the most water is the very time it when rains least. The bigger the storage tank you have, the more rainwater you can use, but also the more difficult and expensive the whole exercise becomes. Complete systems usually involve an underground tank for storage, a pump and a filter system. The leading supplier in the UK of complete systems is Rainharvesting Systems Ltd. Most people use rainwater like grey water for flushing the toilet and watering the garden, but you can go the whole hog and filter it to drinking quality. To do so requires a water-treatment system, which is both expensive and high maintenance. The American company Spectrapure is a specialist in this field.

If you have a lead roof, this isn't an option for you since the filter won't clean out the toxic lead salts from the water. Some horticulturists say that you shouldn't use water from a lead roof on the garden either, which is certainly good advice if you're planning to grow your own fruit or vegetables.

At the other end of the scale, water butts are a cheap and easy way to collect rain with which to water your garden. Simply site one under a shortened downpipe and add a diverter valve to prevent it overflowing when full. If you have the room, even a massive water butt that can hold 2,000 litres or more is not very expensive. You probably won't find one this big at your local hardware shop, so try the suppliers in the directory.

Grey water contains scraps of food, grease, body hair – all sorts of things that, after having flushed them down the sink, you have no wish to be reunited with a day or so later.

PART FOUR
FOOTING
THE BILL

In the introduction to Part One I talked about how you might use this book as a kind of 'travel guidebook'. In the preceding pages I have tried to ease your journey through the process of rescuing a house, but just as a guidebook can cover only the main routes and a few popular excursions, this book too can only signpost the major landmarks along the path from finding a property to rescuing it. The order of the foregoing chapters – my 'suggested itinerary', if you will – is to some extent a product of the way my mind works.

I've always been a person who thinks about money last, which is why I've barely touched on the subject before now. But, of course, there's little point in planning a trip of you can't afford the fare, so you should at least have the financial side in the back of your mind all the way through. One of the best arguments for rescuing a house is cost effectiveness: you can get a better house for less. But you'll only do so if you plan your expenditure and work out in advance how you're going to fund it. The two chapters in this final part show you how. Chapter 12 shows you how to estimate what it's all going to cost and how to draw up a realistic budget and Chapter 13 shows you how to raise the money via mortgages, loans, grants, tax incentives and subsidized house-purchase schemes. I also explore there a few other less orthodox (but completely legal) ways of getting enough money together to foot the bill.

Your overall budget cannot be more than the total amount you have available to spend. This might sound obvious, but it's amazing how easy it is to forget.

12 ESTIMATING COSTS

One of the biggest problems that can arise when refurbishing an old property is spiralling cost. If you don't keep a tight control on what and where money is spent, things can easily run away from you. Everything seems to end up costing more than you originally thought and there is always more work to do than you allowed for at the beginning of the project. The good news is that most problems can be avoided by careful planning.

BUDGETING

There is a well-known phenomenon known as budget creep, whereby you're tempted to pay just a little more for each item. This might be a matter of only a few pounds or euros here or there, but before you know it your total budget has shot up by 25 per cent.

There is no fail-safe way to prevent costs from rising, but there is an awful lot you can do to keep them under control. The first is to have a budget, the second is to stick to it and the third is to have a contingency. This is easier than it sounds. True, everybody who works for you will be pushing you to spend a bit more, and they'll often have very good and valid reasons why you should, but if you're strict with your budget they will eventually get the message. To stay in command of your budget you'll need to be well organized, well disciplined and in control.

Your overall budget cannot be more than the total amount you have available to spend. This might sound obvious, but it's amazing how easy it is to forget. Your costs must be dictated by your budget – not the other way round. The first step is to list the money you have and the money you can raise. This includes:

- ➡ Cash
- ➡ Profit from the sale of another property
- ➡ Mortgage/loan offers
- ➡ Grants
- ➡ Other sources

There is a well-known phenomenon known as budget creep, whereby you're tempted to pay just a little more for each item. This might be a matter of only a few pounds or euros here or there, but before you know it your total budget has shot up by 25 per cent.

SUB-BUDGETS

Once you have worked out your total budget, you need to break it down into sub-budgets. I suggest some sub-budgets later in this chapter, but you can break the total budget down in any way that makes sense to you. The very process of doing so provides some structure and discipline and will make it easier to manage and control. My suggested sub-budgets for building work will enable you to separate out costs by trade, but you may find it more useful to break things down on a room-by-room basis. Whatever method you use, list the costs of buying the property separately from the costs of refurbishment and make sure you include a contingency sum as one of the refurbishment sub-budgets.

Next, you need to allocate a figure to each sub-budget, bearing in mind that those figures must be realistic. You can dutifully write down £500 for a new central heating system but this won't be very helpful when you find nobody will install one for less than £4,000, so do some research first. Some costs, such as stamp duty or planning-permission charges, will be fixed or follow directly from the cost of the property, so you'll have no choice in how much you allocate for them. Allocate all the fixed fees first, then move on to your variable costs.

Most variable costs will have upper and lower limits. To replace a rotten window frame might cost £100 for a basic repair, £300 for a cheap replacement or £800 for a replica timber-framed double-glazed unit. Try allocating the minimum costs to each sub-budget first and then see how much is left over. You can then allocate any excess according to your preferences and priorities. The advantage of doing this is that it becomes much easier to see where savings can be made should it become necessary once work is under way.

Remember: Don't guess at how much something will cost; find out for sure. There are many ways to do this. If you're using an architect, a design-and-build builder, a surveyor or other designer, they should be able to provide accurate estimates. If you're managing things yourself you can find out the going rate for building costs using a number of methods:

CALCULATING COSTS

✚ Employ an expert to do it for you. Quantity surveyors calculate costs from drawings according to a standard method of measurement and price books. This is a time-consuming task and, not surprisingly, it's expensive. The fee for a rescued house project will certainly be several hundred pounds and more likely a few thousand. If you're building a large block of flats this is probably a good investment, but it's disproportionately high for a single property development.

✚ A much cheaper alternative is to employ an estimator. Estimators are far less skilled than quantity surveyors, but the latest computer software allows them to do almost as good a job on a small project, calculating quantities and costs automatically from your drawings. The process is far quicker and, although the final estimate may be less accurate than if a quantity surveyor had been employed, the fee of a hundred pounds or so represents a substantial saving. Two of the main estimating companies are Estimators Ltd and HBXL.

✚ Of course, the true costs will be what your builder actually charges. You could ask a couple of general builders to provide itemized quotes for all the works and average out the prices. If you're intending to manage subcontractors directly then knock off 15 per cent (the usual general builder's project-management fee/profit margin). Many people use this method, but it's hardly fair on the builders unless you're intending to use one of them. Many builders refuse to give itemized quotations for this very reason.

✚ Estimating software is available for you to buy. It's quite expensive, usually costing more than a hundred pounds, but some suppliers will sell you a time-limited version for less which you can use for six months or so. The advantage of owning the software over employing an estimator is that you can experiment with different schemes and compare the costs. The main packages are HBXL and Easy Price Pro.

✚ Many builders' merchants will happily provide quotes for materials based on your plans and give you itemized prices. They may do this for free if you appear to be a potentially good customer or they may charge. Some have websites where all their prices are an display. The rather cheesily named 'Build the Dream' is a costing service provided by builders' merchants Travis Perkins. They make a charge, but this is discounted from any materials you purchase through them.

✚ There are several books available that give current builders' prices. The best and most comprehensive is *Spon's Architects' and Builders' Price Book*. It's expensive, but your local library should have a copy. Such volumes can be rather a chore to use, but they are very detailed and comprehensive (builders use them to get their prices, too). They usually list two sets of detailed prices for major and minor works. If your building costs are likely to be less than £65,000, use the 'minor works' listing.

✚ A more readable book is Mark Brinkley's *The Housebuilder's Bible*. Although this is aimed mainly at new self-build housing, many of the costs are transferable to a rescued house project. The author is intending to launch a website in the near future which should be even more useful.

SUGGESTED SUB-BUDGETS

BUYING THE PROPERTY

Your biggest expense is probably going to be buying the property. To budget for this you must first consider how much that property will be worth when you have completed all the works you intend to carry out. Deduct from this your budget for refurbishment and you have your break-even point. The amount you pay for your property must obviously be below the break-even point in order for you to make a profit. If the purpose of your rescue is not to make a profit but, for example, to move to a desirable area in which very few properties come up for sale, you might decide it's worth paying the break-even price, or even a little more. Remember that the price of the property is not the price at which it's being offered for sale. To the asking price must be added sums for the following costs.

CONVEYANCING

Expect to pay between £500 and £2,000, including Land Registry charges, local authority search fees and deed registration fees. Using a specialist conveyancing firm rather than solicitors can be cheaper (see p. 49). Some web-based conveyancing companies offer very low rates, sometimes as low as £250 plus disbursements.

STAMP DUTY

No stamp duty is payable if the property is purchased for less than £120,000 (less than £150,000 in deprived areas) but 1 per cent of the purchase price must be paid for properties costing £120,000 to £250,000, 3 per cent for properties costing between £250,000 and £500,000 and 4 per cent for properties costing more than £500,000. (These figures are for residential property in the UK. The Irish system is horribly complicated and is discussed in the next chapter.)

SURVEY

You have the choice of a basic valuation, homebuyer's report or full structural survey. Usually this will have to be arranged through your mortgage lender and the fee is based on the size of the property. Expect to pay anything between £300 and £1,500. Where the home information pack system is in operation the seller will usually pay for this, but you may choose to appoint your own surveyor in addition.

MORTGAGE ARRANGEMENT FEE

Mortgage companies often charge a fee to arrange a mortgage for you. This is a bit cheeky, considering how much profit you'll be giving them in repayment fees, but some mortgage companies do waive the fee as part of an offer. Otherwise, expect to pay anything between £50 and £500.

Judith Cummings is 50 years old and manages a community mental health group in Liverpool called 'The Advocacy Project'. Based on the edge of Toxteth, its work focuses on mental health issues within the black community in the L8 area. She is currently finishing an MA in Mental Health.

Judith is from Trinidad and came over to Liverpool in the early 1960s with her parents. Judith's father died a few years ago, and she then sold her own house in order to live with her mother.

Her Vision

Judith is now looking to live on her own. She wants a house that is large enough for her extended family to visit, and maybe for her mother to stay. She would like to live in the L8 district, and is enthusiastic about having plenty of space for entertaining. Judith's budget is approximately £150,000. She is blessed by the fact that members of her family can help her fund the project.

The Front Runners
Hartington Road

The building in Hartington Road, which was built between 1872 and 1892, is a large property consisting of two semi-detached houses. The left-hand house is in moderately good external structural condition although the lower windows are boarded up. By contrast the right-hand half has been stripped of all its roofing slate and is no more than a fire-damaged shell.

From the outside it would appear that the left-hand property has been split into two flats, the upper of which has three bedrooms, a bathroom and a kitchen, the ground-floor flat having one bedroom, a living room, a bathroom and a kitchen. According to the Land Registry the property belongs to a man who has been living in Nigeria since last December. He has appointed a local Liverpool friend to act on his behalf. The property has been vacant for more than ten years.

Finding out about the home

A run-of-the-mill Land Registry search reveals that the right-hand house is owned by the Liverpool Housing Trust, who own a large number of properties in the area, many of which had been allowed to fall into considerable disrepair as the city council had, in the past, been undecided about declaring the area a slum clearance zone. It now appears that this will not happen and, as a result, many of the properties are being refurbished by the Trust.

Fern Grove

Fern Grove runs off Hartington Road and was built at the same time as the other houses on Judith's short list. The property is the right-hand half of a large, three-storey, semi-detached house which is professionally boarded up and secured. Judith is most excited by the fact that it has a large south-facing garden.

The Liverpool Housing Trust has owned the property since the 1970s, when they converted it into five small single-bedroomed flats. The Trust has indicated that it would be prepared to sell the property to an owner-occupier for approximately £110,000.

Park Way

Park Way is a pleasant, quiet road which leads on to the impressively wide boulevard of Princes Avenue, which is dramatically punctuated by the abandoned derelict hulk of an impressive Victorian Revival church. The house was built at the same time as the other two on Judith's short list. It is a three-storey end-of-terrace with bay windows on the ground and first floor. There is clearly a small garden at the rear and a large garage, which has access from the side road.

Local enquiries revealed that the house was owned by an academic who is believed to be living in France. The usual Land Registry search brings up his name. A brainwave led to a search on the worldwide web which showed that the owner was a distinguished academic at a university in Lyon with an impressive list of papers and books to his name on matters of politics, China and emigration. But attempts to contact him by telephone, fax and email were sadly to no avail.

What Next?

Judith was shown round Fern Grove by the director of the Liverpool Housing Trust, and loved the property. She's now in negotiations with the Trust.

MORTGAGE INDEMNITY GUARANTEE PREMIUM

If you borrow a high proportion of the cost of the property (in excess of, say, 75 per cent) some lenders charge a fee. This is usually a percentage of the excess, the usual rate being about 2 per cent. This is becoming less common in most of the UK, where the norm now is simply to charge a higher interest rate instead, but it's still usual practice in Ireland. The Irish government has got in on the act, too, and charges a further 2 per cent levy on top of this as a tax.

MORTGAGE PROTECTION POLICY

Most lenders will offer you some kind of life assurance to repay the mortgage in full in the event of your death. If you take out an endowment mortgage this is usually included automatically, but with repayment mortgages it's an option that will attract an additional monthly premium. Although advisable, life assurance is far from compulsory in the UK, and you are free to obtain it from any insurer, not just the one your mortgage provider suggests. In Ireland lenders more or less insist on life cover as a condition of offering you a mortgage. You can also opt for other policies that offer some cover in the event of you losing your job or suffering serious illness or incapacity. These are optional and, of course, have an extra monthly premium.

BUILDINGS INSURANCE

Your mortgage provider will require you to take out insurance against the usual risks of fire, flood, impact, subsidence etc. They will probably also offer you a quotation, though you are perfectly at liberty to choose an alternative insurer yourself. If you do so, your mortgage provider will require proof of cover before advancing your loan.

MORTGAGE REPAYMENTS AND BRIDGING LOANS

If you don't plan to live in the property during the development period your mortgage repayments during this time are an expense that has to be budgeted for. If you already have a mortgage on your existing home, you may need to pay for your new property using a temporary bridging loan, a short-term loan that most lenders offer for such purposes. Interest rates are much higher than for mortgages.

REMOVAL COSTS

The cheapest option is to hire a van and move yourself. This will cost £100 or so (plus fuel), but will involve a lot of heavy and time-consuming work. Professional removal firms offer a range of services, the cheapest of which involve you providing boxes and packing up all your possessions yourself. For a little extra you can hire boxes and crates from the removers and for a bit more still they will pack everything up for you. Costs of these services will vary enormously according to how far you're moving and how much you possess. Regional prices vary enormously, so if you're moving far a good tip is to obtain quotes from companies at both ends of the route.

SELLING AGENT'S FEES

Officially, these are paid by the seller, but in reality sellers adjust the asking price so as to cover them. If you manage to buy the property without the seller using an estate agent or an auctioneer you can quite reasonably expect a discount. If you have a property to sell, you must allow for them. Both estate agents' and auctioneers' fees vary from about 1 per cent to 4 per cent of the selling price. If you use an agent to find and buy a property for you, you'll need to budget for this fee as well.

ALTERNATIVE ACCOMMODATION

How much will it cost for you and your household to keep a roof over your heads while the property is made habitable? Keeping your old property throughout the development process could result in expensive double mortgage payments and/or a bridging loan (see above), and renting can be similarly expensive. You need to add your rental or additional mortgage repayments for the duration of the project into your budget as another sub-budget. In order for your budget to be realistic, your estimate of the time the project will take must be as accurate as your estimate of the cost of accommodation.

Other options are to rent a smaller property and put your furniture and possessions into storage, or rent or buy a caravan and live on site. A static caravan will cost between £3,000 and £7,000 to buy and set up, a second-hand holiday caravan perhaps between £1,000 and £3,000. (You may be able to recover some of this outlay at the end through resale). An on-site caravan will save you travelling time if you're working on the house yourself and help keep the site more secure, but such an option has obvious implications for your standard of living and perhaps even your sanity. This is not a decision to be taken lightly. If you budget for living in a caravan and later change your mind you'll suddenly have a big additional expense to cope with.

STORAGE

If you're going to live either on site or in smaller accommodation during the renovation you will need somewhere to store some or all of your possessions. You may be able to get friends and relatives to lend you a bit of loft space, but you'll still be amazed how much you have accumulated and almost certainly will need to rent some storage space. This should be easy to find; our hoarding culture means we all have far too many possessions and a whole industry has developed to store them for us. Most towns and cities have several storage depots where you can hire as much or little space as you want. It won't be cheap and you'll have to pay for moving twice, but at least your treasures will be out of harm's way and secure.

Storing your possessions on site is rarely practical and never advisable. You'll need to move them round as your refurbishment programme progresses, which will be both time consuming and a source of irritation to your builders. You'll also have the very real problem of security, and it will be difficult to obtain insurance cover for the contents of an unoccupied house undergoing building work.

VAT

It is very unlikely that the property purchase itself will attract VAT. The only exception is on a commercial building in Ireland built after after 31 October 1972, for which VAT is payable at a rate of 12.5 per cent of the purchase price. VAT is, however, payable on all professional fees at the standard rate. Your major VAT concerns are likely to arise regarding building costs. The rules are complex, but some guidance is provided in the next chapter (p. 336).

BUILDING COSTS

What you need to budget for will, of course, vary according to the condition of the property and what you're aiming to achieve when it's all finished. It's useful to try to break-down your project on a trade-by-trade basis. This will make it easier to tally your budget with your invoices when they arrive, to keep track of costs and to identify those areas in which extra costs are arising. Another approach is to budget on a room-by-room basis. Any such breaking down makes it easier to adjust costs and budgets if you need to.

The following list is a selection of sub-budgets you might need. Only in the most major refurbishment will you need them all, but some are sure to apply to your project. One sub-budget vital to every project is the last one: contingency.

➡ Connecting services: gas, electricity, water, landline telephone
➡ Roofing work
➡ Guttering and external pipework
➡ Underground drainage
➡ Chimneys
➡ Underpinning
➡ Brickwork, repointing
➡ Heating system
➡ Electrical wiring, telephone and television connections
➡ Light fittings
➡ Smoke detectors and automatic fire detection
➡ Kitchen units and fixed appliances
➡ Bathroom appliances
➡ Tiling
➡ Windows
➡ External doors
➡ Wall plaster
➡ Ceilings
➡ Timber floor repairs

➡ Staircase
➡ Structural timber work: floor and ceiling joists, roof timber repairs
➡ Other interior woodwork: doors, skirting boards, architraves
➡ New partition walls
➡ Concrete floor repairs
➡ Fireplace repairs
➡ Extension/loft conversion/basement conversion
➡ Cavity wall insulation
➡ Loft insulation, pipework insulation
➡ Sound insulation
➡ Carpets and floor coverings
➡ Decorating
➡ External boundary walls, fences
➡ Garages and outbuildings
➡ Garden landscaping and planting
➡ VAT
➡ Contingency (see opposite)

In addition, don't forget the following.

ARCHITECT'S FEES

Expect to pay anything from 5 to 15 per cent of the contract sum depending on what you want your architect to do. It's common to negotiate a fixed fee rather than a percentage these days. This means that even if your building costs do rise, at least your architect's fees won't.

OTHER PROFESSIONAL FEES

Any other expert you employ – quantity surveyors or planning consultants, for example – are likely to charge a fee. Their costs will be variable according to whom you employ and what you ask them to do, but try to get an estimate of these in advance and make sure you budget for them. Fees for planning permission, building control, building standards and by-law approval are usually fixed and won't exceed more than a few hundred pounds.

INSURANCE

The type of policy you need will depend very much on the nature of your refurbishment project but may include public liability, employer's liability, and all-risks cover.

CONTINGENCY SUMS

A contingency sum is a reserve amount of money that you can use if you incur unexpected costs. This is essential in any rescued house project. You'll commonly be told that you should allow a contingency of around 10 per cent of the budget for the building works, but in my experience this is far too little. However well you plan and however well you manage, extra costs will always crop up. If you have no contingency you'll have to find a new source of money every time this happens. Pretty soon you'll end up facing demands you just can't meet. At best you'll have to find savings elsewhere (say bye-bye to the nice kitchen units, or forget the loft conversion); at worst the whole project could fail.

I'd suggest a minimum contingency of 20 per cent, perhaps even 25 per cent in cases where you have not completely worked out what you want or where you're not entirely certain how much work will be required. A good discipline to help you manage your contingency is to notionally put the cost towards an unnecessary luxury: perhaps a swanky bath, an extravagant piece of furniture or even a holiday. This will focus your mind and make you manage your budget well. If you manage not to spend your contingency you can reward yourself for your economy.

The odd person can afford to rescue
a house from their cash savings …
the rest of us need to find ways of
persuading other people to invest
their money in our dream.

13 FUNDING THE PROJECT

You'll probably need to borrow money to fund your rescued
house (a) to cover the cost of purchasing the property and (b)
to pay for the refurbishment or conversion works. You need to
arrange finance for both before you buy the property, otherwise
you could end up saddled with a wreck that you can't afford to
turn into a home. It's quite possible to borrow money to rescue
a house, but you'll need to do more preparation work than you
would in arranging a loan for a ready-to-move-into property.
Fortunately, there are lots of possibilities for grants and
subsidized loans that you may be able to take advantage of.

PAYING FOR THE PROPERTY

SECURING A MORTGAGE

Most people have to borrow money to buy a property, and there is vast industry of lenders and mortgage brokers providing products to cater for them. Unfortunately, not every member of this industry appreciates the excellent business opportunities that exist in the reuse of neglected properties. Many prospective purchasers of old houses have had to change their plans because their chosen lender didn't share their enthusiasm for rescuing a house. The problem is that lenders traditionally think only of themselves. How will they recover the money they have loaned you if everything goes horribly wrong? Their last resort is to repossess the property and sell it, but derelict properties aren't tempting prospects for lenders to try to sell in this situation, so funding for rescued house projects is seen by them as high-risk lending.

There has always been the odd lender specializing in this market, but there was usually the drawback of higher rate interest repayments. Happily, things are improving. A number of high street lenders are laudably seeking to improve their green credentials and are offering products to help developments that have a minimal environmental impact. Some have even launched specialist products for funding the reuse of empty properties (sometimes called brown mortgages). In many cases the interest rates for these products are no higher than standard mortgages. The market is changing fast and new products are being launched almost daily. A new development is the buy-to-renovate mortgage that I discuss later in this chapter. By the time you read this, no doubt other new products will have appeared, but this is a taster of what's available.

You don't necessarily need a specialist lender or a specialist product, but it's always advisable to check out what's available and who might lend you money. As a general rule, the bigger your deposit, the bigger choice you'll have. Some specialist mortgages will be available only for 80 to 85 per cent of the purchase price. The following list is by no means comprehensive, but will give you an idea about the sort of products on offer.

▶ *Norwich & Peterborough Building Society's* brown mortgage is designed specifically for borrowers planning to renovate or convert a neglected property. They positively encourage this as a route into owner-occupation. Borrowers get a free energy survey as part of the deal.

▶ *The Ecology Building Society* has been the saviour of many rescued house projects for years, offering mortgages when nobody else would. The society's mission has always been about environmental sustainability; it's not simply a recent convert. It not only recognizes that rescuing neglected properties makes good sense, it positively welcomes applications to fund empty property schemes. If you're converting a redundant commercial building to residential use, the EBS is likely to be more understanding than most.

▶ *Buildstore* offers a wide range of financial products aimed at self-builders and many are very useful to those wanting to fund a rescued house project. Buildstore's specially designed Accelerator mortgage lends up to 95 per cent of the initial property price or value, whichever is lower, plus 95 per cent of the renovation costs. This is issued in staged payments as work progresses but, instead of releasing funds in arrears as each fixed stage is completed, the money required for each stage is made available before work starts. Borrowers thus have the money in hand to pay for materials and labour. This advance-payment mortgage gives positive cashflow during the building work and lending 95 per cent of the property price and building costs makes it ideal for first-timers who have minimal capital.

▶ *The Co-operative Bank's* green mortgage isn't specifically designed for rescue projects, but could be used to fund such a scheme. The 'green' element is that for every mortgage on its books the bank makes a donation to Climate Care, an organization that works to reduce global warming. With your mortgage you get a free energy survey and an assurance that the bank isn't doing business with organizations that have poor environmental records. The green credentials of this mortgage mean that you should have a receptive ear for your project if you sell its environmental sustainability.

▶ *Tridos Bank* lends exclusively to projects with clear social and environmental objectives, either mortgages with up to 25-year repayment periods or short- to medium-term loans for periods of one to ten years.

HOW TO CHOOSE THE RIGHT MORTGAGE

To find the right mortgage for you, do your research thoroughly. Have a look on the internet; there are a number of excellent websites that make it easy to compare hundreds of mortgages at one time. Watch out, though; many lenders refuse to finance properties such as flats over shops or derelict buildings. An initial search may not highlight these restrictions so you might think you've found the perfect mortgage only to be disappointed when you come to apply.

Another option is to use a mortgage broker. You'll have to pay them a fee, but it could be money well spent. Broker's fees are normally paid on completion of the mortgage, so you shouldn't have to pay them anything if they don't find what you want. Sometimes they charge a flat fee and sometimes a percentage of the amount you borrow. Make sure you get an independent one, and beware of brokers calling themselves independent who may only offer the products of a handful of lenders. A proper independent broker will be able to sieve through the many unsuitable products until they reach the right one for you, which means that the amount you pay them could pale into insignificance compared with the amount of money they save you on your mortgage. What's more, they buy thousands of mortgages so have far more buying power than you could ever have on your own. This means that they may be able to get special deals such as a free survey or even a lower rate of interest.

AND IF YOU STILL CAN'T AFFORD IT . . .

If you're unable to raise enough money through a mortgage to be able afford to buy your property, don't give up just yet. There are three ways you can buy a property with government subsidy in the UK. These are generally intended to assist households on lower incomes into owner occupation, but they can sometimes be useful for those on middle incomes, too.

To find out which housing associations offer shared ownership in your area contact the Housing Corporation, for properties in England. Homepoint is the relevant body in Scotland, and all shared ownership in Northern Ireland is operated by the Northern Ireland Co-ownership Housing Association (whose website is worth a visit wherever you live). Shared ownership is no longer available in Wales. In Ireland, shared ownership schemes are operated by local authorities; to apply, contact the council covering your area.

SHARED OWNERSHIP

A cross between owning and renting, intended to give those who can't afford to get into home ownership a foothold on the property ladder. You buy a share in the property (usually between 25 and 50 per cent) and the remaining share is bought by a housing association. You then pay mortgage repayments to your lender on your share and pay rent to the housing association for theirs. When you can afford to, you can increase your proportion of ownership by buying the housing association's share, either all at once or gradually in a process called staircasing out. On the other hand, if money becomes tight you can staircase-down, selling your equity to the housing association and paying more rent. If you qualify, you may be able to receive housing benefit to cover some or all of the rental payments. Housing benefit is operated by local authorities, so contact yours to find out if you are eligible.

Anybody can apply for shared ownership housing although priority is often given to those currently living in social housing (a collective term for housing association and council housing) and those who have never owned a house before. The housing association will probably want to make a thorough check on your finances to ensure both that you are able to afford the mortgage and rental repayments and that you cannot afford to buy a house at full market price.

Traditionally, shared ownership involves the housing association buying the property itself and then selling you a share in it, but in the case of a rescued house project an arrangement known as do it-yourself shared ownership (DIYSO) would apply. This is where you find the property and both you and the housing association buy it jointly. Shared ownership housing was not designed for such projects, and indeed some local schemes may have conditions that preclude them, but

otherwise there is no reason why it shouldn't work. You might have to persuade your housing association that a rescued-house project is a good idea. Housing associations have strong links with local authorities, so enlist the support of your local authority's empty property officer if the property is empty.

HOMEBUY

An alternative to shared ownership is the UK-based Homebuy scheme under which you buy the property for 75 per cent of the market price and the other 25 per cent is bought by a housing association with a second mortgage (it is, in fact, an equity loan). You don't pay mortgage repayments, interest or rent on the second mortgage, but when you sell the property 25 per cent of the proceeds of the sale go to the housing association. Again, the Housing Corporation operates the scheme.

THE KEY WORKER LIVING PROGRAMME

If you or one of the people who will live in your property is a key worker there is a small chance this scheme could help you purchase the property. 'Key worker' is a curious term describing somebody whose job is key to the local area. In this context it generally means nurses, teachers, police, social workers, occupational therapists and fire fighters (although you should check because there are local variations; town planners are included in London, for example). The scheme operates in London, the south-east and eastern England. It is run by local housing associations or RSLs (Registered Social Landlords, a term more or less synonymous with housing association). It offers equity loans of up to £50,000 towards the purchase of the property (up to £100,000 for some teachers in London) in much the same way as the Homebuy scheme.

PAYING FOR THE WORK

Once you have arranged the finance to buy the property, how are you
going to pay for the work that will turn it into your home? Even if you
intend to do all the renovation or conversion work yourself you will still
need money to buy materials. If you don't have sufficient savings to cover
all the costs there are three main funding options: an extended mortgage,
a loan and or a grant. This is where a house-rescue project can really pay
dividends, because there are some excellent grants and low-interest loans
available to assist you. Grants are the most desirable of the three, so
I'll begin with them.

GRANTS

Rescuing a house fulfils the objectives of a whole raft of regeneration
initiatives up and down these islands. Many of them have funding available
in the form of grants, sometimes given as a percentage of the overall cost
of works, at other times restricted to a set limit. In many cases grants are
available for specific items such as installing solar panels or replacing
a thatched roof.

Some grants are available for one-off projects while others form
part of wider regeneration initiatives. The latter won't be available if
no regeneration schemes are under way or planned in your area, but
it's always better to be informed about what's out there.

Most grants originate from government departments, local authorities,
public sector quangos and voluntary sector organizations such as trust
funds. There are also a few private companies that provide money for
regeneration schemes. A guide to the main grant schemes is in the
appendix on p. 342. These are the main national ones, but many local
schemes exist too. A good place to enquire is your local authority; most
have regeneration officers and empty property officers who should
be able to provide details.

Locating sources of funding is fiendishly difficult and the application
process can be painfully slow and bureaucratic. But be persistent; the
money is there, and if you can convince the funder that your project will
assist the initiative's aims you could well be successful – eventually.

HOW TO APPLY FOR A GRANT

Your chances of making a successful application will depend as much on the way you present your application as on the merits of the project itself. The following are some tips that should help maximize your chances of success.

✚ Apply at the right time
Most funding bodies can't offer improvement grants once the work is under way, and it's practically impossible to get a grant for work that has already been completed. Find out early what the application process is for each grant and make your application part of the project planning process rather than an afterthought. Some grants can be made only at certain times of year. Contact the funder and find out when you should apply.

✚ Apply for the right grant
Find the funding body that best suits your project. This approach is much more likely to be successful than trying to design your project to fit in with a funder's requirements. If you don't meet a fundamental requirement of the grant, don't simply apply and hope for the best: you'll be wasting your time as well as theirs. If you're unsure whether your project is eligible, phone and ask.

✚ Follow the application procedure
Most funding bodies have strict application procedures. You might find this bureaucratic and irritating, but funders must be able to account for their spending fully. Most funders have experienced attempted fraud, and their procedures are in place to avoid people making off with what could have been your money.

✚ Make a good application
Take the time to complete your application well. Read the criteria of the grant and make sure your application addresses them all. Make sure you understand the objectives of the organization and why it's offering the grant. Some organizations are interested in enhancing the external appearance of a property, others in providing homes for low-income households. Tailor your application to address the important points. Make sure you include with the application all the information you're asked for.

✚ Don't expect a grant to pay for everything

Grant funders often have limited financial resources, and some (not all) prefer to offer a large number of small grants rather than a small number of large ones. Some will expect you to at least match the grant from other sources of funding.

✚ Do your feasibility study first

In all but the most straightforward renovation projects, some form of feasibility study will probably be required at an early stage. If you need to prepare a feasibility study, use the guidance in Chapter 4 to help. Many funders will insist on it as part of your application. More complex projects may also require a conservation plan, a business plan and a maintenance plan for the project after completion. Some funding bodies offer financial assistance to cover the preparation of these essential plans, as well as grant-aiding the work itself.

✚ Get support from others

Many projects can have an impact on the wider community: improving the look of a run-down part of town, creating short-term employment for builders or saving a building of architectural importance. Potential funders are more likely to support projects that can demonstrate these sorts of benefits, especially when the benefit meets one of the organization's objectives. If you can enlist public support by raising awareness and seeking the endorsement of groups and individuals with a voice in the local community this is bound to help your application. Some funders actually require evidence of public support to be submitted with your application.

Your chances of making a successful application will depend as much on the way you present your application as on the merits of the project itself.

LOANS

Most people need to borrow money not just to buy a property but to do it up, too. In fact, the renovation costs for many rescued houses are greater than their initial purchase price. On the face of it, getting a loan has never been easier. If your postbag is anything like mine you'll receive almost daily offers to lend you thousands, though I suspect that many of those would-be benefactors might be rather less enthusiastic once they learn what you want the money for.

Rescuing a house is something of a specialist area, so picking the right lender is important. You need to find one who is prepared to advance sufficient funds on the right terms for the project you have planned. There are a number of organizations who might do just that, and on far better terms than many high street banks would consider. A few options worth pursuing are listed below. Details of all organizations mentioned can be found in the directory.

MAXIMIZE YOUR MORTGAGE

When arranging your mortgage for the purchase of the property, put down as small a deposit as possible and use any cash you have to pay for the renovation work. Obviously, this will result in a larger mortgage, but the repayments will still probably be lower than the combination of a small mortgage and a separate commercial loan to cover the cost of refurbishment. Having said that, many banks and building societies impose penalties if a mortgage represents a very high percentage of a property's value (see p. 314), so do your sums first.

BUY-TO-RENOVATE MORTGAGES

If you need to borrow money both to buy the property and to pay for the costs of renovation, it can make sense to package your loans in one product. Most lenders aren't too keen on this idea for the reasons discussed on p. 320, but there are a few providers of specific buy-to-renovate mortgages. These lenders are largely the same ones offering brown mortgages (see p. 320–21). There may be a small interest-rate penalty, but the repayments are unlikely to be more than for a separate mortgage and loan. Those offering buy-to-renovate products include the Norwich and Peterborough Building Society, the Ecology Building Society and Buildstore.

LOCAL AUTHORITY LOANS

The UK government has long been promoting alternatives to grants to help owners pay for improvements to their property and local authorities are getting the message. Some councils have abandoned housing grants altogether in favour of loans; others offer both. Loan schemes vary from council to council, and there are often conditions attached, but there can be some real advantages over commercial lenders. You may be offered a below-market or even a zero rate of interest. The loan period is usually five years and most councils will allow you to borrow up to £20,000, though schemes vary from one local authority to another. The loan application procedure is very similar to that for local authority housing grants (see p. 340). Loans are available for renovating houses in Ireland, too, targeted at low-income households. Application should be made to the Housing Grants Section of the Department of the Environment.

ARCHITECTURAL HERITAGE FUND LOANS

The Architectural Heritage Fund offers grants for projects involving the repair for reuse of buildings that are listed, are in a conservation area or are in some other way acknowledged as being of historic interest. Currently the fund offers loans only for projects involving buildings owned by charities. Before you dismiss your project as ineligible, consider setting up your own charity specifically for the purpose. Many people have formed building preservation trusts and have been awarded grants. This isn't a devious fiddle; the fund positively welcomes such as approach and will offer advice and help on setting up a trust.

The fund can lend up to £500,000 per project, usually subject to the loan amount not exceeding 70 per cent of the estimated open market value of the property. Interest rates are well below market lenders' rates and the loan period is normally two or three years. Applications are considered at quarterly meetings and should be submitted at least six weeks before the meeting at which the decision will be taken.

THE CHARITY BANK

Another option if your project could be classed as a social enterprise is the Charity Bank. It was set up in 2002 to provide finance to communities or organizations that commercial lenders either couldn't or wouldn't assist. In fact, being turned down by a commercial lender is almost an eligibility criterion, since the bank will lend only in cases where other banks or building societies either won't make a loan at all, or will only do so on unacceptable terms. Jointly regulated by the Financial Services Authority and the Charity Commission, the Charity Bank is the first combined charity and bank in the UK.

Organizations eligible to borrow from the bank include registered or exempt charities, community and voluntary associations, community businesses, social enterprises and social landlords. The loan must be for exclusively charitable purposes. The bank will also lend to for-profit companies if the loan is for exclusively charitable purposes.

Loans are generally between £3,000 and £250,000, although as a first-time borrower you should expect to be offered an amount nearer the lower end of that range. Loan periods are generally between three months and ten years.

CASE STUDY_7 Maxwell's notes from the frontline

Sally and Barry Walshe and their two children live together in a first-floor flat in Kensal Green in North London. Sally is a nursing sister, and Barry an ambulance driver. They met at work and have been together for twenty-five years. Their son is a semi-professional footballer and their daughter works at a London taxi showroom.

The family have a budget of £240,000; in London terms a small sum for a family of four.

Their Vision

In order to give their son a proper adult life, Barry and Sally have vacated the master bedroom and sleep on a bed jammed into one of the two smaller bedrooms. These arrangements have been in place for seven years, and it is clear that both Barry and Sally are finding this increasingly intolerable.

Quite simply, they want three proper bedrooms and a garden. This is a lot to ask for on their budget, and for this reason they all believe that an empty property could give more for their money.

The Front Runners
Upper Edmonton, London

A typical late Victorian, two-storey brick property with a back garden. Although it's small, most of the adjoining properties, which are in a good condition, have substantial rear extensions, and there is little doubt that, with imagination, the property could provide what the family are looking for.

The area

Upper Edmonton started life as a hamlet. In 1842 the Edmonton Workhouse was built in Silver Street, and in 1872 the station at Silver Street opened on a direct line to Liverpool Street, leading in the 1880s and 1890s to large-scale developments of terraced houses similar to the one Barry and Sally are interested in.

This house first appears in an 1893 street directory, at which time it was occupied by Hubert Merling. It is currently owned by Harry Lucas, whose parents moved into the house in 1921 and who bought it in 1952. Harry was born in the house in 1925. When his parents died they left the property to him and his sister. Harry married and moved out. His sister stayed, later moving to a nursing home before her death in 2005, leaving the property empty.

Harry Lucas was clearly very keen to dispose of the property and had already generated a great deal of local interest.

Golders Green, London

The obviously vacant ground-floor flat that caught the Walshes eye is part of an early 1930s semi-detached house that has been converted into two flats. A glimpse through the window shows that building work had been left unfinished.

The flat would provide the family with the accommodation they need, if planning consent could be obtained for an essential extension. There have been similar extensions to adjoining properties and there is certainly enough garden space and no issues of overlooking neighbours. Until building work started a year or so ago, the house was a dental surgery with space for two dentists, a reception area, a waiting room, a toilet and a small kitchen.

The flat is owned by a professional property developer, who met Barry and Sally and talked about the property. He was surprisingly forthcoming in explaining that as the property was now a building site he did not have to pay any Council Tax, which was why the refurbishment was only half completed. He was happy to sell, but wanted to obtain planning consent for an extension first.

The area

Golders Green was a small hamlet six miles North of London. Throughout the sixteenth, seventeenth and eighteenth centuries it was a popular destination for day excursions, allowing Londoners to escape from the over-crowding and pollution of the city. The underground station on the Northern Line opened in 1907 and paved the way for a new smart suburb of large semi-detached houses and luxury flats, which, in the 1920s, became popular with the city's Jewish community.

What Next?

The house in Golders Green was a real possibility. The rub was the budget: the project would undoubtedly cost more, and on exploring the government's key-worker loan scheme they discovered that the property did not qualify for any of the £50,000 loan because it required so much work. This is sheer stupidity, as by granting a loan for this empty and semi-derelict property the government would kill two birds with one stone: putting a perfectly good flat into use and providing key workers with the accommodation they need. We can only hope the government changes its mind in the future, and expands the loan system. Barry and Sally continue to explore alternative ways of purchasing the property and negotiating the price with the owner.

OTHER FORMS OF FUNDING

FAMILY AND FRIENDS

Even if your friends or relatives have money that you could borrow, approaching them can be difficult. Unlike other forms of borrowing, this one has all sorts of emotional complications. If things go wrong, you potentially have more to lose than money. The advantage, of course, is that relatives may be prepared to trust you when commercial lenders wouldn't, and possibly on more favourable terms. There are financial advantages for your relatives, too. Investment in property has seen fantastic returns over the last twenty years (with only the occasional blip), but it's a difficult market to enter unless you can buy a whole property. This way, your lenders can buy a smaller share of a potentially profitable enterprise.

TELEVISION PRODUCTION COMPANIES

It can hardly have escaped your notice that property renovation is a popular subject for television (*How to Rescue a House* included). Some series are simple reporting, but others offer design advice and funding to help owners achieve their (or the programme makers') objectives. If you're happy for the world (or at least one channel's viewing audience) to see what you're up to you can apply to the programme production company to see if your project is suitable for inclusion in the next series.

SPLIT YOUR PROPERTY INTO TWO

A popular way of subsidizing the cost of refurbishing a large house is to turn part of it into another dwelling and then let it or sell it. The most practical option is to turn a basement into a self-contained flat, although all sorts of other options may be possible. You'll need planning permission to create a new dwelling, and your costs will increase with the extra plumbing, insulation, kitchen and bathroom required. You'll also need to arrange for separate service supplies, a new postal address from the Post Office and a council tax valuation for separate billing. Despite all this, the income from letting or selling will usually more than outweigh the additional costs. Before you begin, get some advice from local estate agents on the likely rental income or sale price you might expect and what local demand is for. You can then plan a new dwelling that will have most appeal to the local housing market.

It can hardly have escaped your notice that property renovation is a popular subject for television.

SELL SOME LAND

If your property is on a large plot it may be possible to raise some money by selling some of the land. By far the most lucrative way of doing this is to sell it for residential building development with outline planning permission. A plot of land for development needs to be at least 8m x 8m and either alongside or accessible from a road. In some parts of the country, especially in villages, you'll need a bigger plot than this. Minimum sizes for building plots are usually given in the council's borough plan or unitary development plan. Government policy in the UK encourages increased building density, so smaller plots may be acceptable to planners in certain areas.

In some parts of the country building land is in such short supply that land prices are exorbitant and even a tiny plot can command a very high price. Land prices in London are well known, but plots inside the building line of many desirable villages can be even higher. The drawbacks are that you lose some or all of your garden and will almost certainly have another property potentially overlooking you and your neighbours, which probably won't make you the most popular resident of the area.

If you want to sell land, ask your architect about getting outline planning permission. See Chapter 8 for more on permissions.

PLANNING GAIN

Very occasionally you may be able to get some financial help towards your project from local developers. Unlikely as this may sound, the planning gain system is being used in new and innovative ways by some local authorities and some rescued-house projects have been the beneficiaries. Planning gain has already been alluded to on p.183 under 'Conditional consent', but some more detail here may be useful.

The system works like this. A developer applies for planning permission to build, say, a supermarket. The consequences of building it might be both positive (increased choice and convenience) and negative (visual impact, increased vehicle and pedestrian traffic). The local authority would prefer to avoid the negative impacts, so may grant permission with planning gain conditions requiring the developer to pay for changes to the local infrastructure such as an improved road layout or new pedestrian crossings etc. But increasingly planning gain is being interpreted much more widely. For example, a new commercial building would need more employees, but where are they going to live? It's not unusual for local authorities to require developers to either provide housing, or provide money to pay for more housing. In such circumstances it's possible that planning gain money held by a local authority could be used on your project.

It's certainly worth a phone call or two to ask whether any planning gain money exists that you might use. Contact your local authority's empty property officer or planning officer. Agreements are often referred to as 'section 106' or 'section 278' agreements, these being the sections of the Town and Country Planning Act 1990 and the Highways Act 1980, respectively, relevant to planning gain conditions.

GETTING THE MOST FROM YOUR TAX ALLOWANCES

Rescuing a house, like pretty much everything else that involves spending money, provides an opportunity for the taxman to sting you. That might not seem very fair; after all, I've been saying all through this book that the government supports rescue projects. Well, life is never completely fair, but if you know what you're doing you can take advantage of several tax allowances and minimize the tax you have to pay. The UK government has in recent years introduced a number of tax incentives aimed at encouraging people to return empty properties to use. Not all of these incentives are well publicized and it's important that you know which ones apply in your case. Making full use of such allowances can make a substantial saving on the overall cost of the project and could very well be crucial to a project's viability. Allowances are made on stamp duty, capital allowances, VAT, and council tax.

STAMP DUTY

Stamp duty is a tax levied on the purchase of most property and also on shares. The duty is levied as a percentage of the sale price. The current rates for the UK are shown in the table opposite. In 2001 the government removed stamp duty on residential property sales up to £150,000 in so-called disadvantaged areas. Substantial portions of the country are covered, so before you say that your area is far from disadvantaged, pay a visit to the Inland Revenue website. The appropriate page has a search facility; enter the property's postcode to discover whether the area it's in is considered disadvantaged. Disadvantaged-area discounts for commercial property were discontinued in the 2005 budget.

In the Republic of Ireland things are generally more expensive and more complicated. The rates for residential property are given opposite, but if you're converting a non-residential building into a house, different rules apply. If you're buying the property as your main home and the floor area is less than 125 m² (roughly the size of a small four-bedroomed house) you may be exempt from stamp duty altogether. Unfortunately, the government won't just take your word for it. You need to get a floor area certificate issued by your local council.) If the floor area is more than 125 m² then stamp duty is paid on the site value or 25 per cent of the full value of the property, whichever is the greater.

Unlike in the UK stamp duty in Ireland is levied on the whole cost of the transaction. This precludes adoption of the practice, widespread in the UK, of underpaying for a property and overpaying an equal amount for fittings.

The rates apply only to residential property or to the value of the residential component of a property. A different set of stamp duty rates applies to non-residential property (see bottom table, opposite).

If you're buying a property that is part residential and part commercial – a flat with a shop below, for example – you'll need to apportion a value to each part and pay the appropriate rate of stamp duty for each. There is also a small duty payable on mortgages in Ireland that is additional to stamp duty.

UK-stamp duty rates

Sale price	Disadvantaged area	Other areas
Up to £120,000	0%	0%
£120,001 to £150,000	0%	1%
£150,001 to £250,000	1%	1%
£250,001 to £500,000	3%	3%
£500,000 or more	4%	4%

Irish residential property stamp duty rates*

Purchase price*	First-time buyers	Other owner-occupiers	Investors
Up to €127,000	0%	0%	9%
€127,001 to €190,000	0%	3%	9%
€190,001 to €254,000	3%	4%	9%
€254,001 to €317,500	3.75%	5%	9%
€317,501 to €381,000	4.5%	6%	9%
€381,001 to €635,000	7.5%	7.5%	9%
Over #eu635,000	9%	9%	9%

Irish commercial property stamp duty rates

Purchase price	
Up to €6,350	0%
€6,351 to €12,700	1%
€12,701 to €19,050	2%
€19,051 to €31,750	3%
€31,751 to €63,500	4%
€63,501 to €76,200	5%
Over €76,200	6%

* The odd amounts
in the first column of the
table result from the fact
that it was originally
compiled in Irish punts
but has subsequently been
converted to euros.

CAPITAL ALLOWANCES

Capital allowances permit taxpayers to write off the costs of capital assets they have acquired against their taxable income. In the UK not all capital expenditure is allowable and until recently residential property was one of the exceptions. Recent changes mean that the costs of refurbishing an empty property can now be set against taxable income, but only if the property is made available for short-term letting. Hence it's unlikely that capital allowances will be helpful to you in creating your own home. There are many other conditions, but tax law is really outside the scope of this guide. Further information can be found on the Inland Revenue website.

VAT

We're all familiar with this one. VAT is charged on many goods and services at the point of sale. At the time of writing the standard rate is 17.5 per cent in the UK and 20 per cent in Ireland. VAT isn't charged on most property transactions (although in Ireland transactions of commercial property that were built after 31 October 1972 and have been altered or extended since are subject to a VAT rate of 12.5 per cent). In general, however, you will have to pay VAT on refurbishment and building costs. Both the UK and Irish governments have in recent years made many changes to VAT rates associated with building work and more could follow, so check the latest position before you start.

In Ireland most building costs are subject to VAT at a reduced rate of 12.5 per cent, although some are fully rated at 20 per cent. In the UK currently no VAT is payable on building costs associated with new-build property and conversions of non-residential properties to residential use, but until recently costs associated with most conversion and refurbishment work were charged at the full 17.5 per cent. Following a successful campaign by the Empty Homes Agency, the government has made changes aimed at encouraging the reuse of empty properties. The longer your property has been empty, the less VAT you pay.

With most of these exemptions and discounts, VAT is initially charged at the full rate and a rebate is claimed at the end of the project. The rebate process isn't complicated, but needs to be planned for properly to avoid losing out. You can only claim once, so you must get it right first time.

If you employ a VAT-registered builder to carry out the construction work, your builder should, in theory, simply charge you the reduced rate. In practice, your builder may be unaware of these VAT discounts so you should enlighten them beforehand to ensure that you are invoiced correctly. You'll probably still end up buying some materials directly yourself, even if just the odd tin of paint. You can still reclaim the VAT discount on such items.

In general, VAT is payable on construction materials, labour costs and professional fees. The owner of the property usually pays it to the provider of the goods or services. To qualify for a discounted rate the onus is on you to prove how long your property has been empty. You could contact the utility providers and ask them to confirm when utilities were disconnected, or you could contact your council's empty property officer. Customs and Excise will usually accept a letter from either of these sources as sufficient evidence. The reduced rates are shown in the table on p. 338.

HOW TO RECLAIM VAT

You reclaim your VAT all in one go from UK Customs and Excise at the end of the project. Before you do this, request a copy of the DIY Builder's Refund System Guidance Note from Customs and Excise, which provides all the information you need. Ask also for VAT Notice 719 (available on the Customs and Excise website or on request by phoning the advice line). Do this at the beginning of the project, not the end, because if you don't do things right at each stage it's virtually impossible to correct mistakes retrospectively. You must make your claim within three months of completion. This doesn't necessarily mean three months from the day you move in – Customs and Excise appreciate that you might move in before everything is finished – but a delay of more than six months is likely to arouse suspicion.

You will require valid VAT receipts for all the goods and services on which you want to reclaim VAT. Collect these as the project progresses and keep them in a safe place. Photocopies aren't accepted. A valid receipt is one made out to you with your name and address and the supplier's VAT number on it.

The rules concerning what you can reclaim VAT on are a little complicated, but are based on a simple principle. If the cost relates to a permanent fixture in the property then you can reclaim the VAT but if it's for a movable item then you can't. So, for example, a new roof is reclaimable but a new cooker isn't. For guidance on exactly what's included and what isn't see the Customs and Excise Guidance Note 719. It's a good idea to discuss any 'borderline' items with Customs and Excise before you buy them, ideally at the planning stage before you start work.

VAT cannot be reclaimed on professional fees for architects, surveyors and the like, but if you pay for a design-and-build package the VAT can be reclaimed on the total bill, including the design element.

If the property is a listed building the rules are different. Illogically, alterations to listed buildings are zero-rated, but repair work isn't, which is hardly an incentive to preserve the character of our historic buildings.

One last tip: if you buy materials in other EU countries you can still reclaim VAT in the same way. A number of French and Belgian building suppliers have set up large outlets in the Channel ports to tap into the market for cross-Channel shopping. Their prices are very competitive, and if you have time to make the trip you can make some big savings. On a more practical level, this is helpful for projects in both Irelands, since supplies may be purchased on either side of the border.

These tax allowances really aren't very well known, but making full use of them can be crucial to the viability of rescuing a house.

Reduced UK VAT rates on empty property conversions

Period property has been empty	Conversion of non-residential properties to residential use	Repairs and alterations to residential properties	Repairs to residential listed buildings	Alterations to residential listed buildings	Sub-dividing a residential property
Up to 3 years	0%	no reduction	no reduction	0%	5%
3 to 10 years	0%	5%	5%	0%	5%
Over 10 years	0%	0%	0%	0%	0%

COUNCIL TAX

Council tax is charged on most properties in the UK as a means of funding local authority expenditure. There are various exemptions and discounts and some of these apply to empty property. Originally empty properties were exempt altogether, but this was quickly perceived as an incentive to owners to keep their properties empty. The current position allows local authorities to set an empty-property discount if they consider one appropriate, or indeed not to offer a discount at all.

If you find yourself to be the owner of an empty property, albeit temporarily, you're entitled to claim exemption from council tax payment for up to six months. After this period you can apply for a discount, if available.

If the property is in such poor repair that it's uninhabitable you may be entitled to an exemption for up to twelve months. You'll need to supply documentary evidence such as a builder's schedule of works or surveyor's report showing the repairs required to make the property habitable. The local authority will then decide how long it should reasonably take to carry out the repairs and grant an exemption for that period up to a maximum of one year. If you think that a year is unreasonable (frankly, I can't think of many circumstances when it might be), you can appeal to the Valuation Office Agency and request that the property be made exempt from council tax altogether, although this is hardly the action of somebody who intends to rescue a house.

As your refurbishment project nears completion you need to let the local authority know so that they can adjust the council tax to the normal rate. When exactly to do this is a moot point. Most local authorities will expect you to notify them when the property is more or less complete, i.e. when everything is done bar a few snagging items. You could delay until the day you move in, but don't forget that the exemption is claimed on the basis that the property is uninhabitable, not uninhabited. The day on which it becomes reasonable to live in it again is really the day you should start paying council tax.

Ireland has a system of local authority rates but most residential property is exempt. Instead, local authorities charge levies for individual services such as water connection and rubbish collection. Whilst a property is unoccupied you probably won't need these services, so can apply for exemption.

CONCLUSION: A GUILT-FREE HOME

I promised you that by following the advice in this book you could create a guilt-free home for yourself. In today's society, freedom from guilt is a pretty rare feeling.

This is why I really wanted to tell you about the one thing in life I've discovered to which the usual rules don't apply: rescuing a house. For once, the option that is right for the environment is the one that's good for you too. As you'll have gathered by now, rescuing a house is a hard-work option, but we're pretty remarkable individuals when you think about it, and most of us are quite capable of completing this project.

I hope that this book has opened your eyes to a wider choice of houses to find and buy than you had thought possible before, given you more options for altering, redesigning and restoring old properties and shown you more ways to save money and meet the costs of creating your home. I hope also that you have learned something about where to go for help, who to ask for advice and the pitfalls to avoid. And, lastly, I hope you'll have learned how the choices you make really do make a difference. By rescuing a house you can ease your conscience about all the other things in your life that you know you ought to do — but don't.

APPENDIX: GRANTS

Trying to list all the grants available to help with rescuing a house is a bit like trying to explain the price of fish. Grants come and go, conditions are imposed and removed, eligibility criteria change, money becomes available then dries up again. The grants set out here are the main nationally awarded incentives that at the time of writing were available to assist with the costs of rescuing a house, but you should keep your eyes open for new grants and locally available funding. Not everything listed here will be available to everyone, but just as the fish market always has something for sale, there's bound to be something here for you too. Contact details for all bodies mentioned are in the directory.

LOCAL AUTHORITY HOUSING RENEWAL GRANTS

Approximately half of all UK local authorities offer some form of grant to help private owners get empty properties back into use. The amounts on offer and the conditions of the grant are set locally by each authority. It's a common condition that property is let out for social housing for a few years after the grant has been paid, but in most cases you're free to do what you want with the property after this period has elapsed. Grant conditions rarely last more than five years. Some councils offer grants specifically designed to help people renovate empty property to live in themselves, though very rarely to buy and renovate property that is currently occupied. A subsidy is sometimes available to help first time buyers in Ireland, but in the UK it's more common for local authorities to offer low-cost loans instead.

In theory, all local authorities publish a housing renewal policy stating what grants, loans and other assistance is on offer to help property owners, and how to apply for them. It should be obtainable from their website or by phoning their private sector housing or regeneration services section. For properties in Scotland, see the Empty Homes Initiative opposite.

COUNTRYSIDE STEWARDSHIP SCHEME

This is operated in England and Wales by DEFRA (Department of Farming and Rural Affairs), part funded by the EU. It aims to sustain landscape beauty and diversity, protect wildlife habitats and conserve archaeological sites and historical features. Refurbishing a neglected property may attract funding if it is of architectural importance. Applications are invited annually with a deadline of 30 April each year. There is a handbook published yearly which you can obtain from your local DEFRA rural development service office.

HERITAGE COUNCIL BUILDINGS AT RISK PROGRAMME

This scheme is operated by the Heritage Council in Ireland and covers the whole of the Republic. The council maintains a database of buildings at risk and grants are available only for buildings on this list. Grants are normally 50 per cent of the cost of works. The programme is an annual one and the amounts available may differ from year to year. The register is reviewed and published around September each year and applications can be made up until February of the following year.

HERITAGE LOTTERY FUND

This is one of the National Lottery 'good causes'. It aims to assist with repair and regeneration of the historic environment in towns and cities throughout the UK. The fund has helped return many empty properties to use. If you have a historic property in a prominent town centre location, there is a good chance of assistance. Usually the fund asks that you display a plaque on the building to acknowledge its contribution. Grants are available from £50,000 upwards and there is no upper limit. This is a rolling programme so you can apply at any time.

MILLENNIUM AWARD SCHEME

Another National Lottery 'good cause', this is a scheme with broad aims. There is no typical recipient but successful applications all demonstrate a benefit to the community. Building a house for yourself doesn't immediately seem to fit, but remember that empty and neglected properties have an adverse impact on the environment and the community. If you're unsuccessful elsewhere, this one might be worth a try. Grants are offered from £1,000 to £10,000 and again it's a rolling programme, so you can apply at any time. Millennium awards are offered across the UK by the Millennium Awards Fellowship.

EMPTY HOMES INITIATIVE

This scheme is funded by the Scottish parliament and offered through many Scottish local authorities. Local authorities make annual bids to the parliament for funding, which is awarded on the basis of how good their local scheme is judged to be. At the time of writing the scheme has been suspended, and some local authorities operate their own schemes. When in operation, the application procedure is much the same as that for a local authority housing renewal grant in England and Wales (see above).

ENGLISH CITIES FUND

This is a scheme operated by the government's regeneration agency, funded by English Partnerships and two private sector partners, AMEC and Legal and General. It aims to regenerate areas on the fringes of towns and cities that have found it difficult to compete with the town centre. A major objective is to bring brownfield sites back into use. (Empty properties count as brownfield sites.) It's unlikely that you'd be granted funds as an individual, but as part of larger regeneration scheme you may qualify. There are phased bidding rounds and you'll need to contact English Partnerships to find out how and when you should apply.

ENERGY DISCOUNT SCHEMES

When the electricity supply industry was privatized in the UK the government introduced regulations requiring energy suppliers to reduce CO_2 emissions by its customers. This led many suppliers to offer discounts and incentives on insulation and energy saving appliances. What is available to you will depend on who your supplier is, but here are a few examples:

⇒ Most suppliers offer discounts on cavity wall insulation. Some will offer up to 90 per cent.

⇒ Low energy light bulbs sell in high street shops for about £5 to £7 and can reduce your electricity bill by a similar amount. You can often buy them from your electricity supplier at their cost price of about £2 each.

⇒ Some suppliers offer discounts on energy efficient appliances such as fridges and washing machines.

HERITAGE ECONOMIC REGENERATION SCHEME

A scheme funded by English Heritage and a number of local authorities with the aim of regenerating run-down urban and rural conservation areas. The grants are normally given in conjunction with a local authority grant. The local authority grant funds internal works and the HERS grant funds external and structural repairs and reinstatement of lost architectural features. Application should be made to your local authority, who will then apply to English Heritage for the matching funding. (You should apply to your council's conservation officer or planning department. For further details of the scheme, contact English Heritage.)

GAP FUNDING DERELICTION AID

Provided by English Partnerships, these grants are normally available only for large-scale regeneration schemes, but if your property falls within a scheme you could be eligible. Grants are available to support projects including the reclamation of economically damaged land or buildings, so that they can be made suitable for new uses. You'll need to apply to your local regional development agency. There are nine regional development agencies in England and one covering the whole of Wales. For contact details see the RDA website www.englandsrdas.com.

ENERGY EFFICIENCY GRANTS

These grants are available across the UK for a huge number of different applications, but they tend to be regional. In one part of the country you may be able to apply for a grant to pay for a condensing boiler and in another for one to pay for cavity wall insulation. Grants also tend to be offered only for a limited time. This is because funding for such grants is often for specific initiatives, so when the money runs out the grants are no longer offered. Grants are offered by local authorities and utility suppliers, but they are usually coordinated through local energy advice centres. These centres are usually located in council offices but are independently run. You'll be able to find out which one covers your area by looking in the phone book or Yellow Pages under energy advice. Your local centre may be located in the offices of a council outside your immediate area because advice centres often cover more then one local authority area. An easy way to discover what energy grants you might be eligible for is to use the grant finder tool on the Energy Saving Trust website, www.saveenergy.co.uk.

GAP FUNDING HERITAGE AID

As with dereliction aid, this is offered by English Partnerships for large-scale regeneration schemes. The scheme aims to secure repair, rehabilitation and restoration of historic buildings and conservation areas.

LOCAL AUTHORITY CONSERVATION GRANT SCHEME FOR PROTECTED STRUCTURES

Grants are available for repair and renovation of protected structures in the Republic of Ireland. Usually the grant is 50 per cent of the cost of works up to a maximum of €13,000, although 75 per cent up to a maximum of €25,000 is awarded in special cases.

NEW DEAL FOR COMMUNITIES (NDC)

There are thirty-nine NDC schemes operating in England and Wales. Funds are provided by the UK government's Neighbourhood Renewal Unit as part of its larger New Deal programme. The aim is to tackle deprivation in the poorest neighbourhoods in the country, bridging the gap between them and the rest of the population by giving local people the resources to address their problems. The precise objectives vary from one scheme to another, but if your property is within one of the NDC areas it may be worth contacting them to see if there is any potential for funding your project. You'll need to apply to your local NDC board. Bidding arrangements vary but they'll be able to advise you how to proceed. If you're local to the area you have a greater chance of success. To find out whether your property is within an NDC area contact the Neighbourhood Renewal Unit or your local council's regeneration department.

SINGLE REGENERATION BUDGET

This is a series of schemes funded by the UK government. The aim is to enhance the quality of life of people in areas of need by reducing the gap between deprived and other areas and among different groups. The SRB schemes have now been subsumed into a new funding arrangement for the regional development agencies but existing schemes that were started before this merger will operate for their duration as planned. Like NDC programmes, SRB schemes operate on a geographical basis. You'll need to find out whether your property is an area that is covered. To do so contact your local regional development agency.

SOLAR PANEL GRANTS

The UK Department of Trade and Industry (DTI) offers two different grants to encourage people to install solar panels. The first, the photovoltaic demonstration programme, subsidizes the cost of installing photovoltaic solar roofs. Grants of up to 50 per cent are available. You must use an accredited contractor and must supply two estimates. For a directory of accredited contractors contact the British Photovoltaic Association.

The DTI also offers grants for solar hot water panels under its clear skies programme. This pays a subsidy of £500 towards the cost of a system. Details on both schemes are available through the Energy Saving Trust, the government's energy advice agency.

THATCHING-GRANTS

Available only in the Republic of Ireland, these grants are awarded for the renewal or repair of thatched roofs. Applications must be made to the Housing Grants Section of the Irish Department of the Environment.

DIRECTORY

All the organizations, suppliers, funders, books and magazines mentioned in the text are listed here with their contact details. The first section is a general contact list, followed by a list of funders and other providers of money to help you pay for your project, a list of suppliers and products, and lastly a reading list of books and magazines referred to in the text.

USEFUL CONTACTS

An Taisce – Irish National Trust
Tailors Hall, Back Lane, Dublin 8
+353 1 454 1786 / info@antaisce.org
www.antaisce.org

Asbestos Removal Contractors Association
ARCA House, 237 Branston Road, Burton upon Trent,
Staffordshire DE14 3BT
01283 531126 / www.arcaweb.org.uk

Association of British Investigators
48 Queens Road, Basingstoke, Hampshire RG21 7RE
01256 816390 / abi@globalnet.co.uk
www.assoc-britishinvestigators.org.uk

Bat Conservation trust
15 Cloisters House, 8 Battersea Park Road, London SW8 4BG
020 7627 2629 / www.bats.org.uk

British Hydropower Association
Unit 12 Riverside Park, Station Rd, Wimborne,
Dorset / BH21 1QU 01202 886622
info@british-hydro.org / www.british-hydro.org

British Institute of Architectural Technologists
397 City Road, London EC1V 1NH
020 7278 2206 or 0800 731 5471
info@biat.org.uk / www.biat.org.uk

British Photovoltaic Association
National Energy Centre, Davy Avenue, Knowhill,
Milton Keynes MK5 8NG
01908 442291 / enquiries@pv-uk.org.uk
www.pv-uk.org.uk

British Wood Preserving and Damp Proofing Association
1 Gleneagles House, Vernon Gate, Derby DE1 1UP
01332 225100 / www.bwpda.co.uk

The Council for Registered Gas Installers (CORGI)
1. Elmwood, Chineham Park, Crockford Lane, Basingstoke, Hants
RG24 8WG / 0870 401 2300 (registration validity check)
enquiries@corgi-gas.com / www.corgi-gas.com

Countryside Council for Wales
Maes Y Ffynnon, Fford Penrhos, Bangor, Gwynedd
LL57 2DN / 01248 370444
enquiries@ccw.gov.uk / www.ccw.gov.uk

DEFRA
Lower ground floor, Ergon House, c/o Nobel House,
17 Smith Square, London SW1 3JR
helpline@defra.gsi.gov.uk / www.defra.gsi.gov.uk

Draught Proofing Advisory Association
PO Box 12, Haslemere, Surrey GU27 3AH
01428 654011 / dpaaassociation@aol.com
www.insulationassociation.org.uk

Drink Water Inspectorate
Ashdown House, 123 Victoria Street, London SW1E 6DE
020 7082 8024 / dwi.enquiries@defron.gsi.gov.uk
www.dwi.gov.uk

Empty Homes Agency
195–197 Victoria Street, London SW1E 5NE
020 7828 6288 / info@emptyhomes.com
www.emptyhomes.com

Energy Saving Trust
21 Dartmouth Street, London SW1H 9BP
0800 298 3978 / www.set.org.uk

English Heritage
PO Box 569, Swindon SN2 2YP / 0870 333 1181
customers@english-heritage.org.uk / www.ehsni.gov.uk

English Nature
Northminster House, Peterborough PE1 1UA
01733 455000 / enquiries@english-nature.org.uk
www.english-nature.org.uk

Environment Agency
Rio House, Waterside Drive, Aztec West, Almondsbury,
Bristol BS32 4UD / 0945 93333111
enquiries@environment-agency.gov.uk
www.environment-agency.gov.uk

External Wall Insulation Association
PO Box 12, Haslemere, Surrey GU27 3AH
01428 654011 / incaassociation@aol.com
www.inca-ltd.org.uk

Federation of Master Builders
Gordon Fisher House, 14–15 Great James Street,
London WC1N 3DP / 020 7242 7583
central@fmb.org.uk / www.fmb.org.uk

Friends of the Earth
26–28 Underwood Street, London N1 7JQ
020 7490 0881 / info@foe.co.uk / www.foe.co.uk

Forest Stewardship Council
Unit D, Station Buildings, Llanidloes, Powys SY18 6EB
01686 413916 / info@fsc-uk.org / www.fsc-uk.org

H M Customs and Excise
New Kings Beam House, 22 Upper Ground, London SE1 9PJ

National Advice Service – 0845 010 9000
Email – regional; see website for details
www.hmce.gov.uk

H M Land Charges Registry
Plumer House, Tailyour Road, Crownhill, Plymouth PL6 5HY
01752 636666 / www.www.landreg.gov.uk

H M Land Registry
32 Lincolns Inn Fields, London WC2A 3PH
020 7917 8888 / www.landreg.gov.uk.

Heritage Council Buildings at Risk Programme
Rothe House, Kilkenny / + 353 56 7770777
info@heritagecouncil.ie / www.heritagecouncil.ie

Inland Revenue
Somersert House, Strand, London WC2R 1LB
(or regional offices; see website for details)
020 7667 4001 / stamp duty helpline 0845 6030135
www.inlandrevenue.gov.uk

The Institution of Structural Engineers
11 Upper Belgrave Street, London SW1X 8BH
020 7235 4535 / mail@istructe.org.uk
www.istructe.org.uk

National Radiological Protection Board
Chilton, Didcot, Oxon OX11 0RQ
01235 831600 / nrpb@nrpb.org
www.nrpb.org.uk

The Planning Inspectorate
Customer Support Unit, Room 3/15, Eagle Wing,
Temple Quay House, 2 The Square, Temple Quay, Bristol BS1 6PN
0117 372 6372 / www.planning-inspectorate.gov.uk

The Quality Mark Scheme
PO Box 445, Tower Court, Foleshill Enterprise Park,
Foleshill Road, Coventry CV6 5NY
0845 3008040 / qualitymarkscheme@capita.co.uk
www.qualitymark.org.uk

Radiological Protection Institute of Ireland (RPII)
3 Clonskeagh Square, Clonskeagh Road, Dublin 14
+353 1 269 77 66 / rpii@rpii.ie / www.rpii.ie

Radon Protection Hotline
BRE, Garston, Watford WD25 9XX
01923 664707 / radon@bre.co.uk / www.bre.co.uk/radon

The Royal Institute of the Architects of Ireland
8 Merrion Square, Dublin 2
+ 353 1 676 1703 / info@riai.ie / www.riai.ie

Royal Institute of British Architects (RIBA)
Construction House, 56–64 Leonard Street, London
EC2A 4LT / 020 7307 3700 / www.architecture.com

RIBA bookshop:
Construction House, 56–64 Leonard Street, London
EC2A 4LT / 020 7251 0791 / www.ribabooks.com

Royal Institution of Chartered Surveyors (RICS)
12 Great George St, London SW1P 3AD
020 7334 3776

RICS bookshops:
Surveyor Court, Westwood Business Park,
Coventry CV4 8JE / 020 7222 7000 x698
7 St Andrews Place, Cardiff CF10 3BE
029 2022 4414 / bookshop@rics.org.uk
www.ricsbooks.com

SAVE Britain's Heritage
77 Cowcross Street, London EC1M 6BP
020 7253 3500 / save@btinternet.com
www.savebritainsheritage.org.uk

The Scottish Civic Trust
42 Miller Street, Glasgow G1 1DT
0141 221 1466 / bar@scottishcivictrust.org.uk
www.scottishcivictrust.org.uk

Scottish Natural Heritage
12 Hope Terrace, Edinburgh EH9 2AS
0131 447 4784 / info@snh.gov.uk / www.snh.gov.uk

Shelter
88 Old Street, London EC1V 9HU
020 7505 4699 / info@shelter.org.uk / www.shelter.org.uk

Ulster Architectural Heritage Society
66 Donegall Pass, Belfast BT7 0BU
028 9055 0213 / info@uahs.co.uk / www.uhas.co.uk

FUNDERS

The Co-operative Bank plc
PO Box 101
1 Balloon Street, Manchester M60 4EP
0800 0288 288 / customerservice@co-operativebanck.co.uk
www.co-operativebank.co.uk

Co-ownership (Northern Ireland Co-ownership Housing Association Ltd)
Murray House, Murray Street, Belfast BT1 6DN
0800 333644 / nicha@co-ownership.org / www.co-ownership.org

Department of Environment – Eire
Housing Grants Section, Government Offices, Ballina,
Co. Mayo / 096 24200 / info@environ.ie / www.environ.ie

**Department of Trade and Industry
(clear skies programme)**
Clear Skies, BRE Ltd, Building 17, Garston,
Watford WD25 9XX / 08702 430 930 / info@clear-skies.org
www.clear-skies.org

Energy Saving Trust
21 Dartmouth Street, London SW1H 9BP
0800 298 3978 / media@est.co.uk
www.solarpvgrants.co.uk

English Partnerships
110 Buckingham Palace Road, London SW1W 9SA
020 7881 1600 / mail@englishpartnerships.co.uk
www.englishpartnerships.co.uk

Heritage Lottery Fund
Various regional addresses (phone or visit website for
more info) / 020 7591 6044 / www.hlf.org.uk

Homebond
Construction House, Canal Road, Dublin 6
+353 1 491 0210 / info@ezhome.ie / www.ezhome.ie

Homepoint
Communities Scotland, Thistle House, 91 Haymarket Terrace,
Edinburgh EH12 5HE / 0131 313 0044
homepoint@communitiesscotland.gov.uk
www.homepoint.communitiesscotland.gov.uk

DIRECTORY

THE HOUSING CORPORATION – AREA OFFICES

London
Waverley House, 7–12 Noel Street, London W1F 8BA
020 7292 4400 / london.info@housingcorp.gsx.gov.uk

South
Leon House, High Street, Croydon, Surrey CR9 1UH
020 8253 1400 / southeast.info@housingcorp.gsx.gov.uk
Beaufort House, 51 New North Road, Exeter EX4 4EP
01392 428200 / southwest.info@housingcorp.gsx.gov.uk

Central
Attenborough House, 109/119 Charles Street,
Leicester LE1 1FQ / 0116 242 4800
east.info@housingcorp.gsx.gov.uk
31 Waterloo Road, Wolverhampton WV1 4DJ
01902 795000
westmidlands.info@housingcorp.gsx.gov.uk

North
1 Park Lane, Leeds LS3 1EP
0845 230 7000
northeastern.info@housingcorp.gsx.gov.uk
Elisabeth House, 16 St Peter's Square, Manchester M2 3DF
0845 230 7000
northwest.info@housingcorp.gsx.gov.uk
Colonial Chambers, 3–11 Temple Street, Liverpool L2 5RH
0845 230 7000
merseyside.info@housingcorp.gsx.gov.uk

The Housing Corporation Corporate Services
Maple House, 149 Tottenham Court Road, London W1T 7BN
020 7393 2000 / enquiries@housingcorp.gsx.gov.uk
www.housingcorp.gov.uk

Millennium Awards Fellowship
The Millennium Commission, Freepost LON10626,
London SW1E 5YP / 020 7880 2072
starpeople@millennium.gov.uk / www.starpeople.org.uk

Neighbourhood Renewal Unit
Office of the Deputy Prime Minister, 3rd floor, Eland House,
Bressenden Place, London SW1E 5DU / 020 7944 3000
neighbourhoodrenewal@odpm.gsi.gov.uk
www.neighbourhoodrenewal.gov.uk

Norwich and Peterborough Building Society
Peterborough Business Park, Lynch Wood, Peterborough PE2 6WZ
0845 300 6727 / info@npbs.co.uk
www.npbs.co.uk

An Bord Pleanála
64 Marlborough Street, Dublin 1
01858 8100 / bord@pleanala.ie
www.pleanala.ie

The Architectural Heritage Fund
Clareville House, 26–27 Oxendon Street, London SW1Y 4EL
020 7925 0199 / ahf@ahfund.org.uk / www.ahfund.org.uk

Buildstore Mortgages
0870 870 9991
Buildstore Ltd, Kingsthorne Park, Nettlehill Road, Houstoun
Industrial Estate, Livingston EH54 5DB
0800 0185740
acceleratorenquiry@buildstore.co.uk
www.buildstore.co.uk

Charity Bank
PO Box 295, 25 Kings Hill Avenue, West Malling, Kent
ME19 4WD / 01732 520029

enquiries@charitybank.org / www.charitybank.org

Ecology Building Society
18 Station Road, Cross Hills, near Keighley, West Yorkshire
BD20 7EH / 0845 674 5566
info@ecology.co.uk / www.ecology.co.uk

Northern Ireland Co-ownership Housing Association Ltd
Murray House, Murray Street, Belfast BT1 6DN
0800 333 644
nicha@co-ownership.org / www.co-ownership.org

Tridos Bank
Brunel House, 11 The Promenade, Clifton, Bristol BS8 3NN
0117 973 9339
business@triodos.co.uk / www.triodos.co.uk

SUPPLIERS AND PRODUCTS

Aquaco (grey water systems)
Denndale House, Rectory Drive, Bidborough, Kent TN3 0UN
01892 506581
sales@aquaco.co.uk / www.waterdynamics.co.uk

Arcon (computer-aided design software)
Unit 2 Benley Stores, Bentley, Farnham, Surrey GU10 5HY
01420 520023
sales@3darchitect.co.uk / www.3darchitect.co.uk

Auro Organic Paints
Unit 2 Pamphillions Farm, Purton End, Debden, Saffron Walden
Essex CB11 3JT / 01799 543 077
sales@auroorganic.co.uk / www.auroorganic.co.uk

Balmoral Environmental Enginering (large water butts)
Balmoral Park, Loriston, Aberdeen AB12 3GY
01224 891000
tanks@balmoral.co.uk / www.balmoral-group.com

Bauder Ltd (planted roof systems)
Broughton House, Broughton Road, Ipswich IP1 3QR
01473 257671 / systems@bauder.co.uk / www.bauder.co.uk

Blackdown Hortcultural Consultants Ltd
(planted roof systems)
Street Ash Nursery, Chard, Somerset TA20 3HZ
01460 234582
jcw@blackdown.co.uk / www.blackdown.co.uk

Construction Resources (flax and cellulose insulation)
16 Great Guildford Street, London SE1 0HS
020 7450 2211
info@ecoconstruct.com / www.ecoconstruct.com

Easy Price Pro (DIY quantity surveying services
and software packages)
4 Chapel Road, Wattisfield, Suffolk IP22 2PS
01359 253463
services@easypricepro.com / www.easypricepro.com

Ecos Organic Paints
Unit 34 Heysham Business Park, Middleton, Heysham Lancashire
LA3 3PP / 01524 852371
mail@ecospaints.com / www.ecospaints.com

Estimators Ltd (estimating services)
12A High Street, Cheadle, Cheshire SK8 1AL
0161 286 8601
mail@estimators-online.com / www.estimators-online.com

Green Building Store (sustainable building products)
11 Huddersfield Road, Meltham, Holmfirth, West Yorkshire
HD9 4NJ / 01484 854898

info@greenbuildingstore.co.uk / www.greenbuildingstore.co.uk

HBXL (DIY quantity surveying services
and software packages)
City Point, Temple Gate, Bristol BS1 6PL / 0870 8502444
sales@hbxl.co.uk / www.hbxl.co.uk

John Brash and Co. (timber merchants)
The Old Shipyard, Gainsborough, Lincolnshire DN21 1NG
01427 613858
info@johnbrash.co.uk / www.johnbrash.co.uk

Lochplace Building Conservation Ltd
(specialist supplier of traditional building materials)
The Forge, Innishannon, Cork / +353 21 477 6677
mail@lochplace.com / www.lochplace.com

Norske Interiors (UK) Ltd (suppliers of Mermaid panelling)
Estate Road One, South Humberside Industrial Estate, Grimsby
DN31 2TA / 01472 240832
sales@norske-int.co.uk / www.norske-int.co.uk

Plotsearch (building-plot search agency)
Buildstore Ltd, Kingsthome Park, Nettlehill Road, Houstoun Industrial
Estate, Livingston EH54 5DB / 0870 8709994
plotsearchenquiry@buildstore.co.uk
www.buildstore.co.uk/findingland

Property Spy (building-plot search agency)
Chaucer House, 4–6 Upper Marlborough Road, St Albans, AL1 3UR
01727 817310 / enquiries@propertyspy.com / www.propertyspy.com

Rainharvesting Systems Ltd
Cheltenham Road, Bisley, Stroud, Gloucestershire GL6 7BX
01452 772000
info@rainharvesting.co.uk / www.rainharvesting.co.uk

Respatex International Ltd
The Gatehouse, Chesham, Buckinghamshire HP5 2JW
01494 771242
websales@respatex.co.uk / www.respatex.co.uk

Salvo (auction website for used building materials)
PO Box 333, Cornhill on Tweed, Northumberland TD12 4YJ
01890 820499 / admin@salvoweb.com / www.salvoweb.com

Self Build Land UK (online building-plot search agency and
self-build resource)
sales@selfbuildit.co.uk / www.selfbuildit.co.uk

Solarcentury (PV roofs)
91–94 Lower Marsh, Waterloo, London SE1 7AB
020 7803 0100 / enquiries@solarcentury.co.uk
www.solarcentury.co.uk

Spectrapure (water purification systems)
215 S. Industrial Drive, Suite 2A, Tempe, Arizona 85281–2941, USA
+1 480 894 5437 / spectra@spectrapure.com / www.spectrapure.com

Stramit Industries Ltd (composite board manufacturer)
Yaxley, Eye, Suffolk IP23 8BW / 01379 783465
speeddeck@eleco.com / www.speeddeck.com

Thermafleece (wool thermal insulation)
Second Nature UK Limited, Soulands Gate, Soulby, Dacre, Penrith,
Cumbria CA11 0JF / 01768 486285
info@secondnatureuk.com / www.secondnatureuk.com

Thermia Varme AB (also known as Eco Heat Pumps –
geothermal power systems)
Box 950, SE-671 29 Arvika, Sweden / +46 570 81300
jan.falck@thermia.com / www.thermia.com

Windsave Ltd (mini wind turbines)
27 Woodside Place, Glasgow G3 7QL / 0141 353 6841
info@windsave.com / www.windsave.com

Wood Recycling Project (recycled wood supplier)
Unit 32–36, Municipal Market, Circus Street, Brighton BN2 9QF
01273 570500 / info@woodrecycling.org.uk
www.woodrecycling.org.uk

FURTHER READING

Books

1001 All Time Best-Selling Home Plans, Jan Prideaux (Home
  Planners, 2000). A book for those contemplating a new build home
  from scratch, but the plans can give inspiration when considering the
  design of a recycled house. The floor plans and detailed text give you a
  clear idea how each of the homes will look.
Architecture in a Climate of Change, Peter Smith (Architectural Press,
  2005). An excellent guide on designing houses to minimize their
  demands on fossil fuels.
Beating the Property Clock, Ajay Ahuja (How To Books, 2004). An
  excellent guide on how to be a successful property developer. You may
  not be or want to be a property developer, but those in competition
  with you for the properties you want to buy are. This book teaches you
  some of their tricks and contains a lot of advice useful to those buying
  property for themselves.
Building Regulations in Brief, Ray Tricker (Harcourt, 2004). An easy
  to understand book that gives good practical advice on how to comply
  with the UK Building Regulations.
Buying Bargains at Property Auctions, Howard Goodie (Law Pack
  Publishing, 2003). A comprehensive guide on buying property at
  auctions. There aren't many books on this subject, which is why I've
  devoted so much space to it in this book. But if you want to know
  more, this is the place to go.
Buying a Home in Britain, David Hampshire (Survival Books, 1999).
  This book is one of a series explaining how to buy property in different
  countries. I think it's really aimed at those outside Britain wanting
  to buy here, but even if you are a resident this book is very useful. It
  explains how the process works and has a good section on mortgages.
Concise DIY Guide to Project Management, Leonard Sales
  (Construction Management Services, 1992). This book is the one to
  have if you're planning to project manage your own site and employ
  your own subbies and contractors directly.
Country Plumbing, Gerry Hartigan (Eco Logic Books/Worldly Goods,
  1986). A fun but informative guidebook on sewage and sewage
  treatment for any property not connected to the mains sewage
  system. All you need to know about septic tanks is here.
Defects in Buildings: Symptoms, Investigation, Diagnosis and Cure,
  Mike Billington (Stationery Office Books, 2001). Not the snappiest
  title ever, but a comprehensive volume on identifying and diagnosing
  building defects.
Do It with an Architect, Barbara Weiss and Luis Hellman (Mitchell
  Beazley, 1999). This book covers a lot more than its title suggests.
  Not only does it advise you how to appoint an architect but guides you
  through the design and construction stages of refurbishing a house.
Don't Throw It Away, Sarah Finch (Friends of the Earth, 2004).
  A guide to domestic recycling, giving advice on reducing the amount
  you throw away.
Eco Refurbishment, Peter Smith (Architectural Press, 2003). An
  accessible and comprehensive book on converting a house into
  a green home.
Eco Renovation, Edward Harland (Chelsea Green Publishing, 1993).
  Sadly now out of print, this guidebook shows how you can renovate a
  property to minimize its effect on the environment.
Empty Property: Unlocking the Potential, Office of the Deputy Prime
  Minister (ODPM, 2003). Available free from ODPM free literature,

PO Box 236, Wetherby, West Yorkshire LS23 7NB (0870 1226236; odpm@twoten.press.net), this is a comprehensive guide for developers and local authorities to assist them in bringing empty properties back to use.

The Energy Saving House, Terry Salomon and Stephane Bedal (Centre for Alternative Energy, 2003). An all-round guide to saving energy in the home. Includes useful chapters ome renovation.

Going with the Flow, Bill Langley and Dan Curtis (Centre for Alternative Energy, 2004). The best book I can find on small-scale hydropower. Tells you how to generate power from a stream running through your garden.

Green Building Handbook, T. Wooley, S. Kims, R. Harrison and P. Harrison (Spon Press, 1997). A comprehensive guide to the environmental impacts of different building materials.

The Green Guide to Housing Specification, J. Anderson and N. Howard (Construction Research Communications Ltd, 2000). Rather than just listing building materials this book goes one stage further. It contains over 150 commonly used specifications such as walls, roofs, floors and rates them against a simple environmental rating scale running from A (good) to C (poor).

Hazardous Building Materials, Steve Curwell and Bob Fox (Spon Press, 2001). A comprehensive reference work on building materials that are known to be harmful to health or the environment. The book suggests more friendly alternatives

Home Conversions, Paul Hymers (New Holland Publishers (UK), 2003). Possibly the best guide on how to convert a loft, basement or garage into additional living space.

Home Extensions, Paul Hymers (New Holland Publishers (UK), 2003). Expert advice on how to extend a property, whether you're intending to build one as a DIY project or hire contractors.

Home Renovations, Paul Hymers (New Holland Publishers (UK), 2004). A practical hands-on guide to renovating houses. Covers everything from small repair and improvement projects to a full-scale refurbishment.

The Housebuilder's Bible, Mark Brinkley (Rodelia Books, 2004). There are lots of self-build guide books, but this one is different. It contains sixty-five comparison cost tables that enable you to make decisions about design and materials. The latest edition includes a chapter on refurbishing properties.

Introduction to Architectural Science, Steven V. Szokolay (Architect Press, 2004). A detailed but readable guide on the science of buildings. If you want to know more about how sound, heat and light work in buildings, this is the book for you.

Natural Home Heating, Greg Pahl (Chelsea Green Publishing, 2003). Everything you need to know about fuel systems including the costs, advantages and disadvantages of each. Be aware, though, that the book is written from an American perspective, so some of the economic and legal points are different from those in the UK and Ireland.

The New Autonomous House, Brenda and Robert Vale (Thames and Hudson, 2002). In its field, this book's predecessor, *The Autonomous House*, first published in 1975, is something of a classic. Many credit it with kicking off the green movement in domestic buildings. This follow-up reviews a practical example of a house built by the Vales. As its title suggests, the book shows how houses can be designed so that they aren't dependent on external resources.

The New Complete Book of Self Sufficiency, John Seymour (Dorling Kindersley, 2003). This book is something of a classic, telling you everything you need to know to live off the land from slaughtering a pig to generating your own electricity. You'll probably only ever need 5 per cent of it, but it's great to read and dream.

Ortho's all About Windows, Doors and Skylights, 'Ort' (Meredith Books, 2001). A slim but comprehensive book on repairing, upgrading and installing new windows, doors and skylights. The book is good on detailed how-to instructions and includes sections on enlarging window openings and improving energy efficiency.

Photovoltaics in the UK, Christian N. Jardine and Kevin Lane (Environmental Change Institute, 2003). A slim, factual book that provides an introduction to photovoltaics, how to use them and how much electricity they produce.

Power Plants, Brian Horne (Centre for Alternative Energy, 1996). A good overview of the many different types of bio-fuel and how to use them.

The Return of the Solar Cat, Jim Augustyn (Chelsea Green Publishing, 2003). Cats instinctively know where to lie to get the maximum boost from the sun. This book explores what we can learn from our feline friends about solar power. A light-hearted but informative read.

Sewage Solutions: Answering the Call of Nature, Nick Grant, Mark Moodie and Chris Weedon (Centre for Alternative Technology, 2000). A comprehensive guide to environmentally sustainable small sewage treatment covering compost toilets, reed-bed filtration, septic tanks, cesspits and waste stabilization ponds.

The Slate Roof Bible, Joseph Jenkins (Chelsea Green Publishing, 2003). An American book that tells you everything you need to know about slate roofs. Lots of design information along with guidance on construction.

Smart Homes for Dummies, Daniel D. Briere and Patrick Hurley (John Wiley and Sons, 2003). A great guidebook on how to wire your house to make best use of new technology. Wireless local area network, Broadband and X10 (a system using electrical wiring to transmit information). This is the sort of book that it goes out of date almost immediately, so look out for new editions.

Solar Water Heating: A DIY Guide, Paul Trimby (Centre for Alternative Energy, 1998). A short guidebook on how to build your own solar panels (not quite as batty an idea as it sounds).

Spon's Architects' and Builders' Price Book 2005, ed. Davis Langdon (Taylor & Francis, 2004). The best and most comprehensive guide to pricing any building project.

Stanley Complete Wiring, Linda Raglan Cunningham (Merdith Books, 2003). This is an American guide, so the voltage and the legislation are different from here, but I haven't managed to track down a good UK-published book on domestic wiring. My theory is that it's all a conspiracy to stop you doing it yourself.

The Whole House Book, Pat Borer and Cindy Harris (Centre for Alternative Energy, 1998). Primarily written for the self-builder, this book none the less provides lots of useful information for the house rescuer. There are good chapters on layout and building materials.

Windows and Skylights, Fine Homebuilding (The Taunton Press, 1996). This is a collection of articles previously published in *Fine Homebuilding* magazine covering choosing and installing new windows and repairing old ones.

Windpower Workshop, Hugh Piggot (Centre for Alternative Energy, 2000). A DIY approach to windpower: how to design and build a home wind-generator system from scrap and recycled parts.

Magazines

There are no magazines aimed exclusively at rescuing houses but the best self-build magazines cover renovation to a greater or lesser extent. These magazines can all be ordered through your newsagent, or you can contact them directly for a sample copy.

Build it (published monthly)
19th floor, 1 Canada Square, Canary Wharf, London E14 5AP
020 7772 8440 / www.buildit-online.co.uk

Grand Designs
Media 10 Ltd, National House, High Street, Epping CM16 4BD
01992 570030 / granddesignsmagazine.com

Homebuilding and Renovating (published monthly)
H&R subscriptions, Freepost BM2127, 2 Sugar Brook Court, Ashton Road, Bromsgrove, Worcestershire B60 3BR
01527 834435 / www.homebuilding.co.uk

Self-Build and Design Magazine (published monthly)
151 Station Street, Burton on Trent, Staffordshire DE14 1BG
01283 74973 / www.selfbuildanddesign.com

INDEX